*A Practical Handbook
for College Teachers*

A Practical Handbook for College Teachers

Barbara Schneider Fuhrmann
Virginia Commonwealth University

Anthony F. Grasha
University of Cincinnati

Little, Brown and Company
Boston   Toronto

Library of Congress Cataloging in Publication Data

Fuhrmann, Barbara Schneider, 1940–
    A practical handbook for college teachers.

    1. College teaching—Handbooks, manuals, etc.
I. Grasha, Anthony F. II. Title.
LB2331.F76   1982   378'.125   82-17997
ISBN 0-316-29558-2

Library of Congress Catalog Card Number 82-17997

ISBN 0-316-29558-2

9 8 7 6 5 4 3 2 1

ALP

Published simultaneously in Canada
by Little, Brown & Company (Canada) Limited

Printed in the United States of America

85-1642

To all of those patient people in our seminars, workshops,
and consulting experiences who cooperated with us
in our attempts to help them and us
unravel the complexities of
the teaching-learning process.

Preface

This book is for everyone who teaches above the high school level. If you are a teaching assistant experiencing the many anxieties common during the first year of teaching, or if you are a seasoned veteran who wants to enlarge an already vast stock of techniques, or if you are teaching in a community college or in a highly specialized graduate or professional program, you will find in this book a sound integration of theory and practice.

The goal implicit in our writing was to provide you with a fresh approach to the concerns college teachers face in the 1980s. We sought to help you become more at ease with the challenging tasks of instruction and at the same time to aid you in building a rich repertoire of skills and ideas so crucial for successful and rewarding teaching. In selecting each topic that makes up this book we were guided by one prime consideration: Did our experience with college students and faculty verify its usefulness? Two correlate criteria were whether the topic contained both conceptual and practical relevance, and whether the theory and practice could be integrated to provide both a consistent rationale and practical applications.

With these criteria in mind, we blended traditional and non-traditional topics. Traditional topics such as testing and grading, leading discussions, making presentations, using media, and organizing a course make up an important part of the book. To add breadth of coverage we chose also to include less traditional topics like: a concise look at salient events in the history of higher education but with a focus on how your current teaching fits into a historical context; the role of personal values and belief systems in influencing teaching; the specification of teaching procedures based not only on behavioral but also on humanistic and cognitive learning perspectives; methods for designing classrooms based on teacher and student skills, creative thinking processes, and developmental theory; student learning styles and their implications for instructional processes; the use of group dynamics concepts and interpersonal communication theory to get students involved in the classroom; and multiple approaches to assessing instruction and enhancing your ability to make changes in your instruction. We have also written a chapter that helps you define for yourself what effective teaching is and suggests ways in which you can work toward achieving your goals.

The design of the chapters recognizes that people often need a bridge to take them from theories and concepts associated with teaching to an appreciation of their personal relevance and use in their own classrooms. In workshops and seminars on college teaching, we have used various methods to help people translate theory into practice. Within each chapter you will find activities and planning processes, key questions about personal relevance and application, and numerous examples of how concepts are successfully employed by others. In our experience, such things often stimulate ideas for bridging the gap between theory and practice.

The practical application of theories that makes this book unique comes from our experiences in working with faculties in two-year, four-year, graduate, and professional programs throughout the United States and Canada. We have both led seminars and workshops and have consulted extensively with both individuals and groups of faculty. We have interviewed faculty, students, and administrators, have observed teachers in all settings, have videotaped and evaluated our own teaching and that of others, and have experimented extensively. Moreover, the research on teaching and the professional literature have yielded much valuable information. We feel confident that what we present to you is timely and tested, fresh and responsible. We thank each of the individuals who reviewed the manuscript and made thoughtful comments and suggestions: Robert Menges (Northwestern University), Mary Lynn Crow (University of Texas at Arlington), and Carol Zion (Miami-Dade Community College). Their experience and perspective broadened our own.

Table of Contents

*A Practical Handbook
for College Teachers*

Chapter 1
The Past, Present, and Future in College Teaching: Where Does Your Teaching Fit?

In the three hundred years of college teaching in the United States, the teacher's role has remained, until quite recently, relatively stable. Development has certainly occurred, and we will detail that development in the remainder of this chapter. However, in comparison to the upheavals experienced in the development of books and educational technology, the deeper insights into learning processes reached by a tremendous amount of research, and the vast physical and social changes taking place on campuses, the teaching role has changed remarkably, and quite regrettably, little. Undoubtedly, this cannot continue. This book and others that highlight college teaching as a vital and evolving profession are but one bit of tangible evidence that teaching must and will change to meet better the needs of students in the last decades of the twentieth century. For such changes to occur, we must begin to think actively about the changes in teaching that are possible for the future. Alvin Toffler notes that our current teaching activities could be enhanced by modifying them to meet our personal images of the future. To break with the past, each of us must bring new ideas into our current instructional practices.

What are the new ideas in teaching that we must take into account? We obviously have no crystal ball that will accurately outline the details of such things. To suggest that we know for sure would certainly be pretentious. Several of our ideas are incorporated into the content of other chapters of this book, but they are only our best guesses regarding the future. What is more important is that everyone who teaches begin to speculate about the future. Each of us must examine our current teaching-learning assumptions, goals, values, and methods to determine whether they will help our students and us meet the challenges of the future. To begin this analysis, it is important first to determine the origins of some of our current educational ideas and practices. Such insights may help us decide whether we are hopelessly buried in the past. And a careful review of why we hold various beliefs and use particular methods may help us find ways to free ourselves from whatever binds we find ourselves in. This is not to suggest that all traditional goals, values, and methods are inappropriate. As we will soon illustrate, there are many beliefs and practices in higher education that have their origins as far back as the sixteenth and seventeenth centuries, and some of these beliefs and practices are still considered useful. Rather, our goal is to identify only those traditions that are producing problems for us in meeting the emerging needs of our students and disciplines. These are typically goals, values, and methods that make our teaching less flexible than it should be. Finally, we must begin to speculate about the future to determine what new beliefs and practices help us modify our current practices. The brief overview we present of past, present, and future ideas in college and university teaching in the United States should assist you in such an analysis.[1]

The Evolution of College Teaching

The Colonial Period (1600–1800)

During the seventeenth and eighteenth centuries, the role of the college instructor in colonial colleges was a paternalistic one in which hearing lessons and supervising conduct were equally important. Higher education was designed for the sons of the elite, with the express purposes of pro-

---

[1] A complete history of higher education is beyond the scope of this book. Instead, we have elected to highlight several trends that have occurred during the development of higher education in the United States since the colonial period. One must keep in mind that the origins of some ideas found in this country during the colonial period and the nineteenth century lie partly in educational goals and practices found in European universities.

moting the Christian religion, training young men for the ministry, infusing moral standards in otherwise temptable young minds, and disciplining the mental faculties. Indeed, as Francis Rosecrance documents, all but one of the first nine colleges founded in the United States were established primarily to train ministers, and secondarily to make higher education available to the sons of the elite. These purposes were approached through a rigidly prescribed curriculum of Greek, Latin, mathematics, and so-called moral truths. All were delivered by a single instructor, who was usually a *tutor*—a recent graduate of the institution. The tutor was not much older than his students and was filling time until he received his call to the ministry—the profession assumed by the vast majority. A hidden, unspoken agenda of the colonial colleges was to maintain a socially stratified society by separating the elite (college educated) from the masses. This tiny elite was created by the development of a strongly cohesive unit—the college class. All the men who entered in any one year became a *class*, a group that took all their instruction together, usually from one tutor who had the total responsibility for delivering the curriculum. Their collective struggle, day by day, year by year, against the inherent rigidity and prescription provided them with a cohesiveness not often matched by any but the most oppressed minorities.

Life in the colonial colleges was bleak—bare, unpleasant rooms and a day that began at sunrise. Following early morning chapel was a class period, then breakfast. After breakfast came alternating periods of class and study time, then lunch and perhaps a short recreational period. The afternoon pattern repeated that of the morning, with a second recreational period before supper time. After supper came more study, then evening chapel and bedtime. John Brubacher and Willis Rudy describe both the students' lot and that of the tutors: "When not attending class or engaged in recreation students were supposed to be in their rooms studying. Indeed tutors made regular rounds to guard against the devil's finding occupations for idle minds" (1958, p. 81).

Being solely responsible for all the activities of a class, including the evening study time, was an impossible burden for young, inexperienced tutors. Most were openly hated by their students, who frequently used every opportunity to retaliate against the unpleasantness of college life by abusing their tutor in all conceivable ways, including breaking his windows and laying traps for him.

The curriculum, which was impractical and expensive, continued the old English tradition of preparing "gentlemen and scholars." It created a learned and cultured group consisting of clergymen and the sons of the rich to lead and develop the fledgling country.

Teaching methods in colonial days consisted of recitation, lecture, disputations, and forensics, with the greatest amount of time and energy being given to *recitation*. Because the purpose of higher education was primarily discipline rather than meaningful learning, the heavy emphasis on recitation served well. In the recitation session, the tutor often sat at a raised desk, on which was a box containing the names of the students. The tutor drew a name from the box and named a passage or specific content for the student to recite.

> The heart of the recitation consisted of an exchange between the tutor and the student, the tutor citing and the student reciting. The citation was usually an assignment in a textbook, but might just as well be a previous lecture or scientific demonstration. In the recitation the student proved he had learned his lesson, at least the portion for which he was called on in class [Brubacher and Rudy, 1958, p. 82].

Obviously, the emphasis was on the lowest order of cognitive skill— pure memory. But the purpose of training in diligence and responsibility was fulfilled. Occasionally a particularly talented tutor raised the level of recitation to approximate a tutor-student discussion, and even more rarely a student might be challenged to interpret or even to offer an opinion. On the whole, however, recitation was mere reproduction and became the battleground between student and tutor where each tried to outwit the other.

During this period, *lecturing* emerged as a supplement to recitation. Books were not abundant, and the ancient lecture method gave students access to information they otherwise could not obtain. The instructor read his notes and students diligently copied them. In turn, the notes were used as another basis for recitation assignments. In the rather rigid atmosphere of the colonial classroom, lecturing periods provided, in addition to new information, a short break from the constant demands of recitation. Those of us who use the lecture method so frequently today may find it hard to believe that it once was a somewhat novel experience for students —and a welcomed one at that.

Colonial college students were required not only to study Latin and Greek, but to converse in Latin as well. Practice was encouraged by the use of the method of *disputations*, in which the tutor assigned a debatable thesis that concerned the nature of the soul or some other abstract concept. The student then had either to agree or disagree with the thesis through a series of syllogisms. Other students were then invited to offer differing views, using the same syllogistic reasoning process. When all students who were called on or volunteered had finished "disputing" the thesis, the tutor summarized the arguments and closed the exercise with his own opinion on the matter. About the middle of the eighteenth century, syllogistic disputations began to be replaced by public debate (*forensics*), including debate over more popular issues. Until the nineteenth century, however, the recitation method remained at the heart of the process of higher education.

Testing in the colonial colleges had each student questioned orally in public by anywhere from five to twenty examiners. The examiners were college personnel and other learned citizens from the local community. Marks were not given, but judgments were passed on both the student and his tutor. The performance of his students was also an evaluation of the tutor. It was therefore to the tutor's advantage that his students performed well. Thus, when it was his turn to question, he was likely to give easy or leading questions to his own students and difficult ones to others. The game between tutors and students continued.

Are there ways in which your current teaching practices reflect some of the general ideas regarding educational practices present in the colonial period? Of course, we do not have the same type of tutor-student relationship. But there are a number of current educational goals, values, and practices that were popular during this period also. Table 1.1 contains several that we have identified. As you review the information in this table, consider whether your current teaching practices reflect some of the same things. Then think about whether those that do reflect the colonial period are still useful. We believe that some of them probably are valuable parts of our current educational environments. But each of us must decide which ones are still useful based on a personal analysis of their current advantages and disadvantages.

The Nineteenth Century

By the end of the eighteenth century, the impracticality and elitism of college became an issue, and a new emphasis was born. New colleges were founded, with a wider appeal, and college began to be "recognized as a means of getting ahead, not just as a means of registering that one's father had" (Rudolph, 1965, p. 36).

Francis Rosecrance also notes that early-nineteenth-century religious awakenings combined with westward expansion to influence the development of many small church-related colleges across the midwestern United States. The vast majority of these failed, but not before their democratizing effect was felt.

Concurrent with this broader appeal and purpose was the influence of scholars who attended German universities, where intellect and scholarly endeavor rather than rote memory were encouraged. Paternalism had been the hallmark of the eighteenth century; democracy became the hallmark of the nineteenth (Brubacher and Rudy, 1958).

The German influence was supported by the rise of science. Both the

---

Table 1.1. General Educational Goals, Values, and Practices from the
Colonial Period

Review each of the statements listed below. They represent several of the goals,
values, and practices that were implicit in our description of the colonial period. Rate
yourself on a scale from 1 to 5, where 1 represents total disagreement and 5 represents
total agreement with the statement. *Sum the ratings for your responses to these items.
We will ask you to do something with them later.* For those items you rated 3, 4, or 5,
how do they appear in your current educational practices? What are their advantages
and disadvantages? What implications do they have for the future if you continue to
use them in your teaching?

- The instructor is an expert and should have the last word in resolving debates
  on content.
- Instructors should prescribe in detail the course content, assignments, and
  methods of evaluation.
- Colleges and universities should serve a highly selected population of students.
- Student learning is facilitated when the students are highly dependent on the
  instructor for information.
- Our capability to think logically and rationally is enhanced by courses in math-
  ematics, ancient languages, and philosophy.
- Recreational activities should be a very low priority in college.
- A student's first obligation is to study what is prescribed and thus build his
  or her mental capacities.
- Learning is hard work and demands personal sacrifice and discipline.
- Students are basically lazy and need to be goaded into learning information.
- Repeating verbatim what they have learned, in class or on a test, is a useful
  activity for students.
- If a student has not learned, then the instructor has failed as a teacher.
- Students should learn what the instructor thinks is important.
- Teachers know what students need to learn.
- The classroom learning process is often a battle between the students and the
  instructor.

---

curriculum and its attendant teaching methodology began to broaden.
Natural philosophy (science) and new methods (increased use of lectures,
demonstrations, and laboratory methods) were added to the curriculum
but were staunchly resisted by traditionalists. The controversy among
lecture, other methods, and recitation dominated much of the century.
Supporters of the recitation method pointed out that in comparison to
German universities, American colleges were mere secondary schools,
and the students in them required discipline and the development of their
"mental faculties" rather than learned wisdom. In addition, they argued,
"natural philosophy" and its methods are practical and popular and therefore do not belong in the classical curriculum. Proponents of the lecture

method suggested it challenged the professor to be prepared and to present material not otherwise available. Further, the artistic possibilities of a good lecture were cited. As it already had in the German universities, lecture eventually dominated the scene in American higher education. It remains a dominant teaching procedure that is fraught with controversy and criticism. The arguments over the lecture method will probably continue into the future, just as they have occurred since its introduction in our colleges and universities.

One particular form of the lecture was associated with the rise in popularity and respectability of science: a form known as the experimental lecture. Here the professor performed an experiment to demonstrate the principle that was the subject of the lecture. These demonstrations eventually led to the development of the laboratory method. Early in the century, the laboratory was viewed as the private domain of the professor. Gradually this domain was opened to students, at first only to watch, but later to participate in the professor's experiments. Involvement of students in this way eventually led to the discovery that students might learn inductively as well as deductively. Thus, the science laboratory as a teaching device was born. Finally, by the end of the nineteenth century, "at every step—definition of the problem, collection of data, formulation of a hypothesis, testing—the professor was sympathetic guide and critic" (Brubacher and Rudy, 1958, p. 88), but the student did the discovering and formulated the conclusions.

Science was responsible also for the introduction of seminars, which were supported by the new influx of German educators. From seminars and laboratories emerged a new relationship between teaching and research, a relationship that virtually changed the nature of higher education in America. Specialized courses were developed, research libraries and significant laboratory space and equipment were constructed, research papers became a popular teaching method, learned societies of earnest, likethinking students and faculty developed, and graduate education was introduced.

Specialization began to appear in the curriculum, with the evolution of the colonial "natural philosophy" into the various scientific disciplines —geology, biology, physics, and chemistry; the colonial "moral philosphy" into the social specialties—economics, anthropology, sociology, and political science; and the colonial "classics" into language and literary specialties. With specialization, the earliest attempts at an elective rather than a prescriptive curriculum also occurred.

Also during the nineteenth century, the so-called collegiate way was born. At first, because colleges were usually located away from populous areas, residence accommodations were required. Later the idea of the ivory tower, isolated from its surroundings and providing all that its students might need, became a tradition, if not a principle, of American higher education. In the residential, often pastoral, college, the extracurriculum developed. Debating clubs and literary societies for intellectual challenge, fraternities and student activities for social needs, and athletics for physical needs became as important as (if not more important than) the curriculum itself.

By the end of the nineteenth century, colleges began seriously to question themselves. Concerns over standards and excellence were raised. There was some anxiety that learning was simply not taken particularly seriously. College education had broadened, deepened, and become popular. Student evaluation had moved from public examination to written exams with marks (0–100) and grades (A–E), but student motivation often remained low. Near the end of the century, emerging institutions experimented with manual labor as a means of teaching educational principles, encouraging interest, and providing financial support for students. This movement, however, was hardly more than a justification for using student labor to construct needed facilities, and it was short lived. The century ended with college education popular, but all too often less than meaningful.

As you did after examining the colonial period, turn to Table 1.2 and assess to what extent your current teaching practices reflect some of the educational goals and practices that were present during the nineteenth century. Think about those that do reflect the last century in terms of how well they serve your needs and those of your students. What are their advantages and disadvantages?

The Twentieth Century

If the seventeenth and eighteenth centuries in higher education are characterized as paternalistic, and the nineteenth century as democratic, the twentieth century is nothing less than revolutionary. The century began with the prospect of an ever-increasing student population, many of whose aims conflicted with the traditional scholarly ones that the colleges had relatively recently adopted. In the early 1900s, social needs outweighed academic ones. As John Brubacher and Willis Rudy note, "Many a twentieth-century father sent his son to college less to sharpen his wits than to polish his manners" (1958, p. 259). Owen Johnson, in his early-twentieth-century novel *Stover at Yale*, criticized educational habits severely, charging that students learned nothing. Colleges, he pointed out, were mere "social clearing houses" organized not only to serve social purposes, but actually to prevent learning. Student dissatisfaction with the curriculum eventually led to significant reforms, particularly those that directed more attention to practical subjects. In attempts to motivate the generally unintellectual student population, innovations of numerous kinds were tried. Preceptors

---

Table 1.2. General Educational Goals, Values, and Practices from the
        Nineteenth Century

Review each of the statements listed below. They represent several of the goals, values, and practices that were implicit in our description of the nineteenth century. Rate yourself on a scale from 1 to 5, where 1 represents total disagreement and 5 represents total agreement with the statement. *Sum the ratings for your responses to these items. We will ask you to do something with them later.* For those items you rated 3, 4, or 5, how do they appear in your current educational practices? What are their advantages and disadvantages? What implications do they have for the future if you continue to use them in your teaching?

- A college education is for more than just a highly selected student population.
- Rote memory should not be emphasized in college.
- Teachers can learn from their students.
- A college education should prepare people to assume a job.
- Lecturing has positive benefits for students.
- Colleges should teach subjects that are practical and popular.
- Students need hands-on experiences in laboratories and other settings to learn.
- Teachers need to take a less directive role in prescribing what students should learn.
- Students know what they need to learn and should be encouraged to pursue such interests.
- Specialization within a field is an important goal of education.
- Colleges must help meet the social, physical, and intellectual needs of students.
- Teachers should help students develop the capacity to become independent learners.
- Students should be taught to think both inductively and deductively.
- Recreational activities should be an important part of the college environment.

---

were used to guide and stimulate students and to personalize the curriculum for them; honors instruction as a reward for excellence was begun; independent study became a way to encourage academic endeavor; and periods of work were alternated with periods of study in an attempt to make learning practical.

On a broader scale, three reform viewpoints or philosophies of higher education developed—the utilitarian or vocational view, which emphasizes job and career training; the scientific or intellectual view, which emphasizes research and the development of new knowledge; and the liberal or general education view, which emphasizes social development as well as intellectual and vocational development. These three viewpoints have remained prominent on university campuses, never completely comfortable in compromise, but rather living in a somewhat strained coexistence— even today.

Early experimental approaches. During the first half of this century, no single reform emerged as the one wave of the future, but the influence of John Dewey led to much experimentation, especially in the areas of lifelong learning needs and inductive rather than deductive methods.

One experimental approach was that of integrating disciplines for the purpose of realistically treating current issues. Thus the survey course was born, designed to interest young people in using their minds to tackle world and national problems. In this way psychology, sociology, and economics might be combined in a course entitled "Youth in Contemporary Society."

Another approach combined the development of divisions, such as physical sciences, social sciences, and humanities, with the idea of *general education*. A student who in colonial days would have followed a single prescribed curriculum, and who in the late nineteenth century might have had a free choice of electives, now had to master the basics (with a combination of prescribed electives) in each division before selecting an area of specialization. General education was seen as the basis for the widely informed and well-educated person. Through the universal adoption of the general education principle, professors began to differentiate standards for majors and nonmajors. Sometimes they even described their professional status by the number of major and nonmajor courses taught.

A third innovation was the Great Books approach to curriculum. Built on the idea that a classic book is always contemporary and relevant, the Great Books concept built anywhere from a year's study to an entire four-year curriculum on the study of specific, identified "classics."

Changes since 1950. Now, in the second half of the twentieth century, revolutionary changes in the world have challenged all previous views. Lewis Mayhew specifies the profound revolutions occurring since World War II as "the revolt of colonial peoples, the revolution in weaponry, the explosion of knowledge, the urbanization and technocratization of the society, and undreamed-of affluence" (1969, p. ix). The veterans of World War II and later wars brought with them to American universities an attitude of sobriety and seriousness. The "rah-rah" days of Joe College, football, and fraternities spawned in the era of extracurriculum began to wane.

The Cold War and the launching of Sputnik created a panic during which all attention was given to academic excellence. Fear led to an emphasis on technology as the only way to progress and excel. The academic boom in the decade between 1958 and 1968 saw many large research grants, curriculum reforms (especially in the sciences and technology), additional faculty positions, and better salaries. New courses and curricula developed, with the emphasis on production and efficiency. Many institutions became intoxicated with growth. New courses and programs of study were added before the long-range implications of the growth were assessed. Cuts in budgets because of declining resources in the 1970s would later eliminate as frills some of the changes of the 1960s. Yet such changes continued during the 1960s without much realization that a temporary boom in money and students was feeding the growth.

It took the Vietnam War and the student protest movement on campuses during the late 1960s to force another reevaluation of the goals and methods of higher education. Students demanded (perhaps somewhat naively and destructively) a greater voice in the affairs of the university and a realignment of the purposes of academe. Now, at least partly because of student radicalism, we are seeing higher education's responsibility to the community increased. Most important, the aim of education is no longer viewed as the study of externals. The traditional views and methods will no longer suffice in an era when the demand by students is for relevance, meaning, and preparation for the work world. Instead of the "pitcher" theory of education, in which the teacher holds the pitcher full of knowledge and pours out what he or she chooses into the receptacles of student minds, a new view is evolving. In this view teacher and student are partners, though not equal partners, in the challenge of learning—learning about the world, each other, themselves, and ways of managing their lives.

The Vietnam War and the campus and societal unrest of the 1960s made higher education systems more sensitive to issues of relevance, meaning, and job preparation, and declining resources during the 1970s and 1980s forced them to focus even more on such issues. Colleges and universities found themselves having to operate with less funding and fewer students than they enjoyed during the boom years of the 1960s. Inflation, high interest rates, cuts in expenditures by foundations, state governments, and the federal government, and fewer eighteen- to twenty-one-year-old students made institutions take a hard look at what offerings and services they could reasonably provide. Some institutions folded; others searched for ways to survive. One part of surviving was opening the doors to what Pat Cross describes as the "new students." Such students were generally older, highly interested in acquiring vocational skills, and either changing careers or, in the case of many women, formulating career plans for the first time. Continuing education and lifelong learning became very important concepts that guided academic programs. At the same time, institutions took steps to eliminate the "fat" and frills from their systems, and a back-to-basics attitude began to emerge. Course offerings and programs that a decade earlier were innovative and creative suddenly were eliminated or cut to conform to new budget realities. Those that survived were the ones considered absolutely essential to preserve the discipline or to meet the immediate needs of the influx of new students. Institutions found themselves needing to extend their reach to new student populations and to develop vocationally relevant curricula while holding the line on costs.

Learning theories. The twentieth century in higher education is also characterized by systematic attempts to develop teaching methods and practices based on theories of learning. The research literature on human learning has been used as a foundation for educational innovations. Three points of view tend to dominate this experimentation. They are the humanistic, behavioral, and cognitive views of learning. In a later chapter, we present in detail their assumptions and methods. For now, let us briefly examine a few of their principles and how they have influenced instruction in the twentieth century.

Instead of assuming that students will learn merely by passively digesting the pearls of wisdom transmitted to them by their professors, the humanistic view recognizes that learning is something that students must do for themselves. Teachers must not merely transmit, but must involve and engage students in the activities of discovery and meaning making. This emphasis on student needs and the study of oneself as part of the study of humanity is sometimes also called student-centered education, or affective education. Teachers are encouraged to guide and direct less and to facilitate or act as a catalyst for students to initiate and take responsibility for their own learning. Personal feelings and values, concerns with minority issues and sexism, and a reexamination of the content of the college curriculum are part of this approach. It is an attempt to personalize education. It represents a reaction against the excesses of the technological emphasis in education during the late 1950s, an emphasis that some people believed tended to dehumanize individuals, to bend, staple, and mutilate the spirits of students who felt left out by the increased structure, cognitive priorities, behavioral orientation and efficiency of the stress on technology.

The behaviorist point of view has also had an impact on educational practices during this century. During the early part of the twentieth century, John Watson introduced the idea that our behaviors are controlled by stimuli in our environments. He believed that anyone could be taught to become anything—doctor, lawyer, merchant, thief—by the proper manipulation of environmental stimuli. B.F. Skinner began in the 1930s to modify the earlier ideas of Watson and develop what he called a technology of operant conditioning. This technology stressed the need to shape behaviors in small steps and to reward each small success a learner had. It also emphasized that organisms learn at different rates and that some custom designing of learning environments is necessary to accommodate such variations. Skinner's work began with pigeons, rats, and other animals during the 1930s, and it was not until the late 1940s and early 1950s that educational applications began to appear. Teaching machines, token economies in the classroom, personalized systems of instruction such as the Keller Plan, learning contracts, and computer-assisted instruction have evolved based on behavioral principles.

Although behaviorism emphasized the role of environmental stimuli in controlling a learner's actions, the student's cognitive capability was not ignored. Procedures were developed to help students solve problems and make decisions more effectively, to use mental images to assist their learning of foreign languages and other subjects, and to develop cognitive procedures to monitor and control by themselves their ability to learn.

Regardless of their merits, the attempts at reforms based on principles of learning have been less than spectacular. To date, it is not a general practice for people systematically to develop their teaching based on principles of learning. In fact, some students and faculty seem to display passivity, apathy, and even overt hostility and cynicism when suggestions are made to substitute new methodologies for the old. One issue is that the nontraditional, unconventional, alternative ideas represent attitudes about education as well as procedures for teaching. They represent attitudes that (1) put the student first and the institution second; (2) concentrate more on the student's needs than the institution's convenience; (3) encourage diversity of individual opportunity rather than uniform prescription; and (4) deemphasize time, space, and course requirements in favor of competence and performance. Such beliefs run counter to many of the past experiences of students and faculty. Thus, they raise anxiety in students who want more structure or are simply afraid of deviating from the ways they learned in the past. Faculty often charge that new methods lack academic rigor or are based on ideas that are not well researched.

The reactions to nontraditional forms of teaching based on principles of learning are simply another reflection of the traditional-nontraditional controversy that has occurred throughout this and past centuries in higher education. But there need not be a quarrel between the traditional, with its emphasis on academic excellence and depth of inquiry, and the nontraditional, with its emphasis on lifelong learning and self-education. The nontraditional approaches can augment, fortify, and enhance more traditional philosophy and methods, can add new perspectives and horizons to educational opportunity and possibility, and will sometimes show that traditional forms have a necessary and perhaps irreplaceable role to play. We think, then, that the prevailing attitude today and for the future is that the traditionalist and nontraditionalist are not adversaries. One cannot supplant or supersede the other; they are inseparable partners in the single purpose of promoting learning. The traditionalist attitude of rigor and discipline is worthy of note by the nontraditionalist, and the traditionalist must take note of the nontraditionalist emphasis on independent study, flexible patterns, and lifelong enrichment. It may even be said that true creativity can come only from a dialectical synthesis of tradition and antitradition. Traditional forms that remain vital must be preserved, while those that have outlived their usefulness must be replaced by creative, relevant ones. This creativeness in the art of teaching is the wave of both the present and the future in higher education.

Earlier we asked you to assess your current practices to determine their origins in the colonial period and the nineteenth century. Whether you continue to endorse current goals and practices that originated during these periods depends on how helpful you perceive them to be. Table 1.3

Table 1.3. General Educational Goals, Values, and Practices from the
Twentieth Century

Review each of the statements listed below. They represent several of the goals, values, and practices that were implicit in our description of the twentieth century. Rate yourself on a scale from 1 to 5, where 1 represents total disagreememt and 5 represents total agreement with the statement. *Sum the ratings for your response to these items. We will ask you to do something with them later.* For those items you rated 3, 4, or 5, how do they appear in your current educational practices? What are their advantages and disadvantages? What implications do they have for the future if you continue to use them in your teaching?

- Students should alternate course work with job experiences related to their major field of study.
- Education is a lifelong process that does not end with formal training.
- Students should learn to study and work on academic matters independently.
- It is important to stress practical subjects in a college curriculum.
- Vocational and career training is an important mission of a college or university.
- Colleges and universities must stress the development of new knowledge as one of their goals.
- Interdisciplinary course offerings should be encouraged in a college curriculum.
- The goal of education is to produce a well-educated person trained in a liberal arts tradition.
- Self-awareness is an important part of what students should learn in college.
- Teachers should be less directive and act more as facilitators of a student's learning.
- Teachers need to personalize their instruction to meet the unique needs of their students.
- Learning proceeds best if students are taught in small, discrete steps and rewarded after each step.
- Teachers should help students develop problem-solving and decision-making skills.
- Teaching methods should be developed based on theories of human learning.

---

contains ideas based on our discussion of the twentieth century. Try a similar analysis with the statements in this table and see if it provides additional insights into your teaching.

The Future

Just as all education springs from some image of the future, all education produces some image of the future [Toffler, 1974, p. 3].

Alvin Toffler, Benjamin Singer, and other futurists argue that we must integrate future possibilities into our current educational practices. To illustrate this need, Toffler describes a mythical South American Indian tribe that teaches its young the old ways. They learn how to build and ride canoes, the types of fish that live in their lakes and how to catch them, as well as other important aspects of their culture. Because they seldom venture beyond the rather immediate boundaries of their tribe, they are unaware of a hydroelectric dam that is under construction upstream from their territory. In a few years the dam will be completed and their lakes will dry up. What has the tribe done to prepare itself for this event? What can it do if it is so tradition bound?

The metaphor is important and timely, because many of us assume that the main features of our present educational, social, economic, and political systems will continue indefinitely. Yet history shows that we can expect upheavals in our current ways of living. In our experiences, we find students and colleagues who say, "That is true, but it won't happen for a while and certainly not in my lifetime." Or they assume that even if some upheavals occur, their personal lives will remain relatively unaffected. In a series of experiments, Toffler finds similar tendencies in the people with whom he has worked. Participants in his research write about future scenarios as if they will happen "out there" to other people. The future is rather impersonal. They describe their lives as continuing much as they are today. For example, people developed scenarios of a future with anti-gravity cars, the destruction of large parts of the earth, cures for cancer, test-tube babies, a United States–Soviet Union alliance against China, accidental nuclear explosions, and robot computers holding political office in the United States. What would happen to their lives? One participant wrote, "I'll move into my own apartment, attend interior-design school, get a driver's license, buy a dog, get married, have children, and die at a ripe old age."

Clearly, there is a need for people to become sensitive to the possibilities of change and the probable effects on their lives. Futurists generally argue that our educational system could do a much better job of integrating the future into current curricula. They suggest that having no image or a false image of the future destroys the relevance of the educational effort.

Yet our present educational systems, including higher education, are not seen as showing much concern. Today's schools and universities are perceived as past and present bound. Technological and social change is outracing the educational system, and our social reality is transforming itself more rapidly than our educational images of that reality. Students apparently are not taught to understand their investment in the future, to transfer classroom learning to future possibilities, to help change immature institutions, or to see themselves as individuals who can influence the future.

Benjamin Singer adds that the concept of the future is closely tied to the motivation of the learner. How people see their future is directly connected to their academic performance and their ability to cope with a high-change society. The future is not so much a subject as it is a perspective. Introducing it into our curriculum helps us to organize our knowledge in new ways. To these ideas we might add that such things will occur only if our current educational goals and practices are flexible and amenable to change. That is, to make use of a future perspective, our teaching methods will undoubtedly have to alter.

How to integrate ideas about the future into our teaching is an issue. The following are some possibilities for how this might occur:

- Developing personal images or scenarios about future developments in a field might help students increase their sensitivity to the future. In classroom discussions, students might sometimes be asked to forecast developments in a field and defend their answers.

- Teachers might ask students to speculate on the future images held by prominent historical figures or people in their field and what role these images might have had in their actions. For example, what images of the future guided Hitler, Nixon, Freud, Skinner, Goffman, Darwin, Sagan, or any other people who are relevant to a topic of discussion?

- Cooperative experiences and job-related courses might be developed in all fields. Thus disciplines like classics, philosophy, and history might have to change dramatically. Disciplines like psychology, education, and anthropology might have to do even more than they currently do. To accomplish such things, more long-range planning and forecasting need to be done in such disciplines than currently.

- To cope with change, students need to be able to go beyond current facts and knowledge. They will need to be able to bring themselves up to date. Thus they need to learn how to learn as part of their formal education. Classroom procedures might stress teaching people how to seek and find resources for solving problems, how to work independently, how to benefit from working with other people, and how to ask the right kinds of questions. Classrooms must stress teaching people skills for learning as well as specific content.

- New classroom materials are needed to help students understand themselves better; to recognize their investment in the future; to help them feel more in control of their lives; to understand the nature of change; and to help them mature so they can help change immature institutions. What they learn needs to be thought about in terms of its personal implications.

- Students and faculty need to be increasingly concerned with moral issues. The future is not predetermined, but is subject to our influence. People need to become more concerned with values. Students must learn to understand their values clearly enough to make consistent and effective choices. Their values must be challenged and students asked to justify them explicitly in the classroom.

- To integrate future possibilities into the classroom and to improve the teaching of subjects that are rapidly changing, new approaches to teaching are needed. The information explosion in the study of human learning needs to be put to greater use in the design of instructional procedures. Institutions might demand that faculty pay more attention to the literature on learning when designing course procedures. Furthermore, the use of new teaching methodologies must be encouraged. Thus, computer-assisted instruction, simulations, role plays, classroom theater, practicum experiences, and "think tank" procedures should increase.

It is important to note that integrating a future perspective into education is not only to suggest what the world will look like next year or in the next hundred years. Such speculation is fun and often the topic of science fiction books and articles. Rather, the task is to have such images but also to suggest things that might be done today to help create desirable parts of those future images. We must remember that the future is something we help to create. It is not something that will occur without our participation.

Thus the question "What is the future of teaching in higher education?" is not answered well by simply describing scenarios of classrooms in the twenty-first century. Rather, we must suggest things that can be integrated today into our educational systems to create a future perspective and foundations for future practice. Based on the discussion in this section, several ideas for what might be done are listed in Table 1.4. As you did with the other time periods, rate the extent to which you agree or disagree with the statements.

Table 1.4. General Educational Goals, Values, and Practices for the Future

Review each of the statements listed below. They represent several of the goals, values, and practices that were implicit in our discussion of the future of higher education. Rate yourself on a scale from 1 to 5, where 1 represents total disagreement and 5 represents total agreement with the statement. *Sum the ratings for your responses to these items. We will ask you to do something with them later.* For those items you rated 3, 4, or 5, how do they appear in your current educational practices? What are their advantages and disadvantages? What implications do they have for the future if you continue to use them in your teaching?

- Speculation about the future is an important topic for discussion in the classroom.
- Students should be encouraged to develop personal images or scenarios about future developments in all disciplines.
- Having no image about the future destroys the relevance of the educational effort.
- Today's educational practices are too past and present bound.
- Technological and social change is outpacing the capacity of the educational system.
- Students should be taught to understand their investment in the future.
- Classrooms should stress teaching people skills for how to learn as well as specific content.
- Students need to learn about how to cope with the changes in the world around them.
- Students need to learn how to become effective change agents.
- Classroom practices need to become more bound to the research data on human learning.
- Teachers should use more of the advances in computers, video recorders, and other new technologies as part of their classroom methods.
- Students need to learn how to work independently to a greater extent as well as how to work better with other people.
- The values that underlie our disciplines need to be discussed as part of classroom learning.
- Education should help students develop a sense of personal control over their lives and their environment.

The History of
College Teaching and You

After each section of this chapter, we suggested that you rate the extent to which you agree or disagree with the statements presented in the tables. Your total ratings should give you a good idea of which historical periods have influenced your current beliefs about education most and least. Most people find that their current beliefs are a composite of each historical period but that each period did not influence them equally. You may want to examine your ratings and the specific beliefs you agreed and disagreed with by answering the following questions:

- How satisfied am I with the beliefs that I have about education?
- What advantages and disadvantages do they have for me?
- How comfortable am I with the time period that seems to influence my beliefs most? Am I old fashioned, or do my beliefs help me to meet the needs of today's students?
- Do I need to change or modify any of the beliefs I hold?

You may want to think about your responses to these questions as you read the next chapter on examining and clarifying your values as a teacher. Your responses should give you a place to begin to examine your personal values as an instructor.

Summary

In this chapter, we have surveyed the landscape of the history of teaching in the United States from its beginning in colonial days to its as yet unheralded future. We have presented this history in terms of the goals, values, and practices that provided the guiding ideas in the colonial period (1600–1800), the nineteenth century, and the twentieth century, and those that will probably influence future developments.

In the colonial period, college instruction was guided largely by paternalistic ideas that college students should be selected, disciplined, dependent upon instructors, taught to develop rigidly prescribed mental facilities, and generally forced to subscribe to academic requirements into which they had no input and over which they felt no control.

The nineteenth century emphasized democracy, both in its attempt to provide higher education for the broad population rather than only the elite, and in its involvement of students in the process of learning. Consistent with this broadly democratic attitude was the emphasis on subjects that were practical, the concept of specialization as a goal of education, the introduction of job training and experiential learning, the mutual intellectual development of student and teacher, and the social aspect of higher education.

In the twentieth century, revolutionary ideas and behaviors sparked experimentation and innovation. The result has been that alongside traditional views now exist views of education based on humanistic concerns, learning theories, and behaviorist notions. Teaching can, and is, viewed from all three perspectives, with the result being a wide variety of approaches from which modern faculty can select.

Our presentation of the dominant ideas from each of these periods, along with our best guess as to prevailing ideas of the future, are offered as a stimulus for you to examine your own values, goals, and behaviors in both an introspective and a historical analysis. It's only with a clear idea of both the past and the present that we can thoughtfully influence the future.

References

Bell, W. Social Science: The future as a missing variable. In A. Toffler, ed., *Learning for Tomorrow: The Role of the Future in Education.* New York: Vintage Books, 1974.

Brubacher, J.S., and Rudy, W. *Higher Education in Transition.* New York: Harper & Row, 1958.

Cross, P. *Accent on Learning.* San Francisco: Jossey-Bass, 1976.

Johnson, O.H. Dink Stover at Yale, about 1909. In S. Bellman, ed., *The College Experience.* San Francisco: Chandler, 1962.

Mayhew, L.B. *Colleges Today and Tomorrow.* San Francisco: Jossey-Bass, 1969.

McDanield, M. Tomorrow's curriculum today. In A. Toffler, ed., *Learning for Tomorrow: The Role of the Future in Education.* New York: Vintage Books, 1974.

Rosecrance, F.C. *The American College and Its Teachers.* New York: Macmillan, 1962.

Rudolph, F. *The American College and University: A History.* New York: Vintage Books, 1965.

Singer, B.D. The future focused role image. In A. Toffler, ed., *Learning for Tomorrow.* New York: Vintage, 1974.

Skinner, B.F. *Beyond Freedom and Dignity.* New York: Alfred A. Knopf, 1971.

Toffler, A. *Future Shock.* New York: Random House, 1970.

Toffler, A. *Learning for Tomorrow: The Role of the Future in Education.* New York: Vintage Books, 1974.

Watson, J.B. *Behaviorism.* Chicago: University of Chicago Press, 1924.

Wilson, L., ed. *Emerging Patterns in American Higher Education.* Washington, D.C.: American Council on Education, 1965.

Chapter 2
The Role of Personal Values in Teaching

I know that lecture has long been the mainstay of American higher education, and most of my colleagues use it successfully, but I just don't like it. How come I'm so different?

The behaviorists have demonstrated pretty clearly that punishment is not as effective in modifying behavior as reinforcement, but I used to perform in classes, when I was a student, out of fear of failing, and I'm convinced that it works. It worked with me and it'll work with my students too.

It may be demonstrable that group discussion can be effective in developing inquiry skills, but my experience has been the opposite. I just get turned off by the pointless banter and would personally be more effective doing the assignment by myself.

What do you mean, lecture encourages passivity! The most dynamic, involving professor I ever had did nothing but lecture. I'm going to do it too.

Group work is really popular, and it seems that those faculty who use it are getting especially good ratings, so I think I'll try it.

It's really important to me to know that I've done something unique. That's why I keep trying new methods and using new ideas. I really need to feel creative.

Comments like these might be heard on any campus, and they demonstrate that personal values play a part in our behaviors as teachers. *Values represent the important and stable ideas, beliefs, and assumptions that affect our behaviors.* Some of our values are ideals that we hope to achieve. As such, they are the hopes and dreams we have learned to pursue. Seldom, however, do we completely obtain them. Although we might believe in justice, democracy, freedom, and equality, they are probably difficult to achieve fully within our teaching roles or in other areas of our lives. Fortunately, we also learn other values that are much more instrumental in our daily lives. Included are personal values that influence our roles as teachers. We might value independence, innovation, and new knowledge. Our classroom might then stress opportunities for independent student projects and the latest teaching techniques and innovations, and we might spend lots of time in class on new directions in our fields.

What do you value? How do these things affect your teaching and other aspects of your instructional role? Are there other values you might like to hold? Sidney Simon, Leland Howe, and Howard Kirschenbaum note that most people have a difficult time answering such questions. Most of us spend relatively little time examining the stable beliefs associated with our actions—at least until we become sensitive to the important role values play and how little we know about them. These authors believe we instructors can benefit from identifying and clarifying the role values play in our lives. The benefits include recognizing how current values affect our choice of instructional methods, our relationships with students, and the degree to which we are willing to experiment with innovative approaches to the classroom. Clearly, they are beliefs we cannot afford to ignore.

Values and Teaching

Have you given much thought to your values as a teacher? Are you aware of how many of your classroom and other teacher role behaviors are affected by your values? John Davis argues that teachers spend relatively little time examining important values that underlie the teacher-student relationship. While values play a crucial role in determining our identity and behaviors as teachers, we often fail to determine which values are most important to us. In addition, we probably seldom stop and ask ourselves whether our beliefs are congruent with our actions. It is difficult to act always in accordance with our beliefs, but we certainly can work toward a healthy integration of the two.

Identifying Personal Values

The following activity can assist you in identifying global values that are important to you and examining your behaviors as a teacher in light of those values.

From the list of words in Table 2.1 that describe our values, select three that imply behaviors you think are most important to you in your class-

---

Table 2.1. A List of Values

Before completing the activity in the text, briefly examine the list of terms in this table and think about what each means to you.

Value Words

achievement	democracy	independence	quiet
affection	dependence	inferiority	rebellion
age	dignity	influence	religion
aggression	discipline	initiative	respect
alienation	disease	integrity	responsibility
anger	disorder	intelligence	rigidity
apathy	disrespect	interdependence	rules
art	dogmatism	intimacy	safety
authority	dominance	intuition	salvation
autonomy	education	isolation	security
beauty	efficiency	justice	self-awareness
boredom	equality	knowledge	self-direction
bravery	excitement	laughter	self-gratification
brotherhood	exercise	leisure	self-improvement
change	expertise	life	selfishness
chaos	exploration	literature	self-respect
charity	fairness	loneliness	sexuality
choice	family	love	sharing
cleanliness	favoritism	money	speed
collaboration	fear	morality	success
comfort	feelings	novelty	time
companionship	freedom	obedience	trust
competitiveness	friends	organization	understanding
compulsiveness	fun	passivity	variety
community	happiness	peace	violence
conflict	harmony	play	war
control	hate	pleasure	winning
cooperation	health	politics	wisdom
creativity	honesty	power	work
culture	ideas	practicality	zest
danger	imagination	privacy	
death	inclusion	progress	

room and other aspects of your role as a teacher. Then select three that imply behaviors you want absent from your classroom. The latter could represent behaviors you currently use but want to cease employing or things you hope never to have as values.

On a separate sheet of paper, list the three words that describe your most important values and those you want absent from your classrooms, as indicated in the sample format that follows.

Values I Want as a Teacher	*Values I Don't Want as a Teacher*
1. _____	1. _____
Behaviors:	Behaviors:
1.	1.
2.	2.
3.	3.
4.	4.
2. _____	2. _____
Behaviors:	Behaviors:
1.	1.
2.	2.
3.	3.
4.	4.
3. _____	3. _____
Behaviors:	Behaviors:
1.	1.
2.	2.
3.	3.
4.	4.

Having done this, list three or four specific, observable behaviors that would support the presence of that value in the classroom and in other aspects of your role as a teacher. For example, the following might be used as indicators of the presence of the value *freedom*:

1. Students have an open reading list and read books of their own choosing.

2. Students interact with one another without direction from the instructor.

3. I resist attempts by my dean to make decisions for the faculty.

4. I think I have the right to turn down a committee assignment if I want.

Once you have listed observable indicators of the values you most support and those you most abhor, ask yourself the following questions:

1. How many of the behaviors that represent your most dearly held values are regularly present in your classes? Which do you want to incorporate?

2. What steps might you take to ensure the presence of the behaviors that support your values, and the absence of those you don't want?

3. Which values are too important to you to compromise? Why? Are there any that would be worth risking your job for?

The Effects of Values

The last activity had you select several of the words that describe the global values you hold and behaviors that reflect them. Typically we find that people respond to the exercise primarily by listing activities they engage in during class sessions. Yet our values affect a much wider range of our behaviors as teachers. In particular, our choice of classroom goals, our emotional reactions in educational settings, and our perceptions of the classroom environment are related to our values. In the following paragraphs, we briefly describe the broad role our values play. After our discussion, we will ask you to reconsider the types of activities you listed after each of the values you selected in terms of a broader range of behaviors that they might affect.

Choosing classroom goals. The choices we make for particular classroom goals in part reflect choices among our values. We may have chosen group projects over independent term papers for a final course requirement. Or we may have decided to lecture rather than to use group methods. Such choices reflect our personal values. In the former case we chose collaboration over independence, and in the latter we chose personal control and authority over delegation and collaboration.

Influencing our emotions. Personal values play an important role in helping us understand our emotional life in our roles as teachers. This occurs in several ways. *Our positive and negative feelings are sometimes related to whether classroom-related events correspond to our values.* When we encounter things that are in harmony with our values, we usually experience happy or joyful feelings. Teachers who value independence, autonomy, and self-direction are typically pleased, even delighted, with students who demonstrate such characteristics. They are less happy and often dismayed with students who are dependent, take little initiative, and flounder about in the classroom.

Areas of our lives where our values and those of someone else do not mesh are called *value collisions*. Thomas Gordon uses the term to describe situations where different values among people lead to frustration, tension, or anger. Relationships with students, colleagues, administrators, and others often force us to deal with different values. Think about some of the tension-filled interactions you have had with your colleagues and students. Were the conflicts related to the expression of different personal values? Perhaps you valued collaboration and wanted to use group methods in your class. The students resisted and complained because you were not lecturing more. Your dean and department head might value control and dependence more than you do. They might have tried to dictate certain policies to the faculty or otherwise let you know who the boss is. You resisted because you value autonomy and independence for faculty. Many of the issues between teachers, students, and administrators are related to value conflicts. To resolve such issues, both parties need to see the other's beliefs as legitimate and attempt to make compromises.

Our values may also lead to feelings of guilt and anxiety. Basically, guilt is a present feeling of apprehension and concern over our past actions. Anxiety is a present feeling of apprehension and worry over future things that might affect us. Guilt, then, is related to our memory for past events, and anxiety is related to our ability to imagine the future. According to Thomas Oden, both emotions are a problem in value selection. He notes that each of us has certain priorities for our values. Because our behaviors are typically consistent with our values, other people expect certain actions from us and we typically behave in ways they expect. A colleague told us that he values meeting his classes on time, participating on college committees, and doing outside consulting. These were the three priorities for his professional activities, and he ordered his time accordingly—or at least until this year he did. Because he became better known, the requests for consulting and outside speaking engagements increased. He began to do more of them but started to feel guilty. Why? He was occasionally missing classes and was not getting his committee work accomplished. His values had been reordered. He recognized that he was now behaving in ways that were contrary to his past value priorities. Thus, he felt guilty. He also felt anxious. He worried that he might never be able to keep up with his committee work and that he would continue to miss classes. He was concerned that his current value priorities would continue into the future. In Thomas Oden's terms, he was trapped between concerns over violating his past value priorities and possibly making this violation a statement of his future priorities. Can you think of some experiences in your professional life where similar things occurred?

A final way that values affect our emotions is in the discovery of certain inconsistencies related to the priorities we have given our values and behaviors. Milton Rokeach demonstrated this effect in his survey of American values and in an experiment with college students. In his experiment, he asked them to indicate whether they were in favor of civil rights and then asked them to rank eighteen value words for importance. Included in this list were beliefs in "freedom" and "equality." Some gave freedom a high ranking and equality a low ranking. When they were told that this meant they probably believed in personal freedom and not freedom for everyone, feelings of tension occurred.

The tension is sometimes called cognitive dissonance. According to Milton Rokeach, any time two or more personal values are not consistent, cognitive dissonance is aroused. One way to reduce the tension is to change our behavior. In Rokeach's study, students reordered their value rankings, and some later joined the National Association for the Advancement of Colored People and other civil rights groups. These behaviors helped reduce tension. Have you ever experienced tension when your beliefs were shown to be inconsistent? Are there any inconsistencies in the value rankings you made in the last activity?

Perceiving the classroom environment. Arthur Combs indicates that our values play an important part in our perceptions. According to his point of view, perception is a process in which sensory inputs are assigned meanings to help us identify and interpret events in our lives. Our values become important to our perceptions because they help us identify and interpret various events. An instructor who values independence will easily identify students who have similar leanings. A teacher who values collaboration may be attracted to books, articles, and seminar announcements that relate to collaborative and group approaches to teaching. Our values act as filters through which we identify and interpret events around us.

Expanding our awareness. Earlier, we asked you to select three value words and to indicate specific classroom and other behaviors they affected. Perhaps your choices included things like goals, emotions, and indications of how you perceive your environment. If not, reconsider what you wrote. Based on the discussion of values presented in this section, can you also think of ways your classroom goals, your emotional reactions to students, colleagues, and administrators, and your perceptions of the classroom environment are affected by the values you listed? Alternately, are you now aware of additional values that affect these responses?

Personal Values and Our Growth as Teachers

Self-awareness

The suggestions and activities in the last section probably helped you identify several specific values that currently influence your teaching. Perhaps you discovered new things about yourself, or perhaps you simply reinforced ideas you have previously considered. It is also possible that your reflections produced some discomfort. On occasion, self-awareness or knowledge has a tendency to do this. Your self-knowledge may have led you to identify a conflict between a belief you espouse and a behavior you engage in. Or you may have discovered issues related to the priorities you have given your values and behavior. Such discrepancies are a very likely outcome whenever we examine our beliefs and our actions. Chris Argyris has documented their rather common occurrence. His research shows that people have a strong tendency to believe one thing and do another. This is true of teachers as well as individuals occupying other roles in our society. Argyris finds that when people become aware of the discrepancy between what they believe and what they do, several reactions are possible. They may recognize the discrepancy exists but do nothing to change it. Or they may try to rationalize it and may even conveniently forget or suppress it. Such reactions may characterize you. What you do with the conflict between beliefs and actions is entirely up to you. Yet there is a creative strategy for dealing with the conflict. *You can recognize the conflict, accept it as an area that needs attention, and begin to search out ways to become more congruent.*

Bernard Beck, a teacher, looks at his own personality and identifies the kind of conflict that we may experience when we look inward:

> I believe that a large part of a teacher's activity is determined by temperament, and that my own practice is more a product of emergent style than rational intention. Nevertheless, my teaching style is not always a reflection of my personality in other settings, and I sometimes have to handle spontaneous reactions in myself which are at odds with my ideas of how I should behave in class [1972, p. 30].

Value questions like the ones Beck has been asking evolve naturally when we become aware of our values. They are the basis for the self-discovery that leads each of us to respond to the questions:

- Who am I as a teacher?

- What role do my values play in my teaching?

- How can I continue to discover and develop the part of me that is a teacher?

We can approach these questions only from our personal frame of reference, remembering, as Robert Goldhammer reminds us, that where one person sees the upholding of academic standards, another sees biased reactionism. Where one sees creative expression in groups, another sees chaos. We tend to see what we look for, based on our past experiences and the values and other beliefs we have developed as a result of those experiences.

Often, my perceptual distortions arise from my tendencies to understand events as I have understood events previously. I fit new things into old patterns, even when the fits are poor. I frequently fuse inferences with perceptions and believe that I have seen things that are invisible, for example, that people like or don't like me. I even think I see invisible relationships, such as in cause-and-effect, and even more often I see "effects" for which I imagine erroneous causes. Whatever I see as figure, I have made figure. To have shifted my gaze thirty degrees would have generated different figures in different ground [Goldhammer, 1969, p. 290].

The view that it is our perceptions of our experiences and of current events in our lives that determine our behaviors has important implications. Our values and other beliefs are important parts of how we interpret such experiences. They provide some of the meaning we attach to experiences and events and therefore are integral parts of our perceptions. Consequently, to improve our teaching we need information about instructional theory and human behavior, knowledge of the research literature on teaching, familiarity with new instructional methods and technologies, information about student needs, and *information about ourselves*. Our values and other personal beliefs affect our behaviors as teachers and are part of any attempts to enhance our instructional processes. Because each of us is responsible for his or her growth as a teacher, self-knowledge becomes an important part of how we guide and direct our growth. Gerry Weinstein describes what happens as a result of self-knowledge:

First of all, when you know yourself you are essentially claiming to be predictable to yourself. The predictability of self-knowledge is exemplified in such statements as "Well, I know that I anger easily," or "I just can't stand children whispering while I'm talking," or "I get very nervous in the presence of an authority figure." These are all examples of predictable, anticipated modes of response to recurring stimuli. . . . The product of self-knowledge is to create more *response-ability*, more choice. . . . Just being able to describe one's habitual pattern will not necessarily lead to more choice. Understanding, clarifying, and admitting to yourself the structure of your response pattern is a necessary, but insufficient condition for creating alternative responses [in Curwin and Fuhrmann, 1975, p. xix].

O.J. Harvey and H.M. Schroder herald self-knowledge in this way:

It would appear axiomatic that he who knows himself best stands a better chance of controlling his environment and his own fate, in the sense of recognizing more clearly means-ends relationships and being able to reach a desired goal by alternate routes [1963, p. 129].

Finally, Lawrence Kubie describes the psychological freedom that is the result of self-knowledge:

Just as the battle for political freedom must be won over and over again, so too in every life the battle for internal psychological freedom must be fought and won again and again, if men are to achieve and retain freedom from the tyranny of their own unconscious process, the freedom to understand the forces which determine their thoughts, feelings, purposes, goals, and behaviors [1966, pp. 70-71].

Clarifying Our Values and Breaking with Our Past

To recognize how values affect various aspects of your role as a teacher is to gain some of the psychological freedom that Kubie describes. They are one of the forces that determine our "thoughts, feelings, purposes, goals, and behaviors." According to Louis Raths, Merrill Harmin, and Sidney Simon, we must go beyond a simple recognition of the influence of our values in our lives. Personal growth also demands that we let go of values that confine us and acquire values that will promote our development. Again, we must reflect upon our personal values to do this. To break with the past, it is helpful to identify values that were forced upon us by the wishes of other people. Typically, these are some of the values we acquired by imitating others, having them moralize about certain principles to us, and getting rewarded for particular beliefs. To acquire new values that promote our development, Raths, Harmin, and Simon argue that we must choose them from among alternatives, prize our choices, and act upon them. We cannot let other people decide for us.

To break from unexamined past behaviors, it is helpful to identify values that may not serve our interests of growing in our roles as teachers. Some of these values can be identified if we think about how we learned them. Let us examine three of the ways of learning values that sometimes restrict our freedom of choice.

Imitating beliefs of others. People whom we imitate include parents, teachers, ministers, neighbors, colleagues, and friends. The influence of modeling beliefs is most easily seen in families and our peer groups. Brian Hall, for example, reports that family members have a high degree of overlap in the values they hold. This is particularly true of beliefs related to the importance of work and the need to provide for the security of oneself and one's family. Of course, the influence of models extends beyond the family. Perhaps you recall teachers who influenced you as a student. You likely chose an advisor or major professor on the basis of your admiration for a given individual. And there are elements of your current teaching behaviors that you acquired from observing your role models.

You may even have been fortunate enough to have had a mentor, a career role model with whom you could identify and who in addition personally guided you and provided career growth opportunities that you otherwise might have missed. Pat Cross, Daniel Levinson, and Gail Sheehy emphasize the importance of such mentors in the development of a personally successful professional style and career.

A major issue in modeling is that both relatively good and bad values can be modeled. There is no guarantee that the people we imitate will always teach us good things, or that what we are taught will lead us to enhance our personal growth as teachers. In spite of their benefits, role models may also lead us to acquire values that confine rather than promote our development in teaching. In particular, we learn values that lead us to use one method of teaching and not to explore alternatives.

Listening to others moralize. At various times in our lives, we encountered people who were more experienced than we were. They often let us know that they were more knowledgeable. Parents, teachers, deans, department heads, and other authorities at some time in our lives have said in effect, "Experience has taught me that certain values are good for me and they will be good for you." A problem is that moralizing does not teach us how to select the best and reject the worst parts of others' beliefs. We run the risk of following such advice blindly, and in the process we become rather unhappy with our behavior. We might accept the belief of a respected dean or department head that "the only way to get ahead in education is to do research. Teaching should be secondary to your primary goal." Yet we may find our classes unstimulating and become bored with teaching in part because we have made it a low priority.

Getting rewarded for demonstrating certain beliefs. Approval, praise, friendship, money, and the opportunity to engage in pleasurable activities are the incentives used by people to reward certain beliefs. A problem is that there is no guarantee that what is rewarded is in the long run in our best interests. It is difficult to develop your own sense of purpose when you are locked into the "drill" of other people.

Think for a moment of the three important beliefs you selected earlier from Table 2.1. What role did imitation learning, moralizing, and rewards play in your acquiring them? Does Table 2.1 contain other beliefs that you developed in these ways? Was the dislike of any of the values you rejected in that activity learned in this way?

Raths, Harmin, and Simon note that imitation learning, moralizing, and obtaining rewards from others are the primary ways most of our personal values are acquired. This presents a problem for our long-term growth as teachers. Such processes do not permit us to examine or think actively about why we believe certain things. Rather, they essentially get us to believe what others think is important. To overcome this problem, these authors suggest we must begin actively to challenge our current beliefs. We need to become better at *choosing* our values. Of course, we may still select as things we like some of the beliefs we acquired by the processes discussed here. *However, the value then becomes more our choice of how we should believe and act, not simply someone else's.*

Clarifying Our Values and Promoting Our Growth as Teachers

Let us examine in more detail the process that Louis Raths, Merrill Harmin, and Sidney Simon suggest will help us acquire values that will promote our growth. To do this, we must again consider some of our current personal values regarding our roles as teachers. They must be evaluated against criteria that reflect whether they were chosen, prized, and acted upon. These three criteria will help us decide which values are likely to promote our personal growth in teaching.

Choosing, prizing, and acting on our values. Complete the following activity to see how each of the three criteria apply to your values. Fold a piece of paper lengthwise, and write only on the left half of the paper. On the left half, number from one through seven. Following each number, identify and write the following (examples are included in parentheses):

1. Something about your teaching life that you have freely chosen, with no coercion from external influences. (For example, one of our colleagues chose to leave the university setting in favor of a small college. The choice was hers alone.)

2. Something in your teaching that you have chosen, knowing that there are viable alternatives. You have consciously decided that the alternatives are not attractive to you. (A professor might choose to teach several different courses rather than multiple sections of one course.)

3. Something in your teaching that you have carefully chosen after thoughtful review of the probable consequences of your choice. (A colleague we know chose one semester to turn in narrative evaluations on students rather than letter grades. He knew the probable outcry that would ensue, but he felt strongly enough about the current grading system to accept the consequences of his challenge.)

4. Something about your teaching that you are especially proud of. (One teacher might be proud of her well-organized syllabi, another of his positive student relationships.)

5. Something about teaching that you feel so strongly about that most of your colleagues know your opinion because you have made it public. (One faculty member might vocally support more stringent grading standards; another might argue for self-paced modules.)

6. Something about teaching that you have supported behaviorally—you've done something about it. (A person who objects to a particular institutional policy might organize a group of like-minded people to propose changes in it.)

7. Something about your teaching that you have been doing, do now, and will continue to do. (The teacher who believes that personal contact is important might make it a habit to learn all students' names within the first several meetings of a class.)

You have identified seven issues or aspects of your teaching that have at least some value to you. Perhaps you included things you had used earlier in the activity at the beginning of this chapter, or possibly some new ideas emerged. Raths, Harmin, and Simon

> . . . see values as constantly being related to the experiences that shape them and test them. They are not, for any one person, so much hard and fast verities as they are the results of hammering out a style of life in a certain set of surroundings. After a sufficient amount of hammering, certain patterns of evaluating and behaving tend to develop. Certain things are treated as right, or desirable, or worthy. These tend to become our values. . . . Because life is different through time and space, we cannot be certain what values, what style of life, would be most suitable for any person. We do, however, have some ideas about what *processes* might be most effective for obtaining values [1966, p. 28].

The general process involves seven specific subprocesses for developing values. In your responses to the exercise just presented, you have used these seven processes, which can be grouped into three major headings:

Choosing

1. *Choosing freely*: The less coercion, the more important and guiding the choice.

2. *Choosing from alternatives*: Without alternatives, there is no choice.

3. *Choosing after thoughtfully considering probable consequences*: Meaningful, life-guiding choices are not made impulsively.

Prizing

4. *Prizing and cherishing*: A value is something held dear, something we are happy and proud to have.

5. *Affirming*: Those things we have freely, thoughtfully, and happily chosen are likely to be those things we are glad to have the world know about.

Acting

6. *Acting on our choices*: Real values serve as guides to life. Without

action, there are no values. The person who says one thing but does another is dealing in unclear values.

7. *Repeating—making life patterns*: Our strongest values appear again and again, serving to pattern our lives in consistent ways.

The strength of any one value can be assessed by checking it against all seven processes. On the right half of your paper, make seven columns and head each one with one of the criteria/processes as shown below.

	Choosing freely	Choosing from alternatives	Thoughtfully considering consequences	Prizing	Affirming	Acting	Repeating

Now reread each of the seven things about your teaching that you previously listed, and in the columns at the right, check each process that is true for each item listed. After doing so, answer the following questions:

- Which of the seven items meet all seven criteria? Do you agree that these items do in fact represent strongly held teaching values for you? Why or why not?

- For any item that does not meet all seven criteria, ask yourself if you would like to make it stronger. If so, how might you do it? If not, why not?

- Think of several other teaching values that you hold, and put them to the seven-criteria test. Or reconsider those you listed in the activities at the beginning of this chapter. Have you chosen each freely? from alternatives? after careful consideration of its consequences? Do you value each? affirm it? act on it? repeat it?

- If things you thought you valued don't meet the test, is there anything you would like to do to change them? What? How might you begin?

The values that meet the criteria have an excellent chance of helping us to grow and develop as teachers. One reason is that only those values we choose remain after this analysis. Those chosen for us by imitation learning, moralizing, and rewards are likely to be eliminated, particularly those that we do not prize and are thus somewhat ashamed to act on. Such an analysis leaves us with an awareness of beliefs we want to use in our actions. They are the beliefs that help us break with the past and that form a foundation for our future actions as teachers.

The real and ideal me. Reflecting on value choices based on an understanding of the valuing process is one way to discover new beliefs and activities that might enhance your role as a teacher. Another process to clarify important values and subsequent activities is to speculate about your current and your ideal teacher characteristics. Implicit in any set of teacher characteristics are personal values. Thus, a focus on such attributes can help us identify both personal values and specific classroom and other role behaviors that are important to us. Considering your current and ideal or possible future characteristics allows you to identify new things to include in your teaching. As a result, it helps you to break with established but unclarified patterns of behavior. Complete the following activity to see how this process works.

Although characteristics of good teachers have been identified, these characteristics often read like a job description for a saint. They don't give us much in the way of realistic images of good, human teachers with unique personalities and distinctive histories. Taking what you know about teaching and about yourself, make up a list of characteristics that you envision as the *ideal you* as a teacher. This list should not include every positive trait that has ever been identified, but rather should represent what for you is actually attainable, you at your best. For example, if you don't see yourself as ever becoming a great humorist, you wouldn't include the use of humor in your list of ideal traits.

When you have completed a list of fifteen to twenty traits, put the list aside. Then on another sheet list fifteen to twenty traits that you currently see in yourself. When you have completed this list, lay the two side by side to begin to make comparisons. Lay yet another sheet of paper between the two lists, and on it indicate what steps you might take to move from your perception of your real teaching self to your perception of your ideal teaching self. List as many steps as possible. Then sort out the steps. Which are long term? short term? easily achieved? Which require some sacrifice? require help from others? For example, one professor we know identified the ability to facilitate lively discussions as a major characteristic of his ideal. On his "real" list he had put, "interested in discussion, but not very good at it." As steps to move from the real to the ideal, he had the following:

- Read several sources on discussion technique.
- Identify three colleagues who are good at discussion and talk with each about it.
- Visit classes of each person identified above.

- Design a question format for leading a discussion on a particular topic.
- Move students into an arrangement conducive to discussion.
- Confer with key students to obtain their perceptions of good discussion techniques.

He then set dates by which to have each step accomplished, and he kept a journal of his progress and new learnings. He recorded each step, dated it, summarized his progress, and noted new steps. He noted unsuccessful or unrealistic steps, and revised them.

As you compare your real and ideal perceptions and identify steps you can take to come closer to your ideal, set your goals. The quest of the ideal is definitely long term, so be considerate of yourself. Set attainable, realistic goals, chronical your progress, and note your achievements one by one. Don't expect considerable change in a short period of time, but be accepting of slow but definite progress. As Richard and Pat Schmuck note, "Behavioral change is very complex, multi-faceted phenomenon involving cognitive change, emotional involvement, behavioral tryouts, and interpersonal feedback" (1979, p. xv).

Identifying personal motivators/satisfactions. Much of our behavior, both within and outside the classroom, is motivated by our needs. Each of us expends considerable energy to acquire psychological satisfactions. Some of the more common motivators include creativity, knowledge, positive relationships, security, prestige, order, leadership, independence, beauty, self-realization, achievement, social service, cooperation, variety, and endurance. Because these motivators help us achieve fulfillment, we come to value them—to believe they are important to us and to act accordingly. Richard and Pat Schmuck highlight how our personal needs interact with classroom processes:

> In real classrooms with real people, plans are often incomplete, problems are difficult to anticipate, and it is almost impossible to consider the psychological states of students when one's own needs as a developing adult are so paramount. Teaching is a difficult activity, especially when one has authentic hopes, goals, and expectations for both students and oneself [1979, p. xv].

Examining the motivators we have come to value helps us to analyze those we are already good at meeting and which we accomplish less well or might want to accomplish better in the future. A possible outcome is to identify other values that might enhance our roles as teachers. Follow the instructions presented to see how this occurs.

Read the list of motivators in Table 2.2. Remember that to the extent

Table 2.2 Personal Motivators and Our Classroom Behaviors

	Teaching Behavior #1	*Teaching Behavior #2*	*Teaching Behavior #3*
1. Creativity: I want to be innovative; I seek new ways to do things.			
2. Knowledge: I enjoy using my knowledge, insight and judgment. I try to learn.			
3. Positive relationships: I want to work closely with others.			
4. Security: I desire to be certain I can do something.			
5. Prestige: I like respect from others. I want to be recognized.			
6. Order: I want to feel organized and have plans.			
7. Influence: I enjoy getting others to listen and follow.			
8. Independence: I like doing things *my* way.			
9. Beauty: I want to add a sense of beauty to my world.			
10. Self-realization: I try to work up to my potential.			
11. Achievement: I want to feel successful.			
12. Social service: I want to help others meet their needs.			
13. Enterprising endeavor: I want to earn a good income.			
14. Cooperation: I want to work in colleagueship with others.			
15. Variety: I need to try new and different things.			
16. Endurance: I want to persist to the completion of the job.			
17. Other:			
18. Other:			

that you regularly try to live by them, they also reflect things you value. As you read this list, ask yourself which are your strongest motivators. In your teaching, how do you satisfy them? The following activity, adapted from one created by Paul Munson, Cliff Garrison, and Jean Saunders, will facilitate your identifying important needs in your life and their influence on your values.

To begin, think of three teaching behaviors that are a regular part of your unique teaching pattern. For example, you might regularly arrive at class a few minutes early and stay a few minutes late to interact informally with students. Or you might always bring a thorough outline, comprehensive notes, and supportive materials to class with you. When you have identified three behaviors that have become patterns for you, use them as column headings on a sheet of paper, as in Table 2.2. Label the rows as indicated.

Analyze each of the behaviors you identified in the column headings against the list of needs. Check each need that is satisfied by each behavior. For example, the person who seeks student interaction would probably check items 3, 12, 14, and perhaps 7; the person who is always thoroughly prepared might check items 4, 6, and 11.

When you have checked the satisfactions you obtained from each of the three behaviors you choose, answer the following questions:

- Which of the needs appear most frequently? Do you agree that these values are important ones to you? If so, in what other ways do you order your life so as to act accordingly?

- Which of the satisfactions that appear infrequently are things you might like to satisfy better in the future? Which of the motives that you did not check would you also like to satisfy more often in the future? What are some things you could do in the classroom and in other aspects of your role as a teacher to accomplish this?

Discussions with colleagues. Although it would seem obvious that open discussions about teaching among colleagues would provide a fertile means of clarifying and developing personal values around pedagogical issues, many faculty are reluctant to engage in such discussions. Bill Berquist and Steve Phillips suggest that the reticence may come from six different sources: (a) faculty usually identify with a discipline rather than with the teaching profession; (b) "academic freedom" suggests no common ground for discussion; (c) with no formal training as teachers, faculty are often uncomfortable and insecure articulating teaching ideas; (d) there is no formal structure for such discussions; (e) time spent with colleagues is usually spent in work not directly related to teaching; and (f) autonomy rather than teamwork is the rule in higher education.

With the institutional norms discouraging dialogue about teaching, individual faculty or groups of faculty will have to assume responsibility for initiating and encouraging such discussions. The following questions are offered as a stimulus for exploring values and attitudes. They should be used in a spirit of inquiry and sharing, a quest that has no wrong answers. You might use those you especially like in informal discussions over lunch, or some might serve as the basis for a more extensive discussion as part of a departmental meeting or seminar.

- What course is working best for you this year? Why?
- How did you decide to become a teacher?
- What do you most enjoy about teaching?
- What do you least enjoy about teaching?
- If you could change one thing about your current assignment, what would it be?
- What do you think is your most outstanding teaching skill?
- How are today's students different from you as a student?
- If you were not teaching, what would you like to be doing?
- What image do you most want students to have of you?
- Who is the best teacher you have ever known? What makes this person great?
- What is the one thing you most want students to learn?
- What is teaching in this department like for you?
- Describe a really successful class you taught recently. What made it successful?
- How have you grown as a teacher since you began teaching?
- Where would you like to be five years from now? What are you doing to get there?
- What one value do you wish all teachers would hold?

Summary

In this chapter we have explored the role that personal values play in teaching. In order to be in control of the influence that our values have on our teaching behavior, we need to be aware both of what those values are and of where they came from. We have seen that values are not static, but in fact evolve through the life processes of making choices, making positive judgments about those choices, and finally acting on them so as to make them into life patterns. Our values arise from our perceptions of both our real selves and the ideal we might become, from abstract concepts we've adopted as our own, from our past experiences, from influential role models, from our unique personalities, through discussion and thought, and from external pressures placed upon us.

The exercises provided were designed to help you identify the sources of your choices and actions and determine their influence on your teaching. But self-awareness is insufficient for growth. You must now use the self-knowledge you've acquired to move toward the goals you've set for yourself. Remember, though, that your goals themselves are useful only so long as they provide the motivation necessary for continual progress. Goals must never be so low that they provide no challenge, so high that only frustration results, so rigid as to force tunnel vision, with the resultant lack of ability to pursue unforeseen avenues.

Personal values are powerful determinants of behavior. With thoughtful attention, they can be positive rather than negative influences.

References

Argyris, C. Theories of action that inhibit individual learning. *American Psychologist,* 1976, *31,* 636–54.

Beck, B. Toward a poor classroom. In B.C. Mathis and W.C. McGaghie, eds., *Profiles in College Teaching.* Evanston, Ill.: Northwestern University, 1972.

Berquist, W.H., and Phillips, S.R. *A Handbook for Faculty Development.* Washington, D.C.: The Council for the Advancement of Small Colleges, 1975.

Combs, A.W.; Richards, A.; and Richards, F. *Perceptual Psychology.* New York: Harper & Row, 1976.

Cross, K.P. *Accent on Learning.* San Francisco: Jossey-Bass, 1976.

Curwin, R., and Fuhrmann, B. *Discovering Your Teaching Self.* Englewood Cliffs, N.J.: Prentice-Hall, 1975.

Davis, J.W. Must teachers love their students? The value structure of the teacher-student relationship. *Teaching-Learning Issues,* 1978, *36,* 1–16.

Goldhammer, R. *Clinical Supervision: Special Methods for the Supervision of Teachers.* New York: Holt, Rinehart and Winston, 1969.

Gordon, T. *P.E.T. in Action.* New York: Wyden, 1976.

Hall, B. *Value Clarification as a Learning Process.* Paramus, N.J.: Paulist Press, 1973.

Harvey, O.J., and Schroder, H.M. Cognitive aspects of self and motivation. In O.J. Harvey, ed., *Motivation and Social Interaction: Cognitive Determinants.* New York: Ronald Press, 1963.

Kirschenbaum, H. *Advanced Value Clarification.* La Jolla, Calif.: University Associates, 1977.

Kubie, L. The forgotten man of education. In Richard Jones, ed., *Contemporary Educational Psychology.* New York: Harper & Row, 1966.

Levinson, D. *The Psychological Development of Men in Early Adulthood and the Mid-life Transition.* Minneapolis: University of Minnesota Press, 1974.

Munson, P.; Garrison, C.; and Saunders, J. *The Career Motivation Program.* Richmond, Va.: Career Growth Associates, 1976.

Oden, T. *Contemporary Theology and Psychotherapy.* Philadelphia: Westminster, 1967.

Raths, L.; Harmin, M.; and Simon, S. *Values and Teaching.* Columbus, Ohio: Charles E. Merrill, 1966.

Rokeach, M. Change and stability in American value systems. In Rokeach, M., ed. *Understanding Human Values: Individual and Societal.* New York: Free Press, 1979.

Rokeach, M. Persuasion that persists. *Psychology Today*, September, 1971.

Schmuck, R.A., and Schmuck, P.A. *Group Processes in the Classroom*, 3rd ed. Dubuque, Iowa: Wm. C. Brown, 1979.

Sheehy, G. *Passages.* New York: E.P. Dutton, 1976.

Simon, S.; Howe, L.; and Kirschenbaum, H. *Values Clarification.* New York: Hart, 1972.

Chapter 3
Cognitive Perspective on Learning: Classroom Applications

In this and the following chapter, we consider three widely known approaches to understanding human behavior, and examine what they say about how people learn. They are the cognitive, behaviorist, and humanistic perspectives. Associated with each are certain principles and concepts regarding learning, and various classroom practices are often suggested based on them. However, before we consider the implications of each perspective, it is important to note the following points regarding learning theory and teaching regardless of specific viewpoint.

Issues in Developing Theories of Learning and Teaching

A particular learning theory does not and cannot specify all aspects of the practice of teaching. Most theories of learning originally were developed to understand behaviors in laboratory and clinical settings. Principles and concepts were then applied to educational environments. The real life of the classroom is quite different from the rather controlled environment of the clinic or laboratory. In most cases the results in the laboratory or clinical setting will generalize to classrooms, but they are not necessarily completely transferable. William James, in a series of talks to Cambridge teachers in 1892, illustrated this problem quite well.

> You make a great, a very great mistake, if you think that psychology, being the science of the mind's law, is something from which you can deduce definite programmes and schemes and methods of instruction for immediate schoolroom use. Psychology is a science; and teaching is an art; and sciences never generate arts directly out of themselves. An intermediary intuitive mind must make the application by using its originality. . . . A science only lays down the lines within which the rules of art must fall, laws which the follower of the art must not transgress; but what particular thing he shall positively do within those lines is left exclusively to his own genius [James, 1979, pp. 22–23].

Sometimes we need to "stretch" the principles and concepts specified by a particular approach to learning to make them applicable to the classroom.

The validity of an educational practice does not depend on its having a theoretical basis. Certain practices seem to work without theory to support them. Montessori's educational ideas are quite successful and are compatible with Jean Piaget's views of cognitive development—but they preceded the theory. The same is true of certain practices each of us subscribes to in the classroom. We are hard pressed to fine a coherent theory to provide a rationale for fifty-minute lectures, final exams, or term papers. As Frank Murray notes, this issue is with us even when theory may suggest the practice. He states:

> The validity of educational practice is not guaranteed by its plausibility within nor its conformity to psychological theory, even when the builders of the theory have created the educational technique. No better example of this exists than B.F. Skinner's programmed instructions innovation. Although a proven effective teaching technique—often as effective as a classroom teacher—it appears surprisingly not to lose that effectiveness when various theoretical requirements Skinner placed on it are violated [1979, p.32].

There is no single theory of learning that will account for the complexity of the classroom learning environment. The goal of developing a unified learning theory is desirable, but such a theory does not exist today. Instead we have many different theories, or models, to account for how people learn. Grouping them into cognitive, behaviorist, and humanistic categories is convenient, but it is done with the recognition that each category contains great variety. Not all behaviorists, humanists, or cognitive theorists think alike. The information processing approach discussed in this chapter, for example, is one of several types of cognitive theory. In some cases, there may even be some overlap across categories when particular models are considered. For example, the recent developments in cognitive behaviorism extend into two of our convenient categories.

No single perspective will suffice to understand classroom learning processes. Any one position provides less than a completely satisfactory explanation. At the least, all three perspectives in combination are needed to appreciate the complexity of the student learning experience. An eclectic approach is desirable to understand the complexity of human learning.

In this chapter, we present a summary of the principles and concepts of cognitive theory known as the information processing viewpoint. The specific practices that reflect such principles and concepts are also illustrated. Whenever possible, we have included the results of relevant research to support a particular practice. Our presentation in both this and the following chapter is organized in terms of how each perspective treats student motivation and factors that facilitate learning. This will help make comparisons among the three perspectives easier. Finally, to facilitate thinking about the applications of each perspective to your teaching, we suggest you complete the integrative activity at the end of the following chapter.

Information Processing Perspective on Learning

An Overview

One way to examine human learning is to focus on the cognitive processes used within the learner. Such cognitive emphases in the study of human learning are pervasive in the current research literature in psychology and education. As with other approaches to human learning, such as the behaviorist and the humanistic, there are variations on the cognitive perspective. Glenn Snelbecker, and Bruce Joyce and Marsha Weil, note that each approach differs in the aspects of our thought processes emphasized in describing how learning takes place. Yet all of them agree that thinking, language, decision making, and problem solving are important parts of the learning process.

In this chapter, we will emphasize the cognitive approach sometimes identified as the information processing point of view. According to Glenn Snelbecker, this point of view is concerned with how sensory input is transformed, reduced, elaborated, stored, recovered, and used. The use of this information is defined as the ways in which it helps us solve problems and make decisions. To understand information processing, we need to know something about the effects on learning of such things as the organization of information, our ability to attend to sources of information, and the functioning of our memory and thought process in the storage, organization, and retrieval of information.

To apply ideas from the information processing point of view, it is necessary to remember two things. One is that just as cognitive theory has several variations, so too does the information processing point of view within cognitive theory. Thus it is necessary to choose apsects of various positions before one can talk about applications. Second, the study of how we process information is typically a highly theoretical enterprise, and practical applications are not always spelled out explicitly. This is particularly true when the intent of the research is to refine a theoretical idea about how some part of our information processing system operates. Thus a concept must sometimes be "stretched" a bit to suggest application. We have both stretched concepts and selected applicable theories in this section.

In doing so, we have identified a general view of information processing that is held by a variety of theorists. In line with such concepts, we note that people are active seekers of new information and skills. They do not need a great many external incentives to use their cognitive processes. Individuals rely on attention and memory mechanisms to perceive, organize, store, and retrieve information they need for a given task. How people do such things reflects a certain amount of stability in the preferences they have for processing information. Such stable patterns are called cognitive learning styles, and they are also important influences on a student's behavior in the classroom. Let us now examine each of the factors that affect the motivation of students and those that facilitate students' acquiring information and developing cognitive skills.

Motivating the Students

Information processing, and cognitive theories in general, do not see students as passive learners. Although external incentives may be important, especially in the early stages of learning, people are quite able to monitor their own actions. The most productive incentives are those that are internally controlled. Learners try to solve problems and to make decisions from among alternative points of view or courses of action. Whenever they are faced with a problem or the need to make a decision, they automatically try to resolve the issue. Such challenges help people focus their thoughts to find solutions. The "carrots" provided by external incentives are less important in motivating the learner. People are basically active learners who naturally respond to the challenges and problems they face.

The assumption that we are active learners who respond to challenges is one way cognitive theorists explain the initiation, direction, and persistence of our actions. Another assumption is that our cognitive processes are in themselves responsible for motivating our actions. The things we say to ourselves play an important role in classroom behaviors. Richard deCharms notes that students who see themselves as what he calls "origins" believe they personally cause their behaviors and decide to act from personal commitment; they also have higher levels of academic achievement. Those who see themselves as "pawns"—who think that something or someone else causes their actions—are less effective in the classroom. The former beliefs give students hope that what they do will make a difference; the latter beliefs often lead to a sense of helplessness. Reiling also finds that people with internal orientations think somewhat differently on cognitive tasks than do those with external orientations. People who believe they control what happens to them are better at thinking in terms of hypotheses and propositions than are those who see their rewards in life as dependent on external factors. Thus thoughts about what controls behavior, the value of personal effort in classrooms, and whether we can influence events around us can be important motivating beliefs for students.

Reinforcement is deemphasized by information processing and other cognitive theorists, but it is not completely ignored. Rather than viewing reinforcement as a variable that automatically influences our actions, they are interested in how our beliefs and thoughts modify its influence. Edward Deci and Mark Lepper and David Greene, for example, report that external reinforcers may sometimes undermine a student's interest in learning. When given rewards for performing tasks they find intrinsically interesting, students lose interest once they come to believe that external rewards are controlling their actions. Furthermore, our thoughts affect the value we place on a particular reinforcer. Some students find that grades and the approval of the instructor are extremely important for their ability to learn; others care very little about such things. Varying the reward structure of the classroom will have a much greater effect on the former group of students. Finally, how a particular reinforcer affects us depends on what we tell ourselves it represents. Walter Mischel was able to get hungry nursery school children and graduate students to delay eating marshmallows and pretzels placed in front of them by giving instructions to imagine they were "white clouds" and "logs," respectively. Such instructions had a similar effect on both groups. Nursery school children and graduate students were able to delay eating the treats for an average of six minutes without the instructions, and fourteen minutes with the instructions. One might have expected graduate students to wait longer, but this study and others suggest that beliefs modify the effects of reinforcers regardless of the age of the student.

Learning theorists like Jerome Bruner, Jean Piaget, Guy Manaster, and Jeanette Gallagher argue that teachers motivate students best when they tap their natural ability to attempt to solve problems and make decisions. Students will have a greater interest in learning if instructors create an atmosphere where students are challenged to inquire and discover for themselves the answers to important content questions. In such settings, a teacher's behaviors are oriented towards developing materials and course formats that will maximize opportunities for such learning to occur.

To develop such materials and formats effectively, some knowledge of what cognitive activities students are capable of at a particular time in their lives is helpful. According to Jean Piaget, the cognitive functions we can perform vary with our age. His theory includes a series of invariant stages through which people pass. The childhood stages are universal; although they can be influenced by teaching, everyone of normal intelligence achieves and passes through them. For several years prior to adolescence, people think according to what Piaget calls "concrete operations," and without specific teaching to move out of this stage, individuals will remain at this level for life. In high school and college, then, some students are still at the concrete operational stage, in which the tangible, the real, and the provable are attended to. Simultaneously, however, learners are beginning to be able to think at the next and highest stage, formal operations.

Guy Manaster describes this stage:

> The concrete, clear, tangible basis for thinking about an issue is still available and used, as in the concrete operations stage. However, as formal operations develop, the [learner] finds that new perspectives open as thought operates from the base of possibilities, hypotheses, and propositions. This may be tremendously exciting, but may also be somewhat frightening. It sometimes has the feeling of whole new worlds opening, and, as with all adventures, new cognitive adventures have their pitfalls [1977, p. 38–39].

Formal operations are characterized by three specific thinking processes, but these processes must be encouraged and developed through active teaching, without which they will not grow. First, the formal operational students must be jarred out of tangible thinking into the realm of possibility and improbability. Second, the formal operational student needs encouragement to deduce the consequences from hypotheses, which may or may not be true, as if they were true. Third, the student must be challenged to manipulate ideas, to juggle intellectual relationships, and to consider alternate potentials.

Piaget is a "constructivist," by which we mean that in his theory, every individual creates his or her own knowledge. Learning is neither the acquisition of information nor the discovery of knowledge, but in reality the *re-creation* of them. Learners do not learn by copying the experiences of others, but by reacting to experiences in meaningful ways. Piaget emphasizes especially that training in formal operational processes may be most important for older adolescents and adults, who have developed the physiological maturational structures to become formal operational thinkers but who often have not had sufficient interactive experiences to develop the necessary thinking processes.

Without the ability to reason formally, people are locked into merely repeating the learning of previous generations. It is only by use of formal reasoning that both creative thought and constructive criticism become possible. Thus the teacher becomes responsible for helping students develop the formal reasoning process, not for simply passing on old knowledge.

Along similar lines, Jeanette Gallagher and Illene Noppe note that:

> In sum, the educator must view Piaget's theory as a new stress on the teaching of process whereby the [learner] uses his potential for the search for alternative solutions and the avoidance of quick and obvious solutions [1976, p. 227].

Piaget's ideas remind us that students should be encouraged to take alternate points of view. They need to explore as many sides of an issue as possible and to get into the habit of generating different alternatives and solutions to problems. In this way, their ability to hypothesize, to examine possibilities, and to consider alternate propositions is enhanced. Students must also be encouraged to discover and create rather than merely to assimilate what the teacher gives them. This makes them active learners who challenge the information. Finally, students should be encouraged to attempt new procedures to help them learn. They need to have access to alternative teaching styles and modes of studying and learning.

Piaget, like other cognitive theorists, views the task of motivating the learner as something that is best done by challenging the student to process information in an active fashion. What follows are specific suggestions for motivating students, based on the discussion of cognitive processes in this section.

Integrating critical thinking. Most writers on cognitive approaches to teaching suggest that one way to enhance learners' motivation is to provide them with opportunities for critical thinking—in other words, for developing formal operations. Such opportunities should not be something you provide on an exam or through an occasional discussion question, but should be made available on a consistent basis. There are, of course, many ways to accomplish this. We now present two examples that are applicable to a variety of courses and disciplines.

- *The adversary approach.* John Furedy and Christine Furedy suggest that complex skills like critical thinking do not simply "rub off" on learners as they pass through successively higher levels of undergraduate courses. They propose a course design that used adversaries to challenge a student's ideas. Each student who entered the course was required to do a research project. Initial ideas for the project were selected early, and class sessions revolved around students presenting their ideas and having others in class critique them. Furthermore, each student met with the course instructor who challenged his or her ideas about the initial design of the project and, later on, the specific ideas the student developed. The final project was then sent to a department colleague, who acted as a journal editor and provided another critique of the project. At each stage of the project, students had to respond to the comments of their peers, the instructor, and, finally, the editor-reviewer. Although this model was employed in a psychology undergraduate research seminar, it has much more general applicability. Courses where laboratory projects, term papers, library research, or even short stories are required might find creating the adversary relationship a way to promote critical thinking.

- *Teaching as an inductive activity.* Hilda Taba provides a classroom model that helps students form concepts, interpret data, and think of applications of principles discussed in class. She places a high degree of emphasis on teachers' using questions to elicit responses from students. Whenever possible, with either the entire class or small groups, Taba suggests that teachers encourage students to think for themselves by integrating the following philosophy into their instructional practices.

  Students need encouragement to form concepts. It can be provided by presenting them with a problem, a key statement, or some issue for which there is no correct solution. They would be required to list individually the ideas they have and then to share them, either in small groups or with the entire class. The ideas of the various students would be listed together on the board or on newsprint. The instructor would then ask questions like "What belongs together?" "What criteria do you have for grouping certain ideas together?" "What would you call these groups?" "Which categories you formed seem more or less important as solutions to the problem?" "Which ones would you select as a solution?" The goal is to help students make decisions and organize their thoughts to form concepts that will help them solve problems.

  Students need practice interpreting data. Taba argues that instructors tend to do too much interpreting of the world for students. This does little to encourage students to think critically. As part of teaching, instructors should present ideas and data and have the students make interpretations that are discussed in class. Questions like the following might be directed toward the class or subgroups of students working together: "What did you notice of interest to you in the information I presented?" "Why did you think that the events I listed occurred?" "What picture does it create in your mind?" "What would you conclude about the issues?"

Students should be taught to apply principles. Application might involve discussing the "real world" uses of the information, but it can also involve teaching students to predict events, form hypotheses, explain unfamiliar phenomena, and think of ways to verify their thoughts about the implications of a set of concepts. Appropriate questions directed toward the class or small groups of students working together on issues would encourage this to occur: "What would happen if . . . ?" "Why do you think certain things would occur?" "What would it take for you to be able to verify that your response was generally true or false?"

Taba suggests that questions like these must be used on an ongoing basis in the classroom. When they know they must respond and that the teacher will pay attention to their responses, students begin to think critically. This not only makes them more effective as learners, it also enhances their motivation to learn.

Using problem solving. Cognitive learning theories see the challenges presented by problems and issues we face as an important factor in our motivation. Anything we might do to encourage problem solving and decision making will enhance the interest of the learner in the content of the class. Several things might be tried to accomplish this.

- *Use case studies in the classroom.* Some schools, such as the Harvard Business School, have become famous for their use of the case study approach. Law schools and professional schools in medicine, psychiatry, psychology, and management typically make use of case studies. This gives the student a chance to apply what they already know and learn and develop new principles and concepts related to the discipline. Case studies are not reserved for graduate or professional training; they can be used in any discipline. Students might be given cases that relate to a national emergency or event, or the development of a new electronic product. Newspaper articles, magazine stories, journal articles, the experiences of the instructor, and chapters from books can be combined to provide a case study. Groups of two or three students might be assigned the task of developing cases that are then analyzed by other members of the class. Or the instructor might put several together and use them in class. Although entire classes can be taught using cases, cases are valuable when used on an occasional basis as well.

- *Develop problems for students to solve.* Although this is often done in mathematics courses and those in the physical sciences, every discipline has problems that students might be asked to try to solve. This can consist of taking a position on an important issue, writing a paper on a problem in the discipline, or simply discussing an important unresolved issue in class. In recent years, the EXXON Educational Foundation has funded innovative course designs that are useful across a variety of disciplines. One of them is called Guided Design and employs a problem-solving format for teaching in a variety of areas. The format has students learn how to define problems properly, generate alternate solutions, defer judgments when necessary, and select final responses after considering criteria for a solution. A detailed description of how to do this and suggestions for how to use the process in your discipline can be obtained by writing to the foundation.

External reinforcers alone are unlikely to provide sufficient incentives for students to learn. As we noted earlier in this section, providing incentives for students is a tricky business. Cognitive theories generally have called attention to factors other than external incentives as important motivators of our actions. The things we say to ourselves, our sense of personal control over events, and how we interpret various reinforcers affect our level of motivation. In the literature, there are few specific suggestions for how to take such things into account in college classrooms. Our experiences, however, suggest several things that you might consider doing that are consonant with ideas in the research.

- *"I think I can, I think I can."* A famous children's story has a small train engine haul several stranded freight cars up a steep hill. The little engine accepted the challenge after much bigger engines refused to try. The engine first convinced itself that it could do the job. We find the opposite with certain students. They enter a class convinced that they will do poorly or that they almost certainly will have a difficult time mastering the information. In some respects, they are defeated before they begin. A strategy we have found useful is to make students have a success experience with the material. This is done by simplifying difficult concepts and teaching them at a slower pace in class. Frequent quizzes are also given on the information, with an option to retake them if performance is below a certain level. Such quizzes are five to ten minutes in duration. Thus students can practice mastering important pieces of the information before a major exam occurs. The remedial option gives everyone a chance to learn from their previous mistakes. For some students, this is a confidence builder.

- *Have students participate in course design.* We have had students help us design entire courses or part of a course to meet their needs. This included input on grading procedures, term papers, classroom demonstrations and exercises, and the content of particular presentations. They have even written questions that were included on exams. Using small-group procedures, we have had them teach information to their peers and work on projects that were later presented in class. An important goal throughout was to increase their perceptions of personal control over classroom events. It takes more time to design a course with student input and participation, but we find the results in increased student motivation to learn well worth the extra effort.

- *Deemphasize grades and grading practices.* We are not suggesting that you stop grading students. We find, rather, that too much emphasis is placed on the grade in a course. Instructors tell students, "Your grade depends on this," "Please listen, this will be on the test," "I'm a harsh grader," or "Some of you will not get a good grade in this course unless . . ." Such statements stress a course grade as an important incentive. Yet research suggests that it may undermine the intrinsic motivation some students show for the content of the course. We find it helpful to state a course grade policy the first day of class and not bring it up again. Allowing students to contract for a grade as described in the section on behavioral approaches also lets students select a level of performance that is comfortable for them. Their course performance is oriented around things they "elected to choose" and not simply things the instructor chose for them. Finally, the use of pass-fail options, written assessments of a student's strengths and weaknesses, or detailed ratings of performance instead of letter grades helps to deemphasize the importance of letter grades. The use of written assessments and detailed ratings of performance may also encourage instructors to give specific and detailed feedback to students. Examples of such procedures are presented in Chapter 7.

The practices described in the preceding paragraph can lead students to think less about the controlling influence of grades in their academic lives. Some cognitive theorists suggest that this may lead to students' developing more of an intrinsic interest in the information.

Facilitating the Acquisition of Information

Attention. "I'm about to pull my hair out," a colleague remarked to one of us. "I've a student in my chemistry lab who is unbelievable. She gets good grades in class, but I have to tell her things repeatedly. In particular, her behaviors in the lab section bother me. I gave the class instructions today, and she later called me aside and said she did not hear what I said. So I repeated them for her and assumed she now knew what to do. About thirty minutes later, she was still fumbling around and told me she had missed some of what I said earlier. So I had to explain the task to her all over again. I'm really frustrated."

Most of us would conclude, correctly, that the student was not paying attention. From a cognitive learning point of view, deficiencies in paying attention are extremely important in hindering our ability to learn. Attending to relevant information is a first step in producing relatively permanent changes in our behaviors, yet many of the instructors and students we know tend to overlook how important it is. Teachers tend to assume that much of what they present in class will capture a student's attention. Similarly, students assume that if they attend class, they can't help but focus on important content. Neither view is entirely correct. Although we automatically attend to some kinds of stimulation, we can also miss much of the information that is presented. Our ability to attend to relevant information is not always an automatic event that demands relatively little effort.

The more that students and teachers assume that it will happen without special effort, the less likely students are to obtain the information necessary to learn. As the chemistry lab example illustrates, there are implications for the teacher and student in failures to attend. An instructor may question his or her competence, become frustrated, or constantly wonder "why they don't get it the first time." Students may experience a lower level of achievement in class and feel somewhat helpless to do anything about it. Research in cognitive learning processes suggests that there are things teachers can do to overcome such problems—to present classroom information more effectively and to train students to pay attention. Following are several ideas we have found useful in overcoming attention problems, including characteristics of attention that instructors must take into account when presenting information. Along with them, we make several suggestions to apply in the classroom.

A student's ability to pay attention drifts. People are able to concentrate on almost any stimulus or part of a classroom presentation for short amounts of time, but seldom can we give our undivided attention to anything for extended time periods. Daydreaming, being fatigued, entertaining other thoughts, possessing a low interest in the information, believing the content is not very important, and just needing a break take their toll in classrooms and other areas of our lives. Jane Mackworth notes that twenty to thirty minutes seems to be the maximum amount of time the average person can attend to a task before attention begins to drift seriously.

Although this is a normal reaction, students can be encouraged to enhance their ability to concentrate. We have found the following useful.

- *Give students a break.* A two- to three-minute "stretch break" every half hour and ten to fifteen minutes every hour and a half give a welcomed rest from having to listen to a presentation. Standing up and moving around forces people to attend to other stimuli, and we find that this breaks the fatigue that is building up.

- *Ask students a question.* This takes them from the role of passive receivers of information to a more active role. At least twice in every half hour of instruction, give the class a question to answer. Instead of directing it toward a single student, ask everyone to jot down an idea for an answer and then call on a few people. Specific questions typically work best, because the goal is to help students focus on the content and you don't want to take up too much class time.

- *Have students paraphrase, summarize, ask you a question, or make a comment on what was said.* To keep the class with you and to get them to take a more active role when listening to information, periodically stop and ask a couple of people to paraphrase or summarize what you have just said. Or take a couple of minutes and ask everyone to write a question or comment on a separate sheet of paper regarding your remarks thus far. Then call on selected people. You might ask for a paraphrase or summary a couple of times during a one-hour presentation. Having students ask a question or develop a comment is a good task during a "stretch break" or while on an extended break. They can think about a response, and you can use their responses to lead back into the content presentation.

- *Check notebooks periodically.* We are amazed at the discrepancies that sometimes occur between what was said and what students write in their notes. Lapses in attention are certainly responsible for some of the errors. When we point out inaccuracies, it lets students know that they need to concentrate more in class. Such checks do not have to be done with the whole class at once. Randomly spot checking four or five notebooks a week and concentrating on the past week's notes is usually sufficient. This is particularly true if you announce some of the errors you found. Other people will make the necessary corrections in their notes if they have a similar problem. Spot checking will also help people become more accurate—they may want to avoid the embarrassment of having the instructor find errors in their notes again.

Things that change capture our attention. We typically tire of stimuli that do not vary. Some theorists, such as William Dember, stress that our lives focus around accommodating to (getting used to) certain levels of stimulation and then seeking new levels of stimulation. People prefer variety in their environments, and the classroom environment is no exception. Instructors stand a much better chance of holding their students' attention if the level of stimulation is manipulated. This can be done in several ways.

- *Create movement.* An instructor standing in the same place and presenting information can become monotonous for students. A colleague humorously asked me just before he entered the classroom what I could tell him to do differently in his class. I asked him if he moved around, and he said no. I suggested that he walk around the room, including taking trips up and down the aisles as he talked. Several students reported afterward that it was one of his best classes.

  A similar principle applies to students. They tire of sitting in the same place all the time. Discussion and buzz groups that meet in different parts of the room help. Have people join groups that meet in places removed from their current seats.

- *Use novelty.* There are, of course, various ways to create novelty in the environment of the classroom. The goal is to let students sense that "something's different" today. Several things that are easy to do include: have students stand around in small groups to hold a discussion instead of sitting in their seats; use multicolored chalk instead of white chalk on the board; bring in a guest speaker; role play a famous person in your field while lecturing about that person; hold class for twenty minutes and dismiss everyone except those who want to remain for a discussion; show a movie; videotape a presentation instead of delivering it live. Changing anything from the normal way you do it creates novelty. We have presented simply a few relatively easy things to do that create novelty.

- *Vary intensity.* The goal here is to make the information you are presenting stand out better. Varying the rate, tone, and inflection of your voice will help. Listing major points on a board or handout also helps ensure that people will notice them; this is particularly true if they are printed in large letters so they really stand out. Periodically presenting information that is a bit more difficult than usual will also accomplish this goal. Of course, it also helps to leave enough time for questions afterward.

- *Repeat the information.* Within limits, repetition helps to maintain attention, but too much repetition may have just the opposite effect. Repeating each major point two or three times helps. This is particularly true if you can vary the way you repeat it. Listing the major points in a summary sheet that is passed out after class is another way to build in repetition.

- *Present information that in part meets the students' needs and interests.* People pay attention to things that are personally relevant. Trying to relate course content to the lives of the students or to things in their environment helps. This might range from talking about chemical reactions in terms of environmental pollution issues to helping students apply something to a personal problem. Although not everything we present can and should be made personally relevant, students appreciate it when some attempts are made to do this periodically.

- *Use study guides to orient a student's attention to important information.* A device we have found useful is to give students study guides. Such guides point out key concepts, terms, and issues that they are expected to know. The guides can be developed for the textbook, lectures, or outside readings. Class exam questions are selected from a sample of the information contained in the guides. Such devices help to focus a student's attention on important concepts. An added benefit is that they see themselves as responsible for not doing well on the exam. Instead of blaming the teacher for a "trick" or "unfair" exam, they have only themselves to blame. The content of the exam was given beforehand. Typically, the study guides are passed out at the beginning of a new topic. We have also found that students perform better on exams and appreciate having the course content structured in this way. An example of one study guide for a textbook chapter is presented in Table 3.1.

Memory. How is information retained and later retrieved for our use? The answer to this question is rather complex, because there are many different points of view regarding how our retention system operates. Although all cognitive theorists consider memory a key element in how we process information, they differ in how they describe our memory processes. Variations on two major themes appear in the literature. One point of view, taken by Nancy Waugh, Donald Norman, and Arthur Melton, suggests that people have three interconnected memory systems. They are called the sensory register, short-term memory, and long-term memory.

The *sensory register* typically operates whenever we are presented with information. It is a brief visual or auditory trace of the information we are asked to learn. For example, if during an experiment you were given a brief visual presentation of the stimulus display shown following this paragraph, you would maintain a visual representation of it for about 1.5 seconds. During that time, you could tell someone what letter was present at a particular row and column coordinate (such as row 3, column 3). The sensory register decays rapidly and is thought to represent a preliminary stage of our short-term memory.

Table 3.1. A Sample Study Guide

Introduction to Psychology
Study Guide: Chapter 1—Understanding Psychology: Introduction

After reading the chapter, answer each of the following questions. You will probably find you need to review the text to help you develop appropriate responses.

Briefly identify and/or define the following:

psychology	APA
Wilhelm Wundt	Jean Piaget
1879	developmental psychology
conscious experience	experimental psychology
introspection	psychophysics
Sigmund Freud	industrial psychologist
unconscious processes	psychopharmacologist
free association	personality psychology
Francis Galton	androgyny
individual differences	social psychology
Ivan Pavlov	clinical psychology
conditioned reflex (and its importance to psychology)	basic science
	applied science
behaviorist	psychiatrist
John B. Watson	psychologist
B.F. Skinner	psychoanalyst

Short essay questions

Please answer in a paragraph whenever possible:

What are the "orgins" of psychology (prior to 1879)?

What is the heredity-environment controversy? Offer some examples both from the text and from your own experiences.

Argue both positively and negatively (in favor of and in opposition to) the basic science approach to the study of psychology.

John and Frank, formerly high school friends, run into each other one day after not having seen each other for several years. Frank discovers that John's wife is a psychologist. Frank discloses that he has been suffering from uncontrollable sweating and insomnia (inability to sleep). Frank asks John to ask his wife for an appointment to get a prescription for some tranquilizers. Based on information in the text, what do you think John would say? Why?

P O A D X
M T C Y R
G I O W Q

Our *short-term memory* takes information from the sensory register and transforms it into an acoustic code. Perhaps you have heard the expression "echoes of your mind." This acoustic code stores information for a relatively short amount of time and has limits on how much can be stored. Short-term memory for something that is presented once lasts for about

30 seconds and has a limited capacity of seven plus or minus two units of information. That is, after a single presentation, about five to nine items of information can be retained for a relatively short time period. How long something can be retained and how much is retained can be increased by rehearsing it and forming meaningful categories. Thus, having someone repeat information to you or repeating it to yourself will help increase its short-term retention. Think how you remember a phone number for more than 30 seconds after someone gives it to you and before you write it down. You simply repeat it to yourself a number of times. Along similar lines, if you were given numbers, words, or concepts that exceeded the five-to-nine limits on short-term memory storage capacity, you might form categories. Thus, the digits 345987636974321 become 345-987-636-974-321, or five categories instead of fifteen items. Putting information into meaningful categories helps us overcome the limitations of short-term memory.

Long-term memory is the third memory system that some theorists propose to account for how we retain and later retrieve information. Information is taken from short-term memory and transformed into a memory code that is based on meaning. We assign meaning to information by the labels we assign to it and the use of mental imagery. Thus a concept like *table* has a verbal label and an imagery code to help us remember it. A more abstract concept like *theoretical* might have only a verbal label. Gordon Bower suggests that the presence of both a verbal label and an imagery code helps explain why concrete concepts are remembered better than more abstract concepts. Unlike short-term memory, our long-term memory system is thought to have an unlimited capacity. Once information enters long-term memory, it stays there forever. Our failure to remember something is not due to the information dropping out of the system. Rather, memory losses reflect a problem with our ability to retrieve. We find ourselves with a lack of access to the information.

Think of storage in long-term memory as similar to the storage of books on shelves in a library. We might not find a particular book because we look in the wrong place or it was initially misfiled. Thus we can improve our long-term memories by giving information good "call numbers" (strong verbal and imagery codes) or by searching the "shelves" properly. To do the latter, we need to have good retrieval cues. Forgetting where you took a vacation three years ago might be remedied by reconstructing your vacations over the past two years and the events leading up to your vacation three years ago. Reconstructing the context in which we did something is one way to increase the chances of our retrieving it. Or thinking of a partial cue may allow us to remember the item we have forgotten. Have you tried to remember the name of someone you are seeing again? You say to yourself, "I'm not sure what her name is. Let's see, it sounds like marr but that's not it. Mary—no. Maureen—no. Marylou—yes, that's it."

The second theme used by cognitive theorists to explain memory is called *levels of processing*. For example, Fergus Craik argues that there is no need to think of our retention system as having three interconnected subsystems. Such a view implies that we are rather passive recipients of information and that information is somehow shuttled from one subsystem to another. Instead, it is better to view our ability to remember as an active process in which we analyze information at various levels and, if needed, reconstruct it for later use. How deeply we process the information determines how well we will be able to remember it. For example, the rapid forgetting of information presented once is due to the rather shallow acoustic analysis we give to it. The persistence we notice in long-term memory occurs because the information was processed to a deeper semantic level.

Processing information to a deeper level means two things. One is that we have attached relevant semantic and imagery codes to it. This may occur automatically, or we may need to think about the information in order to do this well. In addition, according to Jean Piaget, we try to assimilate or accommodate new information into our existing memory systems. If new information is relevant to what is already included in our memory, we assimilate it. If not, we create a new structure to accommodate it. In the latter case, the information may not be stored as well, or the retrieval paths may not be as well established or as good. Processing information to a deeper level helps us attach meaning to it and thus enhances our memory for the content over long periods of time. We are then in a better position to reconstruct the information when asked to do so.

Although information processing theorists differ on how to describe the operation of our memory systems, there are implications in the various viewpoints for classroom application. Several applications that follow from the characteristics of our retention system are listed below.

- *Repeat information.* Earlier we suggested that repeating information within limits will aid a student's ability to pay attention. Based on our discussion of memory processes, it should be clear that it also will assist a student's short-term memory. A class session can be viewed as a number of connected but somewhat discrete presentations of different pieces of information. The ability to take accurate notes, to ask a question on the content, to answer a question by the instructor, or to express a comment at any given moment is influenced by how well a student's short-term memory operates. We know from the research that our short-term memory tends to decay rapidly unless there is repetition of the information. An instructor who emphasizes each major point two or three times helps a student repeat it as well. More important, asking students to paraphrase what you are saying in their notebooks would be even more beneficial. It makes them take an active role with relation to the information presented.

Possible benefits include more accurate notes and the ability of the student to use the information in answering or asking questions regarding the content.

- *Suggest organizing devices for the content.* We know that short-term memory has a limited capacity that can be expanded if information is categorized in a meaningful way. Similarly, long-term memory is affected by how much meaning is assigned to information. Having information well organized and placed into convenient categories should enhance a student's both short- and long-term memories. This can be done in class by organizing presentations so that information clusters in particular categories. These might be historical periods, particular theoretical points of view, or key concepts that seem to organize the major points. Encouraging students to use these categories or to form others is helpful. In the latter case, students might be asked to organize the lecture notes, textbook readings, outside readings, or other sources of information into a system in which content from various sources is organized into convenient categories. Because the students form the relevant categories, such a task should help them remember the information better.

Another way to help students organize the information is through the use of objectives. Behavioral objectives are illustrated in the section on behavioral approaches to learning theory. In the process of specifying the things students are expected to learn, we should not overlook the value of objectives in helping students organize the information. Such objectives may be especially useful with learners who are unfamiliar with the organization of the material or who need structure.

Finally, *advanced organizers* help students process and remember information better. David Ausubel defines an advanced organizer as *a device that precedes a presentation on a topic and helps the learner develop a context for the information.* It can be any idea, image, recollection, or abstraction that will help to organize what is to follow for the learner. The organizer can be a statement, a descriptive paragraph, a question, a demonstration, or even a film or slide and tape presentation. The form is less important than that it be clearly and consistently related to the information that is to follow. It provides a broad context for what is to occur in the session. For example, before discussing differences among cultures, you might present an organizer like "Culture can be seen as the way that people within a group try to solve problems. Different cultures solve problems in various ways." Or a presentation on Freud's personality theory might be preceded with a statement that "Freud's personality theory borrowed from the laws of thermodynamics and how energy moves around in a physical system." A presentation would then show how the specifics of a culture or Freudian theory relate to the organizer.

- *Encourage the use of mental imagery.* Our ability to remember things over long periods of time is related to how meaningful we can make them. Research suggests that semantic and imagery codes help us store information. When both are present, our memories are enhanced. Instructors can increase the chances that students will use imagery by building such devices into their presentations. Metaphors or analogies to things students are already familiar with sometimes help make relatively abstract concepts much more concrete. For example, comparing electrical current and circuits to water flowing in pipes of various sizes, using the idea of throwing birdseed over your head in a plaza in Rome to illustrate the mean and variance of a distribution, and having students think of a passenger on a moving train who sees lightning bolts strike objects behind and in front of the train to illustrate a point in relativity theory are imagery devices that help students visualize concepts. Memory research shows that imagery is extremely important to acquiring and retaining information. Yet it is not used as often as it could be in the classroom.

Richard Atkinson developed a clever system for using mental imagery to help students learn a foreign language vocabulary. The idea is to take the foreign word (such as *caballo,* pronounced "cob-eye-yo"), isolate a sound in its pronounciation that has an English equivalent (such as eye), which is called the *keyword,* and then form an integrative image that combines the keyword with the English word that is the translation of the foreign word. In this case, the English translation of the Spanish *caballo* is *horse.* Thus an image is formed of a horse kicking an eye, or perhaps a horse with a giant eye coming out of its head. Several other examples for learning foreign language words include:

Russian	*Keyword*	*Translation*	*Image*
Strana	(strawman)	country	A giant strawman walking across the map of a country.
Linkor	(Lincoln)	battleship	A battleship with a statue of President Lincoln on the deck.
Osen	(ocean)	autumn	A maple tree in fall colors by the shore.

The images can be as wild as one wants to make them. Students form their own images. The keyword does not have to be a single word; a phrase will do as well. Atkinson's research shows that students using this method learn foreign language vocabulary faster and retain it longer than students who use conventional methods to memorize vocabulary.

• *Help students elaborate on the information.* To elaborate, we must process information to a much deeper level than if we only have to repeat it verbatim. Making it more meaningful and assimilating or accommodating it to existing information in our memories are important parts of this process. Many things an instructor does can assist students to do this; consider those listed here from the research literature.

David Ausubel suggests two principles that will help instructors aid students in elaborating. These are *progressive differentiation* and *integrative reconciliation.* In progressive differentiation the most general ideas and most inclusive ideas of a topic are presented first. They are then progressively made more detailed and specific. Students learn best, according to Ausubel, when the most abstract ideas are presented first, so that they can include any material that is to follow. Teaching should proceed from the abstract to the specific. Integrative reconciliation means that new ideas should be consciously reconciled and integrated with previously learned material. Each new presentation should have a link with information that has been presented earlier. A teacher should make such connections explicit. Both these processes help students elaborate on course content.

Paul Hettich suggests that having students keep journals will assist them in elaborating course information. The aim of a journal is to help individualize a course. It helps students connect the knowledge, concepts, and ideas they acquire from a course to their past and present experiences, thoughts, work, self-reflections, other readings, and, perhaps, other courses. Students keep a notebook during a course. They are asked to write two to five entries each week about course ideas they have made outside of class. The students' journals are reviewed by the instructor, who makes comments on the students' ideas.

Roger T. Cunningham argues that the types of questions instructors ask can encourage or hinder a student's elaboration of course concepts. Simple recall questions that ask students to define, name, designate, or identify a correct answer do not assist elaboration. Questions that stress convergent, divergent, and evaluative thinking are much better. Convergent questions ask students to explain, state relationships, and compare and contrast. Divergent questions ask people to predict, hypothesize, infer, or reconstruct something. Evaluate queries require students to judge, defend, or justify a choice.

Robert A. Bjork suggests that instructors make use of variable encoding to help students elaborate or process information to a deeper level. Variable encoding is a phenomenon in which the same information presented in two different contexts is better remembered than if it were presented in the same context. In an experimental setting, a person might have the word *foot* repeated. In the same-context condition, it might be presented in arm-leg-foot and chin-knee-foot. In the different-context condition, it is first presented in arm-leg-foot and then in inch-meter-foot.

Instructors can make use of this facilitative effect in two ways. One is to have students answer questions in class that ask for the implications of a certain concept in different contexts. For example, students might be asked what implications the Watergate break-in had for governmental self-regulation, potential candidates for the presidency, the views of other nations toward our country, and ideas about the nature of humanity.

A second way to use variable encoding is to consider ways of repeating course content in different contexts. Bjork describes how he taught his introductory psychology course to make use of this principle. He taught the course twice in one term to a group of students. Up to the midterm, he used George Miller's text *Psychology, the Science of Mental Life*, plus appropriate reprints. The approach in Miller's text is historical-biographical, with important concepts developed in relation to the careers of famous psychologists. From the midterm on, he used David Hebb's text *A Textbook of Psychology*, plus appropriate reprints. Hebb's book covers similar material but from a physiological, brain-mechanism viewpoint. One caution Bjork notes in this approach is a tendency during the second half towards undesirable repetitions of jokes or anecdotes used in the first half of the course.

Cognitive Learning Styles

Cognitive learning styles are consistent ways in which people differ in how they perceive, encode, store, and otherwise process information. Some students may prefer information that is presented visually; others may prefer an auditory presentation. People may want to analyze information into specific pieces, or to abstract the global features of the content. Students might be differentiated on their reliance on internal versus external cues to process and understand something. There are many different ways to conceptualize our preferred cognitive learning styles. Instructors must recognize that such differences exist and, to the extent possible, orient instructional procedures to include the cognitive syles of their students. In Chapter 5, which deals with learning styles, we discuss the instructional implications of cognitive styles in more detail. For now, it is important to recognize that they are also an important factor in how students acquire information.

Summary

Cognitive, behaviorist, and humanistic theories of learning have suggested a number of classroom applications. Regardless of the theoretical perspective taken, when we consider the uses of learning theory it is important to remember three things: (1) A particular learning theory does not and cannot specify all aspects of the practice of teaching. A lot is still left up to the skill and imagination of the individual instructor, who may need to "stretch" the theory to derive an application. (2) The validity of an educational practice does not depend on there being a theory behind it. Certain practices seem to work although there is no theory to support them. (3) There is no single theory of learning that will account for the complexity of the classroom learning environment. An eclectic approach is desirable to work through the complexity of human learning.

The *information processing perspective* is one cognitive approach to learning. It is concerned with how sensory input is transformed, reduced, elaborated, stored, recovered, and used. The use of this information is defined as the ways in which it helps us to solve problems and make decisions.

Information processing and other cognitive theories deemphasize the role of external reinforcers in motivating students. Instead, they assume we are active learners who naturally respond to the challenges and problems we face. Furthermore, the thoughts people have about how much control they have over their lives, and how valuable personal effort is in getting ahead in the classroom, contribute to their motivation. Thus, teachers can motivate students by integrating critical thinking activities into the course design. Using a problem-solving perspective when presenting information also helps. Finally, helping students develop confidence in their abilities to accomplish things will facilitate student interest. This can be done by providing students with a success experience, letting them participate in course design, and deemphasizing grades and grading practices.

A number of cognitive factors are associated with facilitating a student's ability to acquire information. *Attending* to incoming information is a necessary first step in processing content. Instructors must recognize that a student's ability to pay attention drifts. Giving breaks, asking questions, and having students paraphrase or summarize what is said helps maintain attention. Creating movement in the classroom by changing position; using novelty in the form of guest speakers, role plays, or discussion groups; repeating information; varying the rate, tone, and inflection of one's voice; and presenting information that partly meets students' needs will also increase attention.

Memory systems must be taken into account when designing instruction from a cognitive viewpoint. The characteristics of the sensory register and short-term and long-term memory, and a tendency to process information at various levels, affect how much of what students take in is retained. Some of the other things instructors can do to facilitate students' memory for information is to repeat information; suggest ways that the content can be organized and categorized; encourage the use of mental imagery; and help students elaborate on the information. The latter can be accomplished by ensuring that new information is linked to that which preceded it; asking thought-provoking questions; and giving examples of concepts in a number of different settings.

Cognitive learning styles are also important for students acquiring information. These are the stable ways people differ in how they perceive, encode, store, and otherwise process content. Variations exist among people in cognitive styles, and instructors should orient instructional procedures to take into account the cognitive styles of their students.

References

Atkinson, R.C. Mnemotechnics in second language learning. *American Psychologist,* 1975, *30,* 821–28.

Ausubel, D.P. *Educational Psychology: A Cognitive View.* New York: Holt, Rinehart and Winston, 1968.

Ausubel, D.P. In defense of advance organizers: A reply to the critics. *Review of Educational Research,* 1978, *48,* 251–57.

Bjork, R.A. Information processing analysis of college teaching. *Educational Psychologist,* 1979, *14,* 15–23.

Bower, G.H. Analysis of a mnemonic device. *American Scientist,* 1970, *58,* 496–510.

Bruner, J.S. *Toward a Theory of Instruction.* Cambridge, Mass. Belcamp, 1975.

Cox, W.F., and Dunn, T.G. Mastery learning: A psychological trap? *Educational Psychologist,* 1979, *14,* 24–29.

Craik, F.I.M. Human memory. *Annual Review of Psychology,* 1979, *30,* 63–102.

Craik, F.I.M., and Lockhart, R.S. Levels of processing: A framework for memory research. *Journal of Verbal Learning and Verbal Behavior,* 1972, *11,* 671–84.

Cunningham, R.T. A descriptive study determining the effects of a method of instruction designed to improve the question-phrasing practices of prospective elementary teachers. Unpublished doctoral dissertation, Indiana University, 1968.

DeCharms, R. Personal causation training in schools. *Journal of Applied Social Psychology,* 1972, *2,* 95–113.

Deci, E. The effects of externally mediated rewards in intrinsic motivation. *Journal of Personality and Social Psychology,* 1971, *18,* 105–15.

Dember, W. The new look in motivation. *American Scientist,* 1965, *53,* 409–27.

Furedy, J.J., and Furedy, C. Course design for critical thinking. *Improving College and University Teaching,* 1979, *27,* 99–101.

Gallagher, J.M., and Noppe, I.C. Cognitive development and learning. In James F. Adams, ed., *Understanding Adolescence,* pp. 199–232. Boston: Allyn & Bacon, 1976.

Hettich, P. The journal: An autobiographical approach to learning. *Teaching of Psychology,* 1976, *3,* 55-59.

James, W. Quoted in Murray, F.B., The generations of educational practice from developmental theory. *Educational Psychologist,* 1979, *14,* 30-43.

Joyce, B., and Weil, M. *Models of Teaching.* Englewood Cliffs, N.J.: Prentice-Hall, 1980.

Lepper, M.R., and Green, D. *The Hidden Costs of Rewards: New Perspectives on the Psychology of Motivation.* Hillsdale, N.J.: Erlbaum, 1978.

Mackworth, J. *Vigilance and Attention.* Baltimore: Penguin Books, 1970.

Manaster, G. *Adolescent Development and the Life Tasks.* Boston: Allyn and Bacon, Inc., 1977.

Melton, A.W. Implications of short-term memory for a general theory of memory. *Journal of Verbal Learning and Verbal Behavior,* 1963, *2,* 1-21.

Miller, G.A. The magical number seven, plus or minus two: Some limits on our capacity for processing information. *Psychological Review,* 1956, *63,* 81-97.

Mischel, W., and Baker, N. Cognitive appraisals and transformations in delay behavior. *Journal of Personality and Social Psychology,* 1975, *31,* 254-61.

Murray, F.B. The generation of educational practice from developmental theory. *Educational Psychologist,* 1979, *14,* 30-43.

Piaget, J. *The Origins of Intelligence in Children.* New York: International Universities Press, 1952.

Piaget, J. *The Construction of Reality in the Child.* New York: Basic Books, 1954.

Piaget, J. Development and learning. In R.E. Ripple and V.N. Rockcastle, eds., *Piaget Rediscovered.* Ithaca, N.Y.: Cornell University, 1964.

Posner, M.I., and Keele, S.W. Decay of visual information from a single letter. *Science,* 1967, *158,* 137-39.

Reiling, A. Internal versus external control and formal thought. Paper presented at the Biennial Meeting of the Society for Research in Child Development, Philadelphia, March 1973.

Snelbecker, G.E. *Learning Theory, Instructional Theory, and Psychoeducational Design.* New York: McGraw-Hill, 1974.

Suchman, R.J. Described in Joyce, B., and Weil, M. *Models of Teaching,* pp. 137-51. Englewood Cliffs, N.J.: Prentice-Hall, 1972.

Taba, H. Teaching strategies and cognitive functioning in elementary school children. San Francisco: San Francisco State College, Co-op Research Project No. 2404, 1966. Also described in Joyce, B., and Weil, M. *Models of Teaching,* pp. 123-36. Englewood Cliffs, N.J.: Prentice-Hall, 1972.

Waugh, N.C., and Norman, D.A. Primary memory. *Psychological Review,* 1965, *72,* 89-104.

Wittrock, M.C. The cognitive movement in instruction. *Educational Psychologist,* 1978, *13,* 15-29.

Chapter 4
Behaviorist and Humanistic Perspectives on Learning: Classroom Applications

The debate over the extent to which our actions are modified and controlled by the external environment has a long history in psychology and education. The opposing viewpoint holds that our actions are attempts at self-understanding to achieve creativity and fulfillment in life. The terms *behaviorist analysis* and *humanistic analysis* of behavior respectively, are often used to categorize these positions. Each point of view makes assumptions about the nature of humanity and what influences behavior. And in spite of the different answers each provides, both positions have led to procedures for understanding and modifying behavior. In particular, proponents of each position have specified certain classroom procedures that instructors might use. This chapter presents the assumptions and classroom applications of each position. By putting them together in one chapter, we hope to facilitate the process of comparing and contrasting the positions.

The Behavioral Perspective
on Learning

An Overview

> Give me a dozen healthy infants, well-formed, and my own specified
> world to bring them up in and I'll guarantee to take any one at ran-
> dom and train him to become any type of specialist I might select—
> doctor, lawyer, artist, merchant-chief and yes, even beggar-man and
> thief, regardless of his talents, penchants, tendencies, abilities, voca-
> tions, and race of his ancestors [Watson, 1924, p. 104].

It is hard to imagine the type of classroom or school system that might
effect such results. Yet this boastful, arrogant, and overly optimistic language was part of the early beliefs regarding the potential of behaviorism.
For John B. Watson, the founder of modern behaviorism, and for people
like B.F. Skinner who followed him, the key to understanding and controlling the behavior lay in identifying the stimuli that influence our actions.
This early work began around the turn of the century. It focused on the
role of environmental stimuli and deemphasized or ignored the role of
conscious processes in understanding behavior.

Environmental stimuli were thought to produce their effects in two
ways. According to the classical conditioning model illustrated by John
Watson's approach, such stimuli controlled our behaviors by eliciting responses directly. The organism was seen as somewhat passive and in need
of external stimuli to prod it into action. Thus stimuli that precede our actions were seen as important to learning. In the operant conditioning model
of B.F. Skinner, a different set of assumptions were made. The organism
was seen as much more active, taking action to manipulate the environment. Control over behavior was maintained by the stimuli that followed
the organism's responding. Such stimuli are commonly referred to as rewards or punishments.

Beginning in the late 1940s and continuing today, cognitive processes
have crept into the behaviorists' analysis of our actions. Modern behaviorists
strike a balance between the role of external stimuli and our ability to use
our thoughts to control our actions. They discuss the role of externally
administered rewards and punishments in influencing behavior, but they
also focus on how we self-monitor, self-regulate, self-reward, and self-
punish our actions.

Most of the classroom applications of behaviorist principles have their
roots in principles of learning derived from the early environmental emphasis. In particular, the operant conditioning model of B.F. Skinner has
provided the clearest and most widely used methods for employing behaviorist principles. Teachers are encouraged to structure their classrooms to

facilitate a student's content learning. Although teachers do not ignore our cognitive capabilities, they are by and large not oriented toward manipulating *how* we think. *Instead, they are oriented toward influencing students' learning by making changes in the classroom environment.* A concern with how we think is much more in the domain of classroom principles derived from information processing theories, discussed in the previous chapter. Let us now examine how behaviorist theorists view student motivation and the factors they believe facilitate students' acquiring content.

Motivating the Students

From a traditional operant conditioning point of view, the primary factors that guide and direct our actions are external stimuli. Pleasant stimuli, or *positive reinforcers,* act as incentives to increase the chances that we will respond. Aversive stimuli also control our behaviors, but in two different ways. Some aversive stimuli increase the probability of behaviors that remove the individual from situations. These are called *negative reinforcers.* Familiar examples include closing a window to shut out noise and picking up a crying baby to calm it. Other aversive stimuli, when presented after a response occurs, decrease the chances of an action's repeating itself. This process is called *punishment* and includes such familiar things as getting one's hand slapped, receiving a traffic ticket for running a red light, and running out of gasoline because the gas gauge on your car was not checked. Pleasant and unpleasant stimuli motivate us to take actions.

The traditional view has been modified in recent years. Behaviorists are more willing to consider as reinforcers a wider range of stimuli. Thus, they now believe the chance to socialize with peers and the things we say to ourselves will motivate us to take certain actions. But the emphasis is still on defining such things as objective stimuli. That is, there is not much said about internal needs for achievement, status, or self-actualization as motivators of our actions. Internal and external stimuli are simply described as positive and negative reinforcers, or as punishment.

Of the three types of stimuli that influence our actions, classroom applications stress the use of positive reinforcers or rewards. Aversive stimuli are seen as having too many undesirable side effects to make them useful to teachers. Such aversive stimuli include frustration, anger, and anxiety in students. Also considered are ethical issues regarding the use of unpleasant stimuli to influence a student's actions. As a result, recommendations for the classroom revolve around manipulations of positive reinforcement.

Behaviorists would see high test and term paper grades as positive reinforcers, but their recommendations for administering rewards in the classroom go beyond simply assigning grades. In general, they recommend establishing classroom structures that administer rewards to students on a systematic, on-going basis. Perhaps the most widely used of these systems is the establishment of contracts with students. Contracts involve students' performing certain class-related activities to earn points that are later "cashed in" for a grade. The student's grade depends upon the number of points earned. Alternately, the instructor may specify a certain number of activities for an A grade, and fewer for a B, C, or D grade. There are a variety of possibilities. Examples of the first two are given in Tables 4.1 and 4.2. Several rules for establishing a contract system follow. They are based on suggestions by Homme and Johnson.

Table 4.1. Components of a Point Contract System

Activity	Points Earned
Exams	
90–100 items correct	50 points each exam
80–89 items correct	40 points each exam
70–79 items correct	30 points each exam
0–69 items correct	0 points each exam
Design a research project	20 points
Implement a research project	40 points
Write a book report on as many outside reading books as you want	30 points each report
Run a class session on a topic of your choice related to course content	35 points
Take a field trip and write a report on observations	30 points each report
Write a term paper	60 points
Classroom attendance	3 points each class
Negotiate with the instructor one or more projects of interest to you	Variable number of points per project negotiated with teacher
Points needed for a grade	A = 350 points or more B = 275–349 points C = 200–274 points D or F: No D or F contracts accepted

I have read the requirements for earning points toward a grade in this course. I would like to contract for a _____ grade by earning a minimum of _____ points. The activities I have elected to do to earn points are the following (list activities and corresponding points on a separate page).

I understand that I can change my contract to try for a higher or lower grade until 15 March. This change must be approved by the instructor. All work on this contract must be done to the quality standards set by the teacher. The teacher agrees to give me feedback on a timely basis regarding the quality of all work completed.

Date: _____ Student signature: _____

Instructor signature: _____

Table 4.2. Components of an Activity Contract System

	Grade		
Activities	A	B	C
Midterm exam	90–100%	80–89%	70–79%
Final exam	90–100%	80–89%	70–79%
**Assignments*			
Short essay questions in workbook	Complete 25	Complete 15	Complete 10
Workbook exercises	Complete 10	Complete 6	Complete 3
Outside readings with report	Read 6	Read 4	Read 2
Position papers	Write 3	Write 2	Write 1
Textbook readings	5 chapters	5 chapters	5 chapters
In-class presentation made by students	Make 2	Make 1	None
Research project	Design and implement	Design only	None

*You may take a make-up exam to get the percentage needed if you fail to achieve it the first time. A make-up will be given only once. Failure to achieve a mid-term or final exam score appropriate to your contract will result in your final grade being lowered one letter grade.

**All assignments must be completed to the standards outlined in the syllabus.

- -

(tear off and turn in)

Name: (last) _____ (first) _____ (initial) _____

I.D. number _____

I have read the syllabus and understand the course requirements and the quality standards for each requirement. I have also read the criteria for an A, B, or C grade and would like to contract for a _____ grade. I understand that the instructor will give me feedback on my performance and notify me periodically whether my performance is satisfactory and in line with the requirements of the contract. Failure to meet the requirements for the grade I contracted for will lead to an appropriate lower final grade. I cannot increase or decrease the grade I contracted for without prior discussion and approval of the instructor.

Signed: _____

Date: _____

Rules for Contracting with Students

- **Students should perceive their appropriate actions as leading to immediate positive reinforcement.** There are two considerations important here. One is to ensure that there is a variety of activities included in the contract. Thus as a student completes any given activity, he or she immediately knows the amount of the reward achieved. With a point system, described in Table 4.1, this is easy to accomplish.

- *Students should know exactly what is expected for a particular grade, and their appropriate actions should lead to immediate positive reinforcement.* The two systems described in Tables 4.1 and 4.2 make quite clear what is expected of the student. Furthermore, as the students complete various tasks, they know they have earned so much toward a particular grade. It might be a certain number of points or one-quarter of the requirements for a grade.

- *Reinforce frequently with small amounts.* Grade requirements should be broken into smaller units, with each unit becoming something the student gets reinforced with for completing. Thus a student should not have to complete five activities before getting 20 points. Each activity should be recorded as 4 points when it is completed.

- *A contract must reward accomplishment rather than obedience.* Thus the contract should say, "If you accomplish *x*, then you will receive *y* amounts of reinforcement." It should not say, "If you do what I tell you to do, you will be rewarded with such and such."

- *Use criteria of quality as well as quantity.* There are several ways to do this. One is to establish criteria for each activity—that is, say that it must conform to certain standards. They may be neatness, well-formulated ideas, or, with exams, a criterion of 90 percent of the items completed.

- *Consider negotiating with students the terms of the contract.* Although many instructors using such systems prefer to control the amount of reinforcement given and the activities needed to obtain a reward, both of these are things that can be negotiated. The instructor and student can agree to both of these things jointly, or the instructor might control the amount of reward while letting students set the number of activities or vice versa. Negotiation helps to give the student a chance to include more activities that meet his or her learning needs. But it also involves much more time in the initial stages of a course to establish a contract.

- *Have students sign the contract.* This ensures that they have read the terms and that they understand what they must do for a particular grade. It also helps establish a commitment to perform the actions specified.

Facilitating the Acquisition of Information

Classroom and other applications of behaviorist learning principles have a rather extensive history of laboratory research to back them up. Early work in the behaviorist tradition used rats, mice, and pigeons as organisms of study. This research suggested that learning occurred best when: (1) the learning environment guided the organism's behavior in certain directions; (2) complex responses were broken into simpler components; (3) these components were learned by beginning with the least difficult; (4) variations in individual rates of learning were allowed; (5) sufficient practice was provided until a task was mastered; and (6) immediate feedback and reinforcement were provided. Such findings were eventually transfered to human learning situations. This led to the development of teaching machines, programmed textbooks, and a variety of course designs. Let us now examine how some of the factors listed here are translated into classroom procedures.

Structuring the learning environment. Behaviorists believe that a learning environment should help guide the student toward acquiring particular responses. Having a structured set of course requirements in the form of a contract is one thing that helps. Another is using behavioral objectives to orient the student's content learning. According to Robert Mager, behavioral objectives are statements that guide the student's acquisition of content. They tell the learner what content they are expected to know, the evidence that will be used to judge whether it has been learned, and the level or extent of the acceptable behavior. At all times, the emphasis is on observable behaviors. Four examples of behavioral objectives are listed below.

- For each of the three learning theories discussed in this chapter, the reader must be able to list one way each theoretical perspective accounts for how students are motivated.

- Write a description of the laws of thermodynamics and a hypothesis that is based on each law.

- Students are expected to recognize the principal author of Gestalt, client-centered, and psychoanalytic theory from among other names used on a multiple-choice exam.

- The principles of effective paragraph writing described in the text will be used to write an original paragraph on the midterm exam. Students will label each paragraph sentence in terms of the principle(s) from the text that it illustrates.

There are several ways to list content objectives, as the examples illustrate. The goal is to make it clear to the student what is expected. To do this, some people write several hundred objectives to cover the content in a particular course. Others may write objectives only for the major points students should know. Another use is to list objectives for the content that is presented in a particular class session. We have found in our classes that this helps students to know whether they have attended to the right issues.

If their notes do not allow them to answer the objectives, then they need to check with their peers or the instructor.

The effects of behavioral objectives on learning have been discussed in the research literature. Phillipe Duchastel and Paul Merrill, and Reginald Melton, suggest that the evidence regarding the effectiveness of objectives is mixed. A number of studies using control groups that do not receive objectives suggest that objectives enhance content achievement, but other research shows that students given objectives do as well but not necessarily better than those who are not given objectives. Apparently they do not hurt, and they might help student achievement. More important, the research specifies conditions under which behavioral objectives are ineffective. These include: (1) teaching situations in which students ignore the objectives because they are unaware of them or prior experience suggests that it is not important to take note of them; (2) stating objectives in a very general or ambiguous manner; (3) making them relevant to only a small proportion of the class (for example, the better or the poorer students); and (4) stating objectives with language that is too difficult for the students. In the latter case, the structure or readability of the information may be a factor contributing to the problem. None of these factors appears to be beyond the influence of the instructor to correct.

Providing immediate feedback and reinforcement. As a general rule, behaviorists argue that long delays in providing an organism with a reward or information regarding its progress on a learning task result in poor performance. Thus classroom applications of behaviorist principles stress providing students with immediate feedback and reinforcement for their efforts. In college classrooms, this typically involves giving students information regarding their knowledge of content rather quickly. The examples that follow illustrate some of the ways this can be done.

- Charles Ferster designed an interview technique to provide immediate feedback regarding knowledge of content in the text. The student is asked to respond to questions in several brief (ten-minute) oral interviews on content covered in small portions of a text chapter (ten to fifteen pages).

  The interviewer is a student in the course who has successfully passed the interview the fellow student or interviewee desires to take. The interviewer keeps time, asks questions, and listens to responses without interruption. Both the interviewer and the interviewee can refer to the text or notes during the interview. Afterward, the interviewer comments on the adequacy of the coverage, the points omitted, and the inaccuracies.

  If both the interviewee and the interviewer are satisfied that the material has been mastered, the student is congratulated and then permitted to study the next assignment. If the interview is not successful, the interviewee restudies and tries again without penalty.

After three to five successful interviews, the student takes a brief written quiz that covers material contained in the interviews that were conducted since the last quiz. Each student in the course is required to listen to at least one interview for each one that he or she takes. The latter requirement, of course, helps the students by providing a useful repetition of the information before the next quiz.

- Jack Michael employs a weekly quiz procedure. He divides the course material into units according to the number of weeks in the term. On Monday of each week, optional lectures that cover material not available in the text or clarify material in the text are given.

On Tuesday, all students take the first form of the quiz covering the week's material. Students are given the quiz plus a sheet of carbon paper and a blank undersheet. Students turn in the original but keep the carbon copy. As they leave class, they are given answers to the quiz. On Wednesday, another optional meeting is held, and those who passed the first quiz are allowed to leave immediately. Those who remain have their questions regarding content answered, and an optional lecture is given. On Thursday, all students who failed are required to take a second form of the quiz.

Michael's Tuesday quizzes usually consist of six questions worth 4 points each. If the student loses 5 points or less, a P grade is assigned. This pass grade is worth 10 points toward a final course grade. If a student loses between 6 and 12 points, a grade of Q is assigned (questionable). If the student loses more than 12 points, a grade of F is assigned, which is worth no points toward a final course grade.

The Thursday quizzes use a modified version of the system. Nine questions worth 4 points each are asked. A P is assigned if a student loses 5 points or less. This time a pass is worth only 8 points toward the final course grade. A loss of 6 to 8 points gives a Q or questionable grade that is worth 6 points toward a final grade. A student who loses between 9 and 12 points receives a grade of R (rotten), which is worth 4 points. More than 12 points missed results in a F grade for the quiz.

In a fifteen-week term, fifteen quizzes are administered, for a total of 150 points. A grade of A is given for 140 or more points, a B for 130–139 points, a C for 120–129 points, a D for 110–119 points, and an F for less than 110 points.

- James Johnston and Henry Pennypacker give students performance sessions in which to demonstrate mastery of the units they are assigned. Each unit or module typically consists of a lecture and some portion of the text. Performance sessions have an assigned "manager" or "proctor" present fill-in-the-blank questions to the students on index cards. The managers or proctors are usually advanced majors in the field.

The students sign up for an appointment with the manager. They agree to the amount of time they will spend together, and the manager shuffles the approximately one hundred question cards for that unit and randomly selects the number that reasonably can be covered in that amount of time. When more than one attempt is needed to pass a given unit, the cards are again randomly selected from the item pool. The student is handed the stack and asked to read each question aloud and fill in the blank orally with the correct answer or with "I don't know." Correct answers are provided on the back of each card for immediate feedback. Students turn the card over after responding. Responses are discussed with a proctor if the student disagrees with an answer. Such discussions also help clarify content issued for students. However, these discussions occur only after the student has answered each question.

The manager times the session and computes the student's correct and incorrect response rates (the number of correct and incorrect fill-ins, each divided by the lapsed time). The student's cumulative record is posted on a bulletin board. Grades are determined by comparing the student's overall slope of correct and incorrect rates with predetermined criterion slopes of correct and incorrect response rates. In one course, the performance of graduate students was modified to determine what an appropriately high and low rate of responding might be. Thus 3.5 correct answers per minute and .4 incorrect per minute was used for an A grade rate. This is roughly equivalent to 90 percent correct and 10 percent incorrect. A minimum passing rate, or C grade, might be 1.5 correct and .4 incorrect. Students must hold their rate of responding in order to get a particular grade. Of course, the rate of responding needed for a particular grade can be adjusted depending upon instructor preferences.

Fostering the mastery of information. According to behaviorist principles, the most important goal is to have students master the information. Students often must be able to show that they can obtain a criterion of, for example, 90 percent or better on exams or that they have acquired specified skills (ability to solder an electrical circuit or give a hypodermic injection). Allowing students to retake exams, providing clear learning objectives, and presenting the content in the form of modules are frequently used aids in assisting students to master the information.

Mastery learning is a rather controversial aspect of the behaviorist approach. Critics like William Cox and Thomas Dunn argue that mastery of the content in one course does not guarantee that students have mastered all prior coursework. Because prerequisite skills are often cumulative in their effects, their absence quickly invalidates the effectiveness of mastery learning. Furthermore, retaking exams may lead some students to memorize the information rather than understand it. Finally, some students may use the "least effort principle": They may risk initial failure on an exam to discover the minimal knowledge required to achieve the criterion level on the second attempt.

There are problems with this approach, but it is an alternative to the single exam "sink or swim" philosophy, a system that also has problems in guaranteeing that students have not acquired content by devious means. Sensitive instructors must be aware of the issues with any testing practice and take corrective actions, depending upon how pervasive problems are in their classes.

Using self-pacing. Individual differences in the rate at which people learn are quite apparent in studies of classroom learning. One solution is not to demand that everyone complete a unit of instruction at the same time. If slower individuals need more time, then they should have it—within limits. Instructional procedures based on behaviorist principles usually allow self-pacing by breaking the course up into smaller units, or *modules.* Thus the content might be divided into ten modules. Each module has a set of learning objectives and an exam that allows the student to demonstrate mastery of the information. The information in a module might include textbook and outside readings, short papers, a field trip, and a laboratory experiment. Students are not allowed to take new modules until they have completed previous ones. Modules are sometimes designed so that they progress in level of difficulty. Thus students must demonstrate that they have acquired basic information before they are allowed access to more advanced topics. Grades are often given based on the number of modules completed successfully. Instructors who use this system typically specify a minimum number of modules that must be completed.

When modules are not used, instructors might give five to ten tests on information covered at various times during the quarter. When students believe they are ready to pass a test on the information, they take it. Typically, they are allowed to retake the exam or a parallel exam until they can meet a specified level of competency (70 percent, 80 percent, 90 percent). Thus not everyone is presumed to be ready to take a test at the same time. Individual variations in abilities and time needed for mastery are thus taken into account.

According to Arthur Robin, the research on self-pacing has been directed toward a recurrent management problem in behavioral instruction—procrastination. Two attempts at dealing with procrastination have provided a basis for evaluation of the role of self-pacing in behavioral instruction. One is to impose deadlines on when units must be completed. A second is to give students bonus points for rapid completion or to take away points if they do not complete units within a reasonable amount of time. The research shows that both deadlines and positive incentive systems can combat procrastination and produce steady, evenly distributed rates of completing units or modules. Limiting self-pacing in this way makes instructors' record keeping easier. It also does not reduce academic achievement.

The Humanistic Perspective on Learning

An Overview

The humanistic view of learning emphasizes the development of the whole person. An important part of this development is to bring together the cognitive and affective aspects of the learning experience. Carl Rogers has stated, ". . . if I were to attempt a crude definition of what it means to learn as a whole person, I would say that it involves learning of a unified sort, at the cognitive, feeling and gut level, with a clear awareness of the different aspects of this unified learning" (1975a, p. 104). Content is important, but how people feel about the content and their emotions while learning content are also legitimate aspects of the learning environment.

To become sensitive to the cognitive and affective aspects of learning, students need teachers who facilitate their classroom growth and development. Such instructors are not as concerned with teaching static knowledge as they are with helping students learn how to learn. They encourage students to explore content on their own, to use resources when they need them, and to reflect on the joy, excitement, frustration, anxiety, and other emotions associated with learning. To do this, humanistic teachers interact extensively with students, deemphasize their expert–formal authority roles, allow students to make choices about some of what they learn, and become learners along with their students. In the following sections, we discuss specific principles, attitudes and values, and methods that help achieve these objectives.

Motivating the Students

Like the cognitive approaches to learning, humanistic views place little emphasis on external incentives and stimulation as the forces that motivate individuals. People are viewed as naturally active in whatever environment they find themselves. According to Carl Rogers, no organism passively accepts the environment. We all have the need to maintain ourselves and to enhance our ability to adapt. This is called our *self-actualization tendency* and is the primary force that motivates our learning. The tendency toward self-actualization causes us to seek new experiences, to explore, to learn, to go beyond current levels of stimulation and experience new things that are more complex. In the classroom, Carl Rogers notes, the self-actualization tendency will facilitate a student's ability to learn course content.

Rogers suggests that self-actualization is the major force that initiates, guides, and directs our actions in learning environments. Abraham Maslow suggests several qualifications on this humanistic view of motivation. According to Maslow, there are in reality two sets of needs that motivate people. One is oriented toward their personal growth and allows them to rise above a basic level of existence. Like Rogers, he calls these needs tendencies toward self-actualization. They help to enhance the quality of our lives. The second set of needs consists of those that relate to deficiencies in our lives. They are the ones we cannot leave unsatisfied for long and include our physiological, safety, social, and self-esteem needs. An important part of Maslow's thinking is that such deficiency needs must be satisfied before we will begin to meet our self-actualization needs. Maslow, unlike Carl Rogers, establishes a hierarchy of needs such that those lower in the hierarchy must be satisifed before we pay attention to those at a higher level. Table 4.3 has a summary of the need hierarchy that Maslow proposes.

Instead of suggesting a single need that motivates students. Abraham Maslow indicates that we are better off recognizing that learners have the potential for self-actualization but are often side-tracked by other motives. Furthermore, although Maslow proposes that our needs are satisfied in terms of their rank in the hierarchy, we should see this as only a general tendency. In reality, many of our actions help us satisfy more than one need at the same time. Our jobs, for example, are activities that help us satisfy all the needs in the hierarchy. We earn money to purchase things to eat and to make rent or mortgage payments; we socialize with peers; we obtain status and respect; and, perhaps, we behave creatively. Maslow's system is not simply a ladder that people climb one step at a time; sometimes they climb two or more steps at once.

We see two important classroom implications of Rogers' and Maslow's views of motivation. They are:

- *Encourage students to do things that will help them self-actualize or otherwise achieve their potential.* The classroom is a good environment for helping people meet their needs for self-actualization. Course procedures and requirements can provide an outlet for this need. There are a number of characteristics of self-actualizing individuals that Maslow and Rogers identify. Three that would seem to be facilitated by teachers include the ability to make choices and accept re-

---

Table 4.3. Maslow's Need Hierarchy

Listed below are five categories of needs identified by Abraham Maslow. They are arranged from low to high in terms of the extent to which they allow us to rise above a basic level of existence. Thus physiological needs are considered lower-order needs, and self-actualization needs are of a higher order.

I. *Physiological*

    Food
    Water
    Sex
    Sleep
    Rest
    Exercise

II. *Safety*

    Shelter
    Protection from immediate or future danger to physical well-being
    Protection from immediate or future threat to physical, psychological, or economic well-being

III. *Social*

    Love and affection
    Friendship
    Association with others
    Affiliation

IV. *Self-esteem*

    Self-confidence
    Independence
    Achievement
    Competence
    Knowledge
    Status
    Personal recognition
    Respect
    Influence with others

V. *Self-actualization*

    Realization of one's own potential
    Self-development activities
    Creative behavior
    Problem-centered orientation to life
    Identification with the problems of humanity
    Acceptance of self and others

---

sponsibility for those choices; the desire for new experiences; and the preference for independent thought and reflection. Thus, giving students opportunities to make choices among course requirements, term paper topics, or research projects is something that can be built into a course design. Furthermore, letting students do things for extra credit or assist in teaching the course, or tying a practicum experience to the course, would encourage people to try new experiences. Finally, having opportunities for independent study or projects within a course might encourage less dependence on the teacher. People begin to achieve their potential only when they begin to think and make decisions for themselves.

Becoming self-actualized is, of course, something that none of us ever completely achieves. Nor are classroom experiences alone going to enable people to get to whatever level they eventually reach. But the classroom is one environment in which people spend a good part of their lives. As instructors, we can provide growth-oriented experiences in line with the characteristics of self-actualization that Rogers and Maslow suggest. We can provide a taste of a growth-oriented experience, and for those who want more—we facilitate their development through the classroom experiences.

- *Design a course so that it is relevant to each of the needs in Maslow's hierarchy.* Mary Lynn Crow indicates that instructors can maximize a student's motivation by suggesting ways the course content, procedures, and outcomes will help the student satisfy a variety of needs. She suggests that in designing a course, instructors should first ask themselves what relationship such aspects of the course have to each category of need. For example, how will the course help students earn a living, provide for their psychological and physical safety, meet their social needs, contribute to enhancing their self-esteem, and allow them to achieve their potential? Teachers should be able to indicate how various aspects of the course will help students satisfy such needs and then should directly communicate through course objectives how this will occur. *Crow's system provides one set of criteria for deciding if the course design is adequate.* The results of a colleague trying her system for a psychology of adjustment course are illustrated here:

Physiological needs: Some of the content relates to helping students better understand their sexual needs, how to relax better, ways to increase their physical activity, and how to improve their performance in sports based on research data. The course is part of the major, and, eventually, a successful completion will help them graduate and earn a living. The latter will help them take care of their hunger and thirst needs in the long run.

Safety needs: Course content will help students cope with threats to their psychological well-being. They will learn ways to deal with threats to their self-concept, how to handle stress and anxiety, and how to deal with conflict. Physical security needs will be aided only indirectly by the course—again, when students graduate, their ability to earn a living will help here.

Social: Several group projects and opportunities for small discussion groups in class will help people affiliate with others. We will also have an end-of-course party that should contribute to more of the other social needs people have.

Self-esteem: Students will study in modules. They must pass seven out of ten modules to complete the course. Module exams can be retaken as many times as needed to master the information. This should encourage self-confidence and a sense of achievement. The two best term papers will be read at a special undergraduate symposium of student papers during the spring term. This opportunity will help at least two students gain personal recognition and add to the status they may already enjoy.

Self-actualization: Students will be given the opportunity to participate in a weekend personal growth experience. They will explore how others see them, evaluate the effects of their behaviors on other people, and be able to gain additional insights into how they behave. This should contribute to their overall interpersonal effectiveness.

Facilitating the Acquisition of Information

The behaviorist and cognitive approaches to learning have rather specific, concrete suggestions for what instructors can do to help students acquire information. By our manipulating reinforcers, pacing course content in particular ways, using various types of probing questions, and employing problems in teaching material and other devices, a student's learning is directed in ways that are consonant with behaviorist and cognitive theories. Much of what they suggest are rather mechanical manipulations of the classroom environment. In contrast, humanistic suggestions for instruction are somewhat less specific and concrete. Because the theories propose that instructors must be concerned with a student's cognitive and emotional learning, many of their suggestions demand that instructors adopt certain attitudes and values. Teaching from a humanistic perspective is not so much a matter of using various classroom procedures as it is the transmission of a philosophy of living into the classroom environment. Along these lines, Gene Stanford and Albert Roark note that a humanistic approach does not

. . . provide ready-made techniques or principles [that] if followed guarantee success. Instead, it provides a challenge. The challenge is whether teachers can furnish the conditions in which students can develop to their maximum potential as human beings. To aid in this task, some techniques are suggested, some research findings are offered and a developing body of theoretical knowledge is available, but the teacher is clearly told that the responsibility is his as a human being involved in the lives of other human beings. The message is both implicit and explicit; *help man become that which he can become* [1974, p. 20].

Let us now turn our attention to some of the attitudes, values, and procedures that are consistent with the humanistic view of learning.

Prizing, acceptance, trust, and empathy. Teachers must develop attitudes of prizing the learner, accepting students for what they are, trusting them, and being able to empathize with their thoughts and feelings. Carl Rogers says that these are the foundations for promoting personal and intellectual change in students. "I think of it as prizing the learner, prizing his feelings, his opinions, his person. It is a caring for the learner, but a non-possessive caring. It is an acceptance of this other individual as a separate person, a respect for him as having worth in his own right. It is a basic trust—a belief that this other person is somehow fundamentally trustworthy" (1975a, p. 107). Rogers argues that teachers who possess attitudes of prizing, caring, and acceptance understand the fear and hesitation of a student as he or she approaches a learning task. A teacher also is able to accept the student's satisfaction in achievement. "Such a teacher can accept the student's occasional apathy, his erratic desires to explore byroads of knowledge, as well as his disciplined efforts to achieve major goals. He can accept personal feelings which both disturb and promote learning—rivalry with a sibling, hatred of authority, concern with personal adequacy" (Rogers, 1975a, p. 107).

Such attitudes are sometimes referred to as *unconditional positive regard* for another person. This means that we have a complete, uncensored acceptance of another person. Our interactions with them are warm, non-possessive, and nonthreatening. Unconditional positive regard, according to Rogers, encourages students to take risks, to feel support for their attempts at learning, and to develop their capacities as self-initiated experiential learners.

A further factor that establishes a climate favorable to learning is the instructor's ability to empathize with the thoughts, feelings, and other responses of the student. This kind of understanding is not evaluative. An instructor is not communicating to a student the message "I understand what is wrong with you." Instead, when there is a sensitive empathy, students are likely to react, "Someone really understands how it feels to be me without wanting to analyze me." Rogers believes that teachers who are sensitive to the way education appears to the student increase the likelihood of student growth and learning.

Humanistic views of education emphasize the importance of teachers' possessing unconditional positive regard and empathic understanding toward students, but how people acquire such traits is not clearly spelled out. As one colleague said, "I think I'm a latent humanist. But how do I change myself so I can adopt such attitudes?" Obviously, the answer to that question is rather complex. We doubt if people are born with humanistic attitudes and values. At some point in their lives, they decide to adopt them. They begin to live their lives and behave toward other people in ways that are consonant with such values and attitudes. Research into the components of unconditional positive regard and empathy, for example, suggests the following behaviors that teachers might adopt to begin to experiment with humanistic attitudes and values.

- *Prizing, accepting, and trusting the learner means that students are given room to participate in what they want to learn.* Classroom activities are arranged to provide students with choices—choices about what topics they will study and what projects they will work on, and perhaps the choice to participate in the design and implementation of the course. When this is done, teachers become more facilitators of the student's learning and less experts—formal authorities. Class activities and evaluations are shared with students, and their inputs are used and valued throughout the course.

- *Teachers must show that they are interested in, concerned with, and attentive toward the students.* On a behavioral level, Helen Rausch and Edward Bordon note, this can be conveyed by eye contact, head nodding, a pleasant smile when talking to people, the use of a soft pleasant voice, and as much one-on-one contact as possible. Students are also frequently asked to state what they are thinking and feeling about content issues. When suggestions are made for improving a course, the instructor listens and tries whenever possible to make adjustments.

- *Empathy is conveyed by accurately reflecting the thoughts and feelings of the student.* Charles Truax and Richard Carkhuff note that empathy can be shown by paraphrasing what someone is saying, reflecting their feelings, taking time before responding while maintaining eye contact, and not interrupting a person in the middle of a thought. A student recognizes that you are empathizing when you say something like, "That sounds like a rough experience. You really sound frustrated and down on yourself." People tend to enjoy others who take an interest in them. In turn, they become more communicative toward you.

Self-concept. Teachers must recognize that students' self-concepts play an important role in their satisfaction with and achievement in the classroom. A person's self-concept is an organized set of beliefs and feelings about him- or herself. Because the self-concept helps to guide, control, and regulate actions, it plays an important part in determining how students adapt to the classroom. A student who sees herself as academically competent, intelligent, having interesting ideas regarding course content, and able to work alone will enjoy classes and probably do quite well. Such a student would want to share ideas, not dread taking exams, enjoy class projects, and, more likely than not, look forward to showing teachers what she can do. A student with a negative self-image would not enjoy class as much, nor would he achieve as well. Edward Kifer and Richard Beery report that self-concept and academic achievement are too closely related for teachers to ignore the connection.

A person's self-image develops from personal comparisons with other people and the feedback and reinforcement other people give. Such processes operate in all aspects of a person's life, including the classroom. Thus students who consistently meet various teachers' goals and standards will come to see themselves as successful. Gene Stanford and Alfred Roark emphasize the important obligations this fact places on teachers. "We have," they state,

> an obligation to insure that students have an opportunity to interact extensively in ways that will provide them with accurate feedback and other information about themselves. However, we also have a responsibility to guard against students having experiences that lead them to form negative self-concepts through repeated failure and comparisons that denigrate them. Inevitably, some such experiences will occur, but we must ensure that they are offset by success experiences. [1974, pp. 22–23].

Giving everyone a "success experience" is in some ways an admirable goal, but it is one that is extremely difficult to achieve. Yet there are some things a sensitive teacher might try to do to make opportunities for people to enhance their self-concepts.

- *Learning contracts help students select a level of performance that is in line with their skills and abilities.* Such contracts were described in the section on behaviorist theories, and a humanistic approach is described later in this section. Basically, contracts do not force all students to meet the same standards. Thus, within limits, students can feel that they achieved what they wanted to achieve.

- *Become sensitive to whether you are setting standards and goals that are too high for students to meet.* We find that instructors sometimes slip into believing that students can handle whatever course requirements they develop. We suspect that secretly they want students to be just like them. There are, however, wide variations in the skills and abilities of students. Thus, before setting standards it is important to ask: "How many students do I expect to do well?" "Will these requirements and standards allow this to happen?" "How can I vary my requirements and standards to meet the different levels of ability of my students?"

- *Give students positive feedback.* In most courses, a grade constitutes the major source of student feedback. And when other forms are given, we find that there is an emphasis on negative aspects of what the student did. We suggest that whenever possible, students be given specific feedback orally or in writing regarding their performance. It should include both positive and negative things. Even though sometimes we may struggle to find positive things to say, it is important to the development of a healthy self-concept that they be said.

Teachers as facilitators. Humanistic theorists argue that teachers need to play the role of the expert–formal authority less and the role of a learning facilitator more. The emphasis of the humanist shifts from a teacher stating, "Here is what I can teach you," toward "What do you need from me to teach yourself?" The teacher becomes a catalyst and a resource for the student's learning.

When an instructor takes a facilitator role, it means that a number of things occur in the teacher-student interaction. Carl Rogers suggests that teachers begin to support actively the student's attempts at learning. Students are given the opportunity to make choices about some of the things they learn. The choices may involve content topics, class projects, or other types of experiences relevant to the course. Teachers encourage such choices but also let the student know that he or she is responsible for that choice. In practical terms, it means that assignments must be completed and course-related content must be learned. The student is held accountable for the choices made. An important aspect of this is that the teacher works closely with the student by providing resources (books, self, other people) to assist the student to learn. Teachers also allow students to make mistakes and to learn from those mistakes. Students are given the opportunity to overcome their errors and are not punished for making them. For Rogers, such procedures can be instituted most effectively in a supportive classroom climate where students feel secure to make choices relevant to their learning.

Donald DeLay notes that teachers who facilitate do several additional things. *They try to get students to develop personal meaning from the content.* That is, students are asked to consider how course content affects their lives and the lives of other people. Not only is the course information important, but how it relates to the attitudes and values of the student must be considered. For example, a session on nuclear reactions would not stop with learning the various physical and chemical properties of a fission or fusion reaction. The implications of nuclear energy for students' lives would also be considered. To do this, a facilitator must actively involve the students in learning. Didactic modes of presenting information would not be used exclusively. Teachers might rely on discussion groups, students journals or diaries, or other devices to get students to reflect.

Donald DeLay also suggests that *facilitators of learning must help people learn to inquire.* Students need to be equipped with the tools to inquire properly. A teacher can't present all knowledge to students; there is simply too much of it, and it changes too rapidly. Thus, teachers need to give students opportunities to use resources, to seek things for themselves, and to develop personal ideas about the content. Such teachers might lecture less and use demonstrations, exercises, research projects, position papers, and student-led discussion groups more.

Finally, DeLay says that *students learn best when teachers deemphasize the use of external rewards.* The threat of grades and points earned on papers and tests tends to separate and barricade the learner from the subject matter and from the person directing and issuing the rewards. Evaluation must not be perceived as something an authority figure "does to me." Rather, it must be seen as information that will assist the learner to meet his or her goals. For this to occur, an instructor must begin to get students to monitor and evaluate their progress themselves, or, at least, to rely much less on things the instructor says about their progress. Teachers should shift the focus of classroom feedback toward self-evaluations.

Our discussion suggests several characteristics that are associated with the teacher as facilitator. A few are attitudes and values teachers must adopt; others reflect overt behaviors. Several specific classroom procedures are applicable when teachers want to take a facilitative role. In addition to those mentioned in our discussion in this section, consider the following:

- *Student-teacher contracts.* A form of contracting was discussed in the section on behaviorist learning theories. As we mentioned, the instructor typically selects a variety of things that students can do to earn points in a course. Students select those that will give them the grade they want. In most cases, there is very little negotiation about the activities that will constitute a contract.

  From a humanistic point of view, however, contracting is a little different. Carl Rogers recommends contracting as an open-ended device that helps give students security and responsibility in the classroom. But the process he recommends involves much more negotiation between the teacher and the students. Students take much more initiative in suggesting ideas for activities. To do this, each student first decides what grade he or she wants to receive. Students meet individually with the instructor and present their ideas about activities that they feel would certify them for a particular grade. The teacher makes suggestions, and they talk. Activities in the contract might include exams, papers, projects, teaching part of a class, or any number of other things. It is important to remain flexible. The advantage from Rogers's point of view is that once an agreement is reached, students have less uncertainty about how their performance will be assessed. This removes a great deal of fear and apprehension from class and makes them feel that discussions are possible.

- *Peer teaching devices.* In Chapter 10, we describe the learning cell and the teacher-of-the-day classroom models. Both are excellent devices to get students to inquire about information, develop their own ideas, and learn from each other. Other ideas that fit here are holding classroom symposia to read and discuss student term papers and allowing students to work together on activities.

- *Role playing.* In role playing, students try to experience certain concepts. It helps them "get inside" the information and develop what DeLay terms "personal meaning." Role playing might involve students' playing particular historical characters, the parts of a human cell, molecules in an atom, or participants at a collective bargaining session, or acting out a personal problem. The goal is to enhance the teaching of particular concepts by personal experience. Details on how to set up and run role-playing activities are presented in Chapter 6, Getting Students Involved in the Classroom.

  Regardless of the type of role play used, an important goal of using it, from the humanistic perspective, is to examine how people felt in each role as well as the specific content that was demonstrated. This should be done not only by members of the class who participated but by those members who observed.

- *Student feedback.* Instructors need to encourage students to monitor and assess their progress in a course. Donald DeLay devised a rather clever way to facilitate such assessments. He devised a plan called CRAM, or Comprehensive Random Achievement Monitor. Several times each semester, a rather short test is given in one of a variety of forms. The items represent a sample of the entire subject covered as well as content that has not been presented. The tests are never announced ahead of time, and the questions are sometimes new and sometimes repeated from earlier tests. The tests are always returned and never graded. The only marks are small checks on items students appeared confused about. As the course progresses, students became less hostile toward the procedure and began to realize that they are not being evaluated. Instead, the test procedure lets them know how they are progressing, where they are weak, and what they already know. More important, it gives them some idea of what they might like to pursue next. In DeLay's experience, students began to request the test rather than object to it.

Another device we have found helpful is to ask students to submit periodically a self-evaluation of their strengths and weaknesses in the course. They are asked to indicate what they like and dislike, and what they can do further to meet course and personal learning objectives. They respond to areas of the information, ability to work with other students in discussion groups and projects, participation in class sessions, progress on papers and other course projects, and ability to relate course content to their lives and those of other people.

Teachers as learners. From a humanistic perspective, a student's learning is enhanced when the teacher participates as a partner, perhaps a senior partner, in the learning experience. A course should represent just as much of an opportunity for a teacher to learn as it does for the student, although the content of that learning may differ. For this to occur, a number of traditional barriers to student-teacher interactions must be overcome. Instructors must admit that they do not know everything about the subject matter. Students are told that the course will also help the teacher to learn certain things. Furthermore, teachers must also begin to relate to students on a more personal basis. The expert–formal authority role with whatever status it promotes must be modified toward that of a facilitator of learning. Finally, instructors must lecture less and interact more with students. A lot more give and take will occur when teachers are in the mode of learners themselves. Two approaches to teaching should help illustrate this method.

- Two colleagues in the history department at the University of Cincinnati, Zane Miller and Henry Shapiro, teach a course in historical methods. The focus of the course is the study of the city of Cincinnati. A recent topic was the study of the annexation of the Clifton neighborhood of the city into the municipality. The course explored how this occurred, with students and teachers participating as learners in the process. There were no books, articles, or previous publications by other historians to guide them. Nor did the instructors know much about the way the particular historical event occurred in the city's history. Thus whatever was found was new information for both the teachers and the students. Together they designed the research process, implemented it, and analyzed the findings. Teachers and students were partners in this learning experience.

- Norman Springer, a teacher trained in English literature, decided to teach a course in Euclidean geometry. He wanted to demonstrate that it was possible to understand a subject by one's own effort, through study and discussion, without the help of a teacher who had all the answers. The students at St. Mary's College were at first rather perplexed. How could a teacher who was himself just learning Euclidean geometry "teach" them anything? They soon found out. Springer reports that he would typically try to explain a proposition. His explanations were awkward and at times somewhat confusing. But this generated dialogue with the students. They had to struggle with the teacher to understand the complexities of geometry. He notes: "My being honestly without answers, in the midst of a group of young men who already knew that I was a teacher was electrifying. It had never happened to them before, and it compelled them, sooner or later, to recognize, or at least to consider, that what happened was up to them, that perhaps they could work their own way out, and that it might even be respectable to do so. Through this they might come to see what they had never before believed for one moment, that they did not need a teacher in the accepted sense. . . . I was a learner responsible for my own education, yet, in a special way, at the same time responsible for the students'."

Combining content and affect. With humanistic theory emphasizing the vital role of affect in learning, the humanistic teacher must recognize that there is no emotion without cognition, no cognition without emotion. Sidney Simon describes his approach to combining affect and content in what he calls "third-level teaching." At the first level are *facts,* at the second *concepts*, and at the third *values.* Using the subject of automobile brakes, a level-one (facts) question would be, "Which stops a car more effectively, disc or drum brakes?" At the concepts (second) level, a question might address how brakes work. At the values (third) level, a question might ask whether disc brakes are worth the increased cost over drum brakes.

The relationship of facts, concepts, and values can be viewed as a pyramid, with facts providing the broad base, concepts representing the understandings and generalizations derived from facts, and values, the top of the pyramid, representing the decisions of life that each individual must make based on understanding facts and concepts. Unfortunately, Simon notes, most classroom teaching is done only at the facts level, with some excursions into concepts but, sadly, little in the area of values. Truly meaningful teaching would encompass all three. He suggests that discussions of the value implications of course concepts and topics should be made an integral part of the classroom experience. Students and teachers need to examine and explore the values that underlie course content.

Consider the following examples of the facts, concepts, and values levels of content suggested by Merrill Harmin, Howard Kirschenbaum, and Sidney Simon. Note how each level is taught by the use of certain types of questions and student activities.

- *Chemistry*
  Facts level: How many known elements are there? What elements are inert? What is the special characteristic of radium?

Concepts level: What generalizations can you make about elements when you look at the periodic table? Why are certain elements inert? How did the discovery of radium relate to atomic energy?

Values level: How do you feel about the development of atomic weapons? Have you written your views to your congressman or to the daily newspaper? Under what conditions would you take a job in a defense industry which produces chemical warfare agents? What are the reasons for your decision?

- *Art*

  Facts level: Stretch a canvas. Name three warm colors.

  Concepts level: What is the function of perspective? How is perspective created? Demonstrate how light and shadow are used in painting.

  Values level: What would you like to paint if you could? What would you most like to communicate through painting?

- *Accounting*

  Facts level: What is a debit? Define net return.

  Concepts level: What is the difference between a balance sheet and a profit and loss statement? What is the purpose of an audit?

  Values level: What aspects of accounting give you the most pleasure? The least pleasure? Can you envision any circumstances in which you would steal from a company?

- *Music*

  Facts level: What is a time signature? An octave? A treble clef? What do the following terms mean: allegro, crescendo, adagio, forte, pizzicato?

  Concepts level: Play this piece of music. Transpose this piece from the key of C to the key of G.

  Values level: Write your own music and play it. Interpret someone else's music by playing it in your own way. What do you like most about practicing? What do you like least?

- *Human Sexuality*

  Facts level: How long does it take for a human enbryo to develop? Describe the stages of development. Define the following words: chromosome, gene, ovum, sperm, uterus.

  Concepts level: How does sexuality relate to love? What is the function of the family in facilitating the growth of a human infant?

  Values level: In your opinion, what are three things mothers and fathers should do? Complete the statement: Women's Liberation is . . .

The three levels easily can be extended to any discipline. When you design a course, it is sometimes helpful to determine the amount of time you plan to use on value issues compared to conceptual and factual concerns.

Otherwise, it is difficult to deal with values, because the other two levels typically dominate.

To integrate values into the classroom, Harmin, Kirschenbaum, and Simon state, teachers must adopt certain attitudes and behave somewhat differently than usual. *Instructors must be accepting and nonjudgmental.* They may correct students on the facts level but must understand that there are no right and wrong answers on questions related to values. An instructor's opinion is just that in such discussions, and students must be told it is not a final answer. *The teacher will encourage diversity.* The instructor must reassure students that they will not be censured for expressing an opinion that differs from the teacher's. *Respect for a student's right not to respond to a value issue must be maintained.* Teachers must make this clear to students. It protects the students' privacy but also safeguards instructors from critics who believe students should not respond to value issues. Students' responses are respected. Care must be taken not to put students on the defensive. The purpose of value clarification is to help students clarify and affirm their own values. *Questions should be asked that help students examine alternatives*—questions like "What are your real feelings?" "Are there any other alternatives?" "What are the consequences of your decisions?" It is sometimes necessary to avoid "yes-no" or "either-or" questions. They limit thinking. "Why" questions are also problematic, because they risk punishing students who have no clear reasons for their choices. It is better to ask, "Do you have a reason for your responses?" Finally, *teachers should include questions and activities that help students raise social issues as well as individual concerns.* "You" questions may involve personal concerns—family, money, friends. Students also need to consider broader social, national, and international issues that relate to their disciplines.

Cognitive and emotional learning are obviously interdependent. Based on this understanding, Alfred Gorman identifies the following general objectives for every humanistically oriented teaching situation:

1. Improved interpersonal communication.

2. Sensitivity to the effects of member behavior in group settings.

3. Understanding of the dynamics of working groups.

4. Intellectual and emotional involvement in the learning process [1974, p. 64].

When these objectives are met, "learnings" take place on both personal and interpersonal levels:

Personal	*Interpersonal*
• Understanding one's own feelings	• Understanding feelings of others

- Skill in communicating feelings
- Self-direction
- Self-responsibility
- Intrinsic motivation

- Skill in group task and maintenance behaviors
- Ability to diagnose communication problems
- Full membership participation [Gorman, 1974, p. 65]

Taking group process into account. With the emphasis on affect as well as on content, the humanistic teacher must recognize the vital role that the group itself plays in the learning process of each individual in the group. The teacher alone isn't responsible. If he or she were, there would be no difficulty in transferring a successful teaching episode from one environment to another. The difference is in the group, the differing personalities, past experiences, attitudes, and expectations of the members. The humanistically oriented teacher, more than any other, must take these group and individual variables into account, and, therefore, must detail and use student needs, the classroom communication network, and established behavioral norms as integral aspects of course design.

A detailed discussion of group behavior is beyond the scope of this chapter, but we believe it is important at least to be aware of universal needs in groups. William Schutz identifies three interpersonal needs each of us experiences in every group. The first is the need for *inclusion,* which is expressed in concerns like "How will I fit in here?" "Who will accept/reject me?" "What must I do to be accepted?" Before these questions are answered, it is difficult if not impossible for academic concerns to be addressed. And even after they are answered, academic success is also influenced by the expression of the needs for *control* ("Who has influence here?" "How is leadership determined?") and *affection* ("Who will like and support me?" "With whom do I identify?"). Gerry Weinstein identifies these same concerns, but labels them slightly differently: the needs for *identifying, power,* and *connectedness.* Some of the classroom implications of these needs include the following:

- Devote time, especially in the beginning of a term, to having students learn about one another. A few moments devoted to interpersonal exchange may substantially improve the learning climate.

- Learn students' names and encourage them to learn one another's. This is a personal touch that most students appreciate.

- Negotiate class goals when appropriate. Including students' needs helps them feel motivated. Be specific about *your* minimums; then ask for theirs.

- Identify student resources and use them. Students' interests, hobbies, and occupations make them valuable resources for class sessions.

They can bring their experiences to the classroom to illustrate concepts or to use as starting points for discussions.

- Use small groups in which interaction and articulation are essential. Giving these groups specific tasks to accomplish helps them establish teamwork.

- Identify potential student leadership skills and use them whenever possible. Have students help you by running small groups and suggesting topics and activities for class.

- Group students on the basis of psychological needs. Dick and Pat Schmuck note that "while it may be difficult at times for teachers to put students together primarily on the basis of their psychological needs, on some occasions psychological compatibility may indeed be the best criterion to use. Letting students organize their own ad hoc or task groups is one rather straightforward way to organize students according to their personal compatibilities. We suggest this because students often can be accurate judges of who they, themselves, can best work with, and who in the peer group best satisfy their needs" (1979, p. 34).

- Have students react to one another's work, not in a critical sense, but in the spirit of sharing ideas. Outlines or rough drafts of work might be exchanged, with discussion and questions between students designed as helpful input and reaction sessions.

Criticisms of Humanistic Teaching

It would not be fair to close this section without acknowledging the widespread criticisms of so-called humanistic teaching. The criticisms are primarily that humanistic teaching is "soft," that there are no standards, and that therefore students are simply allowed to "do their own thing" without regard for excellence. Unfortunately, much of this criticism may be well founded, as a result of unskilled and unprepared teachers who use a spurious humanism to rationalize poor performance and laziness. Additionally, many well-intentioned teachers have experimented with humanistic approaches without the necessary understanding of and skill in group process and management, often with disastrous consequences. Dick and Pat Schmuck describe their own experience:

We often work with neophyte teachers who are "turned on" to the idea of democratic teaching or open classrooms, or who wish to make frequent use of small-group instruction. Frequently such teachers will hand over the reins of leadership totally to students, who themselves are unprepared and unskilled in assuming initiatory roles. When the class falls into disunity and disarray, the teacher pulls back the reins of control and explains, "I tried it and it didn't work." But, as all teachers come to see, students cannot change their expectations, behaviors, and skills simply by administrative fiat—behavioral changes in student groups require understanding, planning, and practice over a sustained period [1979, p. 31].

Such unfortunate results can be avoided only when the humanistically oriented teacher both develops sound rationales and approaches cognitively and is emotionally and behaviorally prepared to manage a humanistic environment. Suffice it to say that the task is formidable, and we encourage you to be prepared for the hard work of being a humanist in the classroom.

An Integrated View

Most of us teach using ideas that fit more than one viewpoint about the learning process. Now that you have read chapters 4 and 5, it should be possible for you to fit your current procedures and methods into the theories of learning they seem to agree with. How eclectic or noneclectic you are in your teaching should become apparent. In addition, the information about learning theories should give you some ideas for ways to enhance your teaching, that is, ways to design new classroom procedures or to modify existing ones to make them more compatible with various learning principles. To accomplish such objectives, an analysis of what you are currently doing must be made. The process we now describe is one way we have asked people to do this. Try it and discover what new insights about your teaching it yields. To facilitate your completing the task efficiently, consider using the format described in Table 4.4.

- Select one or two of your current classes. List the methods, processes, and procedures you use to motivate students and to facilitate their acquiring information. If you are not currently teaching, what methods, processes, and procedures might you want to use?

- What behaviorist, information processing, and humanistic concepts and principles discussed in chapters 4 and 5 appear to be associated with those methods, processes, and procedures? In some cases, it is possible for a method to be compatible with more than one view regarding learning.

- Trying to be objective, rate the extent to which the methods, processes, and procedures identified fit a given learning perspective. Use a 5-point rating scale, where 1 = very good fit; 2 = satisfactory fit; 3 = somewhat related; 4 = relatively poor fit; 5 = very poor fit.

- What might you do in the future to modify or change the classroom procedures you currently favor to make them fit behaviorist, infor-

Table 4.4. Suggested Outline for Completing Activity

Methods, Processes, and Procedures	Rating			Modifications	New Principles and Concepts and Possible Classroom Activities
	Beh:	IP:	Hum:		
Motivation of the student					
Facilitation of acquisition of information					

mation processing, and humanistic concepts and principles better? For those you rated as 3, 4, or 5, what is one thing you could do?

- Of the behaviorist, information processing, and humanistic concepts and principles we discussed that you do not use, which ones might you find attractive for the future? What has to change in your teaching to be able to use them?

- Do you think your teaching is too eclectic in the approaches to learning it encompasses? Would you be better off focusing more on one of the three learning perspectives? If so, which one? What has to happen for you to be able to do this?

Summary

Behaviorism had its roots in the study of the ways external stimuli influence various responses. Later, the ways we self-monitor, self-regulate, and self-reward, as well as other cognitive processes, became associated with this viewpoint. Classroom applications tend to focus on how learning environments can be structured to facilitate the learning process.

Motivating students from a behaviorist view means that instructors must understand the external stimuli that will guide and direct students' actions. Typically this means manipulating positive and negative reinforcers and punishment. Of the three, the use of pleasant stimuli is stressed. Positive reinforcement in conjunction with the creation of classroom structures to administer rewards to students on a systematic basis form the elements for motivating students. Perhaps the most widely used system for doing this is the establishment of contracts with students. Contracts basically involve students' performing certain class-related activities to earn points that are later "cashed in" for a grade. The student's grade depends upon the number of points earned. Alternately, the instructor may set a certain number of activities as required for an A grade, and fewer for a B, C, or D grade.

Several factors help students acquire information. A *structured learning environment* where students are guided toward acquiring a particular response is recommended. The use of behavioral objectives helps this to occur. *Self-pacing* is used to accommodate individual differences in the rate at which people learn. Although students are not given unlimited freedom for self-pacing, their course work is divided into units that are allowed relatively flexible amounts of time for completion. *Mastery* of the information is stressed in behaviorally designed courses. This means that students must demonstrate they can obtain a criterion of, say, 90 percent or better on exams or that they have acquired specified skills. Students are allowed to retake exams until they master the information. Finally, *immediate feed-*

back and *reinforcement* of classroom performance are stressed. In college classrooms, this typically involves giving students information regarding their knowledge of content within a few minutes after they have taken a test.

An important part of the humanistic perspective is bringing together the cognitive and affective aspects of the learning experience. Content is important, but how people feel about the content and their emotions while learning are also legitimate aspects of the learning environment. To become sensitive to the cognitive and affective aspects of learning, students need teachers who facilitate their classroom growth and development. Such instructors are not as concerned with teaching static knowledge as they are with helping students learn how to learn.

Humanistic views place less emphasis on external incentives and stimulations as the forces that motivate individuals. *People are seen as active learners, and the tendency towards self-actualization is an important part of their motivation.* Carl Rogers suggests that self-actualization is the major force that initiates, guides, and directs our actions; Abraham Maslow argues that more basic needs also must be considered. People will not try to enhance the quality of their lives unless basic physiological, security, social, and self-esteem needs are first met. The existence of classrooms where students can begin to self-actualize by making choices, seeking new experiences, and being able to work independently and self-reflect is an important motivator. Relating the course to its ability to satisfy a variety of needs should also help increase student interest.

Teaching from a humanistic perspective is not so much a matter of using classroom procedures as it is the transmission of a philosophy of living into the classroom. Factors that facilitate learning are often certain attitudes and values that teachers must adopt. *Teachers must develop attitudes through which they prize learners, accept students for what they are, trust them, and empathize with their thoughts and feelings.* These behaviors are accomplished by allowing students to participate in all aspects of course design, giving them opportunities to explore things that interest them, becoming very attentive to their ideas, and reflecting their thoughts and feelings. *Teachers must recognize that students' self-concepts play an important role in their satisfaction with and achievement in the classroom.* Helping students select a level of performance that is in line with their skills and abilities, becoming sensitive to whether classroom goals are too high, and giving positive feedback are teacher actions that help enhance self-concepts. *Teachers should act as facilitators of students' learning.* To do so, teachers should allow students the opportunity to make choices and to develop personal meaning from the content, help students learn how to inquire, and rely less on external rewards. *Instructors must see themselves as learners.* They should participate as partners in the learning experience. A course should represent just as much of an opportunity for the teacher to learn as it does for the student. *Content and affect must be combined in the classroom.* Instructors are encouraged to teach on the facts, concepts, and values levels to integrate content and affective concerns. *Finally, group processes must be taken into account.* The humanistically oriented teacher must consider both group and individual variables. Individual needs for control, affection, and inclusion affect how students and instructors interact in the classroom. Similarly, group participation activities must be included to give students needed practice in working with others.

References

Beery, R.G. Fear of failure in the student experience. *Personnel and Guidance Journal,* 1975, *54* 191-203.

Cox, W.F., and Dunn, T.G. Mastery learning: A psychological trap? *Educational Psychologist,* 1979, *14,* 24-29.

Crow, M.L. Motivation and student learning. Unpublished presentation made at a teaching-learning conference, University of Cincinnati, October 15, 1976.

Deci, E. The effect of externally mediated rewards in intrinsic motivation. *Journal of Personality and Social Psychology,* 1971, *18,* 105-15.

DeLay, D. Preliminaries of a learning theory. In D. Nyberg and D. DeLay, eds., *Tough and Tender Learning.* Monterey, Calif.: National Press Books, 1971.

Duchastel, P.C., and Merrill, P.F. The effects of behavioral objectives on learning: A review of empirical studies. *Review of Educational Research,* 1973, *43,* 53-69.

Ferster, C.B. Individualized instruction in a large introductory psychology college course. *Psychological Record,* 1968, *18,* 521-32.

Gorman, A.H. *Teachers and Learners: The Interactive Process of Education,* 2nd ed. Boston: Allyn & Bacon, 1974.

Harmin, M.; Kirschenbaum, H.; and Simon, S.B. *Clarifying Values Through Subject Matter.* Minneapolis, Minn.: Winston Press, 1973.

Homme, L., and Tosti, D. *Behavioral Technology: Motivation and Contingency Management.* San Rafael, California: Individual Learning Systems, 1971.

Johnson, K.R., and Ruskin, R.S. *Behavioral Instruction: An Evaluative Review.* Washington, D.C.: American Psychological Association, 1977.

Johnston, J.M., and Pennypacker, H.S. A behavioral approach to college teaching. *American Psychologist,* 1971, *26,* 219-44.

Kifer, E. Relationships between academic achievement and personality characteristics: A quasi-longitudinal study. *American Educational Research Journal,* 1975, *12,* 191-220.

Lepper, M.R., and Greene, D. *The Hidden Costs of Rewards.* Hillsdale, N.J.: Lawrence Erlbaum, 1978.

Mager, R. *Preparing Instructional Objectives.* Belmont, Calif.: Fearon, 1972.

Maslow, A.H. *Motivation and Personality.* New York: Harper & Row, 1954.

Maslow, A.H. Lessons from the peak experiences. In R. E. Farson, ed., *Science and Human Affairs.* Palo Alto, Calif.: Science and Behavior Books, 1965.

Melton, R.F. Resolution of conflicting claims concerning the effect of behavioral objectives on student learning. *Review of Educational Research,* 1978, *48,* 291-302.

Michael, J.L. *Management of Behavioral Consequences in Education.* Inglewood, Calif.: Southwest Regional Laboratory for Educational Research and Development, 1967.

Rausch, H.L., and Borden, E.F. Warmth in personality development and in psychotherapy. *Psychiatry,* 1957, *20,* 351–63.

Robin, A. Behavioral instruction in the college classroom. *Review of Educational Research,* 1976, *46,* 313–54.

Rogers, C.R. *Freedom to Learn.* Columbus, Ohio: Charles E. Merrill, 1969.

Rogers, C.R. Can learning encompass both ideas and feelings? *Education,* 1975a, *95,* 103–6.

Rogers, C.R. Questions I would ask myself if I were a teacher. *Education,* 1975b, *95,* 134–39.

Schmuck, R.A., and Schmuck, P.A. *Group Processes in the Classroom,* 3rd ed. Dubuque, Iowa: William C. Brown, 1979.

Schutz, W. *Profound Simplicity.* New York: Bantam, 1979.

Schutz, W. *Joy.* New York: Grove, 1967.

Simon, S., and Clark, J. More values clarification. San Diego, Calif.: Permont Press, 1976.

Skinner, B. F. *Beyond Freedom and Dignity.* New York: Alfred A. Knopf, 1971.

Springer, N. A teacher in an alien field. In P. Runkel, R. Harrison, and M. Runkel, eds., *The Changing College Classroom.* San Francisco: Jossey-Bass, 1972.

Stanford, G., and Roark, A.E. *Human Interaction in Education.* Boston: Allyn & Bacon, 1974.

Truax, C.B., and Carkhuff, R.R. *Toward Effective Counseling and Psychotherapy.* Chicago: Aldine, 1967.

Watson, J.B. *Behaviorism.* Chicago: University of Chicago Press, 1924.

Weinstein, G. *Education of the Self.* Amherst, Mass.: Mandala, 1976.

Chapter 5

Designing Classroom Experiences Based on Student Styles and Teaching Styles

I've been trying to individualize my Western civilization class by offering the students their choice of topics, but it's sure not working the way I had hoped it would. What's wrong?

I tried organizing my English 101 students into groups so they could discuss their reading more easily, but it seems that just as many students are turned off by that as are by lecture. How can I reach all of them?

You know, every time I offer my composition students a completely free choice of topic and style, the same students hound me for specific directions and assignments. They seem to think I must have a hidden format that they are somehow supposed to find, and they don't want to believe that it's really up to them.

I've tried everything—films, field trips, discussions, lectures, guests, problems, case studies—nothing seems to reach everybody. What can I do?

Comments and questions like these abound in our workshops and throughout colleges and universities when faculty address the question of how best to teach. Unfortunately, there is probably no single way to reach all students, and no amount of testing new ideas is likely to result in a panacea. What we can do, however, is address directly the varieties of ways in which people both learn and teach.

To begin with, it is important to remember that various individual differences exist among students and teachers. Variations in intellectual capacity, emotional level, motivation, personal values, attitudes about learning, and social skills are only a few of the personality characteristics that influence classroom learning. Because of the potential to use knowledge of the variety in personality characteristics to improve classroom instruction, there is an emphasis on this problem in the professional literature. Unfortunately, in our experience, many instructors are relatively unaware of this literature and its implications for teaching, thereby creating a major problem in the classroom. *There is a tendency to assume that students are basically alike.* A teacher typically employs a certain teaching style and methods compatible with that style regardless of whatever personality differences exist among students. An instructor who assumes an expert–formal authority teaching style probably relies on lecture methods. Students who prefer to work alone, or who learn best interacting with others, or who do not value passive learning opportunities may not do their best in such a class. Furthermore, a lack of understanding of what student and teacher styles are possible prevents instructors from developing other instructional options that would better meet the challenges inherent in the diversity among students.

What specific characteristics of students should we consider when designing classroom experiences? What are the implications of such differences for satisfaction with a course and student achievement? How might teaching styles be selected that are more compatible with the personality characteristics of students? Such questions flow naturally from any concern with individual differences among students and teachers, but they are not easy to answer. Research into this area is only beginning to uncover some of the ways instructors can use information about student and teacher styles. This chapter provides some current information about this issue. Thus it provides at least a partial answer to the questions we have listed.

The personality characteristics that distinguish one student or group of students from another are often called *student learning styles.* Pat Cross and Charles Claxton and Yvonne Ralston, in their reviews of the literature, have identified several dozen personality characteristics associated with students. Such characteristics include a variety of attitudes and values students have about learning, how they like to think, and how they want information presented. This represents an abundance of riches—an abundance, unfortunately, that is a mixed blessing. Although it gives us a number of student characteristics to consider when planning our classes, it also makes it difficult to select those that are most important or that might produce the best results. There are no *comparative* studies of this large number of personality characteristics and their relative importance in promoting student learning.

Instead of comparisions among individual personality characteristics, we find that researchers and practitioners in this field have tended to group certain personality dimensions into learning style models. *These models generally emphasize either the cognitive functioning of students, the nature of the social interactions in the classroom, or the instructional preferences of students.* A variety of models exists, but some have been researched and used more than others. Thus we can place confidence in the validity and reliability of some more than others. In this chapter, we present representative models from the cognitive, social interaction, and instructional preference categories. Our selection of models represents our biases regarding which ones have a good empirical base, as well as those models that have been used to help design classroom experiences. As you read, remember that this is a relatively new area and some personal experimentation may be necessary to find an approach that fits your needs. By presenting several different approaches, we hope to encourage some experimentation in using student learning styles that might help you enhance the design of your classroom procedures.

Cognitive Models

Cognitive models of learning style emphasize those intellectual characteristics that function to help us learn. Herman Witkin refers to cognitive characteristics as "modes of functioning that we reveal throughout our perceptual and intellectual activities in a highly consistent and pervasive way" (1977, p. 39). Each of us develops certain preferences or typical approaches for using our cognitive characteristics to perceive, to think, and to remember. Such preferences or approaches constitute our cognitive learning style.

Field Independence and Field Dependence

Based on his early work on perceptual processes, Herman Witkin identified two types of cognitive styles: *field dependent* and *field independent.* When trying to identify target stimuli embedded in a background, field-dependent individuals have a difficult time. They would, for example, have a much more difficult time distinguishing the types of spices used in something they tasted. Field-independent individuals are not confused as easily by background stimulation. They could more easily identify the spices used in the recipe.

With Donald Goodenough and Phillip Oltman, Witkin extended the analysis of these two styles to describe how people learn. It is clear from this analysis that field independence and field dependence refer to much more than an ability to pick out certain stimuli from their backgrounds. They also describe the ways that individuals process information. The two styles are best seen as opposite ends of a continuum that describes how we handle information we must acquire. People who are field independent tend to rely on internal cues for processing information. They try to analyze things into their parts and are able to work independently. Field-dependent individuals rely more on all the external stimuli in a task. They have a much more difficult time separating the individual parts from the whole. They also tend to need other people around them when learning and are more likely to consult with others before making decisions. In Witkin's words:

> The person who, in the laboratory, is strongly influenced by the surrounding visual framework in his perception of an item within it is also likely, in social situations, to use the prevailing social frame of reference to define his attitudes, his beliefs, his feelings, and even his self-view from moment to moment [1975, p. 43].

It is not "good" or "bad" to be more field independent or field dependent. Both sets of characteristics help students adapt to the demands of their educational environments. One way the styles help is to orient students toward particular fields of study. The results of a survey of 1422 students by Witkin, Goodenough, and Oltman illustrate this point. They found that knowledge of a student's cognitive style predicted his or her college major and eventual occupation after formal education. Field-independent students were more likely to major in mathematics and the sciences. These are subjects that require people to be analytical, are not social in content, and do not depend on interpersonal relations. On the other hand, such majors as elementary and early childhood education, speech therapy, nursing, social work, and business personnel work were favored by relatively field-dependent students. Such fields require people to work closely with other individuals. Both types reported a high degree of satisfaction with their majors, and there were no differences in the grades they achieved—they earned similar grades in a different mix of courses.

Neither cognitive characteristic seemed to affect satisfaction with a major or achievement in that major field, provided, of course, the student had selected a major that matched his or her cognitive style. When students had not, their satisfaction and achievement were less. Most such students, however, recognized that the fields they had chosen were not for them. Eventually, most switched majors to one that was more compatible with their field-independent or field-dependent style.

Students with each style also adapt differently to various classroom procedures. Herman Witkin and his colleagues note that classroom procedures that emphasize student discussion and small groups are preferred by field-dependent students. Field-dependent students also like teachers to structure classroom goals and requirements for them. Relatively field-independent individuals are better able to set their learning goals and appreciate the freedom to do this in class. They prefer less structure and guidance from the teacher.

As you might expect, teachers have similar styles. Witkin observes that relatively field-dependent instructors prefer a great deal of interaction with students. They are likely to use more group methods in class. Teachers who are relatively field independent tend to be somewhat impersonal and to lecture more. They also want to structure things for students so they know exactly what is expected. Finally, teachers and students with the same style tend to like each other more. There is less frustration with the class and less tension in the teacher-student interaction when styles are compatible.

Measuring field independence and field dependence. The Group Embedded Figure Test is often used to assess field dependence. You might, however, be interested in how the test works and the results you can expect to obtain from it. Figure 5.1 contains an exercise that uses embedded figures similar to those found in the Group Embedded Figure Test. We have used this activity as a way to sensitize students and faculty to field-dependent and -independent styles. Your task is to find the figure on the *left* in one or more of those on the right. You are allowed one minute to complete the task, so try to spend about fifteen seconds on each set. As you work, glance at your watch to keep yourself on schedule. The correct responses are: item 1: b, c; item 2: a, b, c; item 3: a; item 4: a, b, c.

How many did you get correct? As a rough estimate, if you were able to identify seven, eight, or nine of the illustrations correctly, you are probably more field independent than you are field dependent. Scores of zero, one, two, or three suggest a tendency toward field dependence. Scores of four, five, or six suggest that both of these characteristics are present. Are there any aspects of your behavior as a teacher that correspond to your style as suggested by this exercise?

Cognitive Mapping

Joseph Hill and his colleagues have developed a rather comprehensive approach to assessing the cognitive components of our learning styles. This

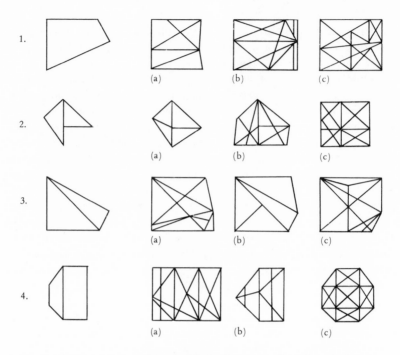

Figure 5.1. In each set of drawings, the figure on the left appears in one or more of the three illustrations on the right. Try to find it. You have one minute to complete the task. Do not trace over the drawings. You must try to identify them visually.

Source: From Anthony F. Grasha, *Practical Applications of Psychology*, 2nd ed., p. 50. Copyright © 1983 by Little, Brown and Company (Inc.). Reprinted by permission.

approach tries to determine certain preferences that each of us has for the processes we use to gather information, think and make inferences, and make decisions and that determine our interest in ourselves, other people, and objects around us.

Gathering information. Of primary concern here are the sensory modalities that we prefer to use. There is no doubt that people vary in their use of physical senses. Some learn best by listening, and it is these we satisfy best with the conventional lecture. For those students who prefer to use their visual sense to gather information, readings and visual aids are important. Students who need tactile and kinesthetic involvement probably like to manipulate objects to help them learn. Some of these eventually go into technical fields like electronics and computer science. Students also may rely on nonverbal messages to gather information from a teacher about what is important or whether the student's response is appreciated.

Thinking and making inferences. An important part of the way we carry out these activities is how we process information. Such things as a preference for deductive reasoning, a tendency to look for similarities and differences, and the use of rules to help us accept or reject information are included. Students who like to look for similarities and differences among things may enjoy classes where they are challenged to compare and contrast aspects of the course content. People who prefer to think deductively may find themselves quite comfortable in a geometry class, but may not like an English literature course as much.

Decision-making processes. A consideration in decision making is the extent to which we like to make decisions for ourselves, rather than consulting other people. The other people may be peers, friends, family members, teachers or other authority figures in our lives. Students who like to think for themselves about content may resent classes where they have to collaborate with other students. On the other hand, students who like to rely on other people when making decisions about answers to problems or other course content would welcome working with others.

Interest in self, others, and objects. Considerations in this area include how well we know ourselves, our ability to empathize with others, our willingness to communicate with people and to enjoy the beauty of the world around us, and our awareness of time and time expectations. For example, a student who is not concerned about time would not enjoy a course that required rigid schedules. Someone who is unwilling to communicate would not be a good candidate for a discussion group or an education or social science major. Someone who can empathize with other people and enjoys the beauty of the environment would probably find satisfaction in courses in art, aesthetics, or humanistic psychology.

A student's cognitive style includes aspects of each of the four categories we have just discussed. When combined, they can be used to suggest classroom procedures and courses that are compatible with a student's style. This could be accomplished by tailoring entire classes to certain cognitive styles or providing variations within a class through modules or other devices. In one study, Joseph Hill and Derek Nunney assigned students to learning tasks that matched their preferences for gathering information, thinking, and making decisions. Some students preferred to gather information visually, to think in a logical, step-by-step fashion, and to work alone to make decisions regarding content. These students took independent study courses with content presented on slides and written materials organized in small, easy-to-understand steps. Other students preferred to gather information by hearing it, disliked highly structured presentations, and enjoyed peer interactions. They were given opportunities for group discussion and other group projects. Students given educational environments compatible with their cognitive styles were much more satisfied with their learning and were able to progress through the information more effectively.

In a related study, Lee DeNike and Sheldon Strother tried to determine the cognitive characteristics of students who benefited the most from classes that used role plays and simulations of real-life events. Students who were most satisfied with and achieved the most after such activities preferred to gather information by listening to others, organized material by applying rules, and preferred peer-group interactions to interpret content and make decisions.

Measuring a student's cognitive map. The four general categories we have mentioned are expanded into twenty-seven specific cognitive characteristics in Hill's Cognitive Style Mapping Inventory. A brief description of these characteristics is included in Table 5.1. The Cognitive Style Mapping Inventory asks students to respond to 224 descriptive statements like "If I hear the daily news on the radio, I understand it better than if I read it in the newspaper" and "I like to figure out the way the parts of a whole fit together." Each of the twenty-seven learner characteristics is rated as Major (true more than half the time), Minor (true less than half the time), or Negligible (rarely true). Figure 5.2 is a cognitive map of one of the authors (AFG).

The Kolb Approach

David Kolb has developed a comprehensive model of learning that takes into account four processes in acquiring information and learning skills. They are:

- *Concrete experience.* Involving ourselves fully in a new experience. Seeking out experiences so we can feel first hand what they're like.

- *Reflective observation.* Observing other people doing things and trying to learn what we can from those experiences, or developing observations about our own experiences in a learning environment.

- *Abstract conceptualization.* Creating concepts and theories to explain our observations about the world around us.

- *Active experimentation.* Using the theories and concepts we have acquired to solve problems and make decisions.

According to Kolb, we can conceptualize each of these processes as being one of four stages in human learning. Most people proceed through the stages of concrete experience, reflective observation, abstract conceptualization, and active experimentation. That is, people have a concrete experience, observe and reflect upon it, and then form abstract concepts and generalizations that, in turn, lead to hypotheses to be tested in further actions. All of this leads the individual to have new experiences. Although this cycle through the four stages is typical, Kolb notes that not everyone follows this sequence all the time. The direction learning takes is also gov-

Figure 5.2. Cognitive map of Tony Grasha from data generated by Hill's Cognitive Style Mapping Inventory. This version was used at Hillsborough Community College in Tampa, Florida. The major characteristics suggest the author prefers to gather information through reading and touch. He enjoys the esthetic qualities of things around him and has a good understanding of himself. In making decisions, he is likely to consult with other people but can also think for himself. When thinking he looks for relationships, categorizes things, and looks for differences among ideas.

No.	Cognitive Characteristic	Score	*Relative Importance of Cognitive Characteristic* 00000 *Negligible* 00000 - - - - - *Minor* - - - - - +++++ *Major*
1.	T(AL)	16	X (Negligible)
2.	T(AG)	19	X (Negligible)
3.	T(VL)	24	X (Major)
4.	T(VQ)	18	X (Negligible)
5.	Q(A)	19	X (Negligible)
6.	Q(O)	23	X (Major)
7.	Q(S)	22	X (Major)
8.	Q(T)	26	X (Major)
9.	Q(V)	24	X (Major)
10.	Q(P)	23	X (Major)
11.	Q(CEM)	22	X (Minor)
12.	Q(CES)	26	X (Major)
13.	Q(CET)	24	X (Major)
14.	Q(CH)	21	X (Minor)
15.	Q(CK)	20	X (Minor)
16.	Q(CKH)	22	X (Minor)
17.	Q(CP)	22	X (Minor)
18.	Q(CS)	27	X (Major)
19.	Q(CT)	22	X (Minor)
20.	(A)	19	X (Negligible)
21.	(F)	25	X (Major)
22.	(I)	26	X (Minor)
23.	(D)	24	X (Minor)
24.	(L)	27	X (Minor)
25.	(M)	25	X (Minor)
26.	(R)	25	X (Minor)
27.	(K)	24	X (Minor)

erned by the needs and goals of the individual. For some people the movement may be from actor to observer, or from specific involvement to general analytical detachment. Or, because our needs and goals make learning a highly individualized process, we may simply emphasize one stage more than another. A mathematician, for example, may come to place a great deal of emphasis on abstract concepts. A poet, on the other hand, may come to place great emphasis on concrete experience. A business manager may be concerned more with active application of concepts; a

---

Table 5.1. Cognitive Characteristics in the Hill System

1. *Theoretical Auditory Linguistics*—T(AL)	Gathering information through words; finding meaning through words; a preference for words.
2. *Theoritical Auditory Quantitative*—T(AQ)	Gathering information through spoken numbers; finding meaning through spoken numbers or nonword symbols.
3. *Theoretical Visual Linguisitcs*—T(VL)	Gathering information through seeing words; finding meaning through reading words; a preference for reading.
4. *Theoretical Visual Quantitative*—T(VQ)	Gathering information through numerical symbols; finding meaning through numerical symbols; a preference for seeing nonword symbols.
5. *Qualitative Auditory*— Q(A)	Gathering information and perceiving meaning through hearing.
6. *Qualitative Olfactory*— Q(O)	Gathering information and perceiving meaning through smell.
7. *Qualitative Savory*— Q(S)	Gathering information and perceiving meaning through taste.
8. *Qualitative Tactile*— Q(T)	Gathering information and perceiving meaning through touch, temperature, and pain.
9. *Qualitative Visual*— Q(V)	Gathering information and perceiving meaning through sight.
10. *Qualitative Proprioceptive*—Q(P)	Ability to use internal cues to gather information or to convey the meaning of something.
11. *Qualitative Empathic*— Q(CEM)	Ability to identify with, or have a vicarious experience of, another person's feelings, ideas, or volitions.
12. *Qualitative Esthetic*— Q(CES)	Ability to view with enjoyment the "beauty" of other people, objects, or events.
13. *Qualitative Ethical*— Q(CET)	Having a commitment to a set of values, or a group of moral principles, and using them to help interpret events.
14. *Qualitative Histrionic*— Q(CH)	Being able to exhibit deliberately an emotion or other behavior to get an effect.
15. *Qualitative Kinesic*— Q(CK)	Ability to communicate and understand through nonverbal means.

naturalist may have highly developed observational skills. Because variations in the direction of learning and the use of various processes occur, each of us has relatively weak and strong points in our learning styles. Knowledge of these strengths and weaknesses can help us enhance our ability to become more effective learners.

Kolb finds that the four abilities described combine to form four learning style clusters. These are shown in Figure 5.3. People who rely on abstract conceptualizing and active experimenting are called *convergers*. They like to find specific, concrete answers, and when presented with a task they

16. *Qualitative Kinesthetic—* Q(CKH)	Ability to perform motor skills in an acceptable manner.
17. *Qualitative Proxemics—* Q(CP)	Ability to judge the acceptable physical and social distance between oneself and other people.
18. *Qualitative Synoetics—* Q(CS)	Having knowledge about oneself.
19. *Qualitative Transactional—*Q(CT)	Ability to communicate with others to sell a product or influence behavior.
20. *Associates—*(A)	Extent to which one is influenced by friends and other people outside the family when drawing inferences or making decisions.
21. *Family—*(F)	Extent to which one is influenced by family members when drawing inferences or making decisions.
22. *Individual—*(I)	Showing independence in making decisions and drawing inferences about the world.
23. *Difference—*(D)	Making inferences by comparing and/or contrasting things.
24. *Appraisal—*(L)	Being able to use with equal weight inferences drawn by relationships, differences, and magnitude.
25. *Magnitude—*(M)	Making inferences by using categorical thinking and using personal norms to accept ideas as true or to reject them.
26. *Relationship—*(R)	Making inferences by considering the relationship between two or more things.
27. *Deductive—*(K)	Using deductive reasoning or logical proof as used in geometry.
[a]28. *Qualitative Temporal—* Q(T)	Being aware of time and time expectations.

[a]This characteristic is included in most accounts of Hill's system. However, it is not included in the cognitive map shown in Figure 5.2 and is not part of the information in the Hillsborough Community College version of Hill's system, on which the map is based.

112

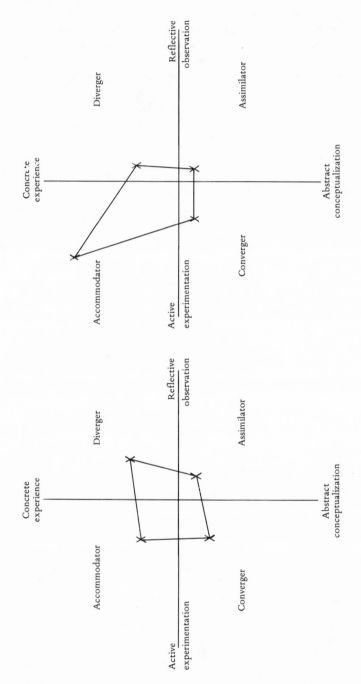

Figure 5.3. Learning styles from the Kolb system. The matrix on the left represents the profile of a flexible learner; the matrix on the right of a learner with a preference skewed toward accommodation.

move quickly to find the answer. They are relatively unemotional and prefer dealing with things rather than people. *Assimilators* rely on the cognitive skills of abstract conceptualizing and reflective observation. They like to assimilate diverse items into an integrated whole. They are more interested in theoretical concerns and have little interest in applications. People who have skills in concrete experience and reflective observation are called *divergers*. They like to generate many ideas and enjoy working with people. *Accommodators* are best at concrete experience and active experimentation. They take risks, focus on doing things and having new experiences, and perform well in situations where they must adapt to new circumstances. They are intuitive and often use a trial-and-error strategy when solving problems.

Kolb finds that each type tends to drift into certain fields. Convergers typically have rather narrow interests and often specialize in an area of the physical sciences or engineering. Math and the sciences attract people who are assimilators. In particular, they are quite good at research and planning activities. Because of their people orientation and ability to generate ideas, divergers enter fields such as counseling, personnel management, and organizational development. Accommodators like a "hands-on" approach, often enter technical or business fields, and prefer action-oriented jobs such as those in sales and marketing.

Besides their implications for specific areas of study, the Kolb styles suggest that certain classroom procedures will fit certain student types better than others. Divergers may benefit more from discussion groups and working on group projects. Assimilators may make observations of concepts in naturalistic settings, watch role plays and simulations in class, and then generate concepts that describe and tie together what has occurred. Accommodators may prefer problem-solving activities and be good candidates for participants in classroom role plays and simulations. Convergers probably would find laboratory experiments and problems that have specific answers satisfying learning experiences.

Measuring the Kolb styles. The Kolb Learning Style Inventory measures an individual's position in relation to the four styles: converger, assimilator, diverger, and accommodator. The inventory requires that a person rank order nine sets of four words each according to the learner's perception of how well they describe his or her learning style. For example, "discriminating," "tentative," "involved," and "practical" would be rank ordered. In this example, each word is associated with a particular preference for learning. Thus, "discriminating" suggests concrete experience; "tentative" indicates reflective observation; "involved" is related to abstract conceptualization, and "practical" suggests active experimentation. The sum of the ranks for the nine sets of four words indicates one's score on each of the four dimensions. A matrix similar to those shown in Figure 5.3 is used to determine to what extent scores fall into each quadrant. Thus it is possible to determine to what degree a person is an accommodator, diverger, converger, or assimilator. Students with profiles that are fairly evenly distributed present no real problems to faculty. It is those with more skewed preferences who provide the real challenge in teaching. Such students tend to fall in the extremes of the quadrants shown in Figure 5.3.

Social Interaction Models

Students do not learn in a vacuum. Teachers, peers, close friends, and family members play a role in what they learn and how they learn. Social interaction models try to identify some of the important features of the interactions that students have and the role they play in learning.

The Fuhrmann-Jacobs Model

Glenn Johnson notes that some students are "dependent prone" and need highly structured settings in which to function, whereas others are "independent prone" and require greater flexibility and freedom. Barbara Schneider Fuhrmann and Ronne Jacobs added to this dichotomy a third category, the "collaborative prone," and developed a logical model that discriminates three classroom learning styles: the *dependent style,* the *collaborative style,* and the *independent style.*

Any one person will learn in all three styles but may prefer a particular style in a given situation, based on both personal preferences and the unique characteristics of the subject to be learned or the activity to be engaged in. In this model, no one style is better than another, although one may be more appropriate for a given individual or in a given situation. Thus, the categories are value-free. Table 5.2 outlines the three styles as they might apply to kinds of classroom experiences, with learner needs identified and appropriate teacher roles and behaviors specified.

Some learning outcomes require that a particular style be used. For example, most beginning skills classes assume that students have little or no prior experience, and a dependent learning style is therefore appropriate. If students are to learn to work with unfamiliar equipment—a computer terminal, for example—neither collaborative discussion nor independent exploration is an efficient, reliable means of learning. Similarly, in a course that focuses on developing skill in group problem solving, a collaborative style is most appropriate. Interaction with others is essential to the learning of the skill.

In addition to our being able to identify certain learner styles as appropriate to certain learning experiences, individuals may find particular

Table 5.2. Student and Teacher Descriptors

Learner Style	Learner Needs	Teacher Role	Teacher Behavior
Dependent (may occur in introductory courses, languages, some sciences, when learner has little or no information upon entering course).	Structure Direction External reinforcement Encouragement Esteem from authority	Expert Authority	Lecturing Demonstrating Assigning Checking Encouraging Testing Reinforcing Transmitting content Designing materials Grading
Collaborative (may occur when learner has some knowledge, information, and ideas and would like to share them or try them out).	Interaction Practice Probe self and others Observation Participation Peer challenge Peer esteem Experimentation	Co-learner Environment setter	Interacting Questioning Providing resources Modeling Providing feedback Coordinating Evaluating Managing Observing processes Grading
Independent (may occur when learner has much more knowledge or skill upon entering the course and wants to continue to search on own. Learner may feel instructor cannot offer as much as he or she would like).	Internal awareness Experimentation Time Nonjudgmental support	Facilitator	Allowing Providing requested feedback Providing resources Consulting Listening Negotiating Evaluating

Source: © Copyright 1980 by Ronne Jacobs and Barbara Schneider Fuhrmann. Reprinted by permission.

styles more than others in keeping with their personalities. Some of us are simply more collaborative (or more dependent, or more independent) than others and, when given a choice of ways in which to accomplish a given objective, are more likely to select the option that allows the greatest interaction (or reliance, or freedom and personal responsibility). In the process of individualizing teaching and learning, some teachers are developing learning packets that allow students to select the method they want to use to reach a particular objective. Table 5.3 details objectives for two hypothetical courses, the student options for reaching the objectives, and the means of evaluation that will be used to measure the students' success.

Note that it is the outcome, not the method, that is important in this example; thus the student has the choice of the *means* of attaining the objective. In an extreme oversimplification of the personality type that would choose each alternative, we envision the options in Table 5.3 being offered to a class composed of Peanuts characters. Linus would undoubtedly select option 1, Charlie Brown option 2, and Schroeder option 3.

In results obtained from over eight hundred undergraduate and graduate students in fifteen different institutions, Fuhrmann and Jacobs found that

---

Table 5.3. Sample Learning Packets

Psychology 101: Objective 15

The student will demonstrate knowledge of the three major schools of psychological thought by passing a multiple-choice exam based on the concepts essential to each.

- *Option 1:* Attend three one-hour lectures and complete assigned readings and worksheets. Worksheets will be corrected by instructor or teaching assistant.
- *Option 2:* Attend discussion groups led by instructor and teaching assistant and participate in dialogue concerning the schools of psychological thought.
- *Option 3:* Use bibliography and text to study on your own.

Exam will be composed of fifty multiple-choice items. Scoring will be as follows: A = 95–100 percent; B = 86–94 percent; C = 78–85 percent; D = 70–77 percent.

English 100: Objective 25

The student will demonstrate the ability to identify and use gerund phrases by successfully passing an objective quiz in which gerund phrases must be both identified and used correctly.

- *Option 1:* Attend the quiz section in which the instructor will explain gerund phrases and their use.
- *Option 2:* Meet with peers and teaching assistant to discuss and practice using gerund phrases.
- *Option 3:* Study the text on your own.

The quiz will include identifying ten gerund phrases and constructing five gerund-phrase sentences.

---

older students are less dependent than younger students, and advanced students less dependent than beginners. The strength of collaboration remains the same. Thus it appears that as students mature through the college years, their need for structure decreases, perhaps as a result of their experiences. Collaboration, however, would appear to be more a function of personality than of learning, at least as this preliminary work suggests.

Measuring the Fuhrmann-Jacobs styles. Based on work with the model of independent, dependent, and collaborative interactions in a variety of settings, Fuhrmann and Jacobs developed the instrument that is shown in Table 5.4. It asks students to classify personally positive classroom learning experiences according to behavioral descriptors of classroom activities.

A student is first asked to identify a personally positive classroom learning experience—a "learning highlight," described on the instrument as "an activity or event that was a positive, rewarding and personally meaningful experience for you. It might be a whole course (e.g., English Literature 205), or one activity (e.g., my research project in Biology 101)." After identifying a highlight, the student reads thirty-six behavioral descriptors of classroom activities and checks those that apply to the highlight. Twelve of the descriptors show a dependent style, twelve a collaborative style, and twelve an independent style. For example, the statement "I achieved goals I set" clearly indicates an independent approach, the statement "I did exactly what was expected of me" characterizes dependence, and the statement "My classmates and I challenged each others' ideas" describes collaboration. The entire process is repeated three more times, and the students' style preferences are measured by noting the specific behaviors that were prevalent in the learning experiences they found most meaningful.

Scores are developed by noting the relative weight of each of the three styles. The interpretation of scores is as follows:

- The D score, indicating *dependence* in the learning situation, refers to the learner's expectation that it is the teacher who is primarily responsible for the learning that occurs. The learner with a high D score has had positive previous experiences in which the teacher assumed total responsibility for content, objectives, materials, learning experiences, and evaluation. The learner perceived the teacher to be the expert and authority.

- The C score, indicating *collaboration,* refers to the learner's expectation that the responsibility for learning should be shared by teacher and learners. The learner with a high C score has had positive experiences in which the teacher shared responsibility and encouraged participation in all aspects of the learning design. Learners have enjoyed interaction and perceive their peers as well as the teacher as possessing expertise or input worthy of consideration.

Table 5.4. Learning Interaction Inventory

	I.	II.	III.	IV.
1. The teacher's frequent quizzes forced me to keep up with the course.				
2. I appreciated the teacher presenting most of the material in the course.				
3. I achieved the goals I set.				
4. I cooperated with my classmates on our work.				
5. I shared my ideas with other classmates.				
6. I appreciated the teacher's having designed all the learning experiences for the course.				
7. I criticized others' ideas and pointed out areas they may not have discovered.				
8. Being able to try out new ideas was important to me.				
9. New ideas stimulated my curiosity, and I worked to satisfy myself.				
10. I used available resources for my own purposes.				
11. I frequently encouraged my classmates to continue working, look for alternatives, move toward goals.				
12. I felt good about the teacher's well-detailed plan and organization of the course.				
13. I created ways to accomplish my goals.				
14. I liked having the teacher assign all the materials we used.				
15. I offered ideas and thoughts which were accepted.				
16. I worked on my own.				
17. I developed the work I wanted to do.				
18. I listened to what others had to say.				

	I.	II.	III.	IV.
19. I evaluated my own learning.				
20. I worked patiently with others.				
21. I worked and talked with my classmates.				
22. I went beyond course expectations to satisfy my own curiosity.				
23. My classmates and I challenged each others' ideas.				
24. I learned from the teacher's well-executed demonstrations.				
25. I appreciated the opportunity to direct my own learning.				
26. I liked the teacher's thorough coordination of in-class and out-of-class activities.				
27. I did exactly what was expected of me.				
28. I'm glad the teacher directed our discussion.				
29. I liked the teacher's assuming full responsibility for assigning grades.				
30. I was warm and open to the people with whom I worked.				
31. I relied on the teacher's expert knowledge of the material.				
32. I'm glad the teacher alone decided on how our work was to be evaluated.				
33. I designed my own experiences.				
34. Class members co-designed parts of the course.				
35. I created a new approach or idea.				
36. I liked having time to work with my classmates.				

Table 5.4. *(Continued)*

In items 37-40, circle the appropriate response(s):

37. For experience number I,
    a) I had the necessary knowledge and skill in the content area to direct my own learning.

    A great deal   Quite a bit   Some   Little

    b) I had the confidence and motivation to direct my own learning.

    A great deal   Quite a bit   Some   Little

    For experience number II,
    a) I had the necessary knowledge and skill in the content area to direct my own learning.

    A great deal   Quite a bit   Some   Little

    b) I had the confidence and motivation to direct my own learning.

    A great deal   Quite a bit   Some   Little

    For experience number III,
    a) I had the necessary knowledge and skill in the content area to direct my own learning.

    A great deal   Quite a bit   Some   Little

    b) I had the confidence and motivation to direct my own learning.

    A great deal   Quite a bit   Some   Little

    For experience number IV,
    a) I had the necessary knowledge and skill in the content area to direct my own learning.

    A great deal   Quite a bit   Some   Little

    b) I had the confidence and motivation to direct my own learning.

    A great deal   Quite a bit   Some   Little

38. In a class where I had a sizeable amount of knowledge and skill and was confident and motivated, I would most want the teacher to incorporate the following approach(es):

    Tell me what to do   Share with me   Let me do it alone

39. In a class where I had some amount of knowledge and skill and was confident and motivated, I would most want the teacher to incorporate the following approach(es):

    Tell me what to do   Share with me   Let me do it alone

40. In a class where I had minimal amount of knowledge and skill and was confident and motivated, I would most want the teacher to incorporate the following approach(es):

    Tell me what to do   Share with me   Let me do it alone

Source: ©Copyright 1980 by Ronne Jacobs and Barbara Schneider Fuhrmann.
Reprinted by permission.

120

- The I score, indicating *independence,* refers to the learner's expectation that he will be encouraged to set and attain his own goals. The learner with a high I score has had positive experiences in which the teacher is perceived as one expert who may be asked to share expertise, but who helps learners develop their own expertise and authority and frequently acts as a resource to the learner.

- No individual style is implicitly better or worse than the others. In fact, each of us has used all three, and each has a current preference. The real key to being effective is to be able to use the one that is most appropriate at the moment. Appropriateness depends on a number of circumstances, most importantly, the individual's ability and willingness to learn the content, and the match between the learner's style preference and the teacher's teaching style preference. The dependent learner responds best to a directive teacher, the collaborative learner to a collaborative teacher, and the independent learner to a delegative teacher.

- A very high score on any one mode may mean only that the learner has been particularly successful with that mode in the past, or it may mean that she tends to overemphasize that mode, thus robbing herself of the opportunity to develop the other styles. A very low score may mean only that the learner has not been successfully exposed to that style, although it may also mean that she has been purposely avoiding learning that way.*

The Grasha-Riechmann Model

Tony Grasha and Sheryl Riechmann have developed an approach to learning styles based on the roles students play in the classroom. These roles show some of the preferences students have for interacting with their peers and the teacher, and their approach to course content. Six roles have been identified: competitive, collaborative, dependent, independent, participant, and avoidant. Each is described in Table 5.5, as are the classroom activities that students who use that role tend to prefer.

Each of the learning styles described in Table 5.5 occurs to some degree in every student. No student plays any one of the roles exclusively. Instead, people are seen as having a learning style profile composed of all roles, with some used more often than others.

It is tempting to assume that the roles a student brings to the classroom are relatively fixed, but research evidence suggests otherwise. How a teacher structures the classroom influences the learning style profile of students. In one study, Grasha reported that students in traditional lecture-oriented

*©Copyright 1980 by Ronne Jacobs and Barbara Schneider Fuhrmann. Adapted by permission.

Table 5.5. Student Learning Styles as Identified by Tony Grasha and Sheryl Riechmann.

Student Learning Style	Description	Classroom Activity Preference Based on Research Data
Competitive	This response style is exhibited by students who learn material in order to perform better than others in the class. They feel they must compete with other students in the class for the rewards of the classroom, such as grades or teachers' attention. They view the classroom as a win-lose situation, where they must always win.	To be a group leader in discussion or when working on projects . . . to ask questions in class . . . to be singled out for doing a particularly good job on a class-related activity. No real preference for any one classroom method over another (lectures, seminars) as long as the method has more of a teacher-centered focus than a student-centered focus.
Collaborative	This style is typical of students who feel they can learn the most by sharing ideas and talents. They cooperate with teachers and peers and like to work with others. They see the classroom as a place for social interaction as well as content learning.	Lectures with class discussion in small groups . . . small seminars . . . student-designed and -taught courses and classes . . . group rather than individual projects . . . peer-determined grades . . . talking about course issues outside of class with other students . . . instructor-group interaction.
Avoidant	This response style is typical of students who are not interested in learning course content in the traditional classroom. They do not participate with students and teachers in the classroom. They are uninterested or overwhelmed by what goes on in classes.	Generally turned off by classroom activities. Preferences include no tests . . . self-evaluation for grading . . . no required readings or assignments . . . blanket grades where everyone gets a passing grade. . . . Does not like enthusiastic teachers . . . well-organized lectures . . . instructor-individual interactions.

Participant	This style is characteristic of students who want to learn course content and like to go to class. They take responsibility for getting the most out of class and participate with others when told to do so. They feel that they should take part in as much of the class-related activity as possible and little that is not part of the course outline.	Lectures with discussion . . . opportunities to discuss material . . . both objective and essay type tests . . . class reading assignments . . . enthusiastic presentations of material . . . teachers who can analyze and synthesize material well.
Dependent	This style is characteristic of students who show little intellectual curiosity and who learn only what is required. They see teacher and peers as sources of structure and support. They look to authority figures for guidelines and want to be told what to do.	Teacher outlines or notes on the board . . . clear deadlines for assignments . . . teacher-centered classroom methods.
Independent	This response style is characteristic of students who like to think for themselves. They prefer to work on their own but will listen to the ideas of others in the classroom. They learn the content they feel is important and are confident in their learning abilities.	Independent study . . . self-paced instruction . . . problems that give the student an opportunity to think independently . . . projects that the student can design . . . a student-centered classroom setting rather than a teacher-centered one.

classroom environments tended to approach the learning situation with competitive, dependent, and avoidant student styles. Classroom environments that included group activities, individual projects, and requirements for extensive student participation led to students' adopting collaborative, independent, and participatory roles.

Besides the shift in styles often seen with regular exposure to particular classroom methods, a study by John Andrews suggests that students actually may benefit more from classroom methods that closely fit their styles. He found that students high on the collaborative scale reported a strong benefit to their learning from participating in a peer-centered chemistry discussion section. In contrast, students with a strong preference for the competitive style reported being helped to learn by instructor-centered classes and not to benefit as much by interacting in a peer-centered section. Andrews also found syle differences regarding which aspects of the sections were particularly helpful. Students with "impersonal" styles (independent, avoidant, competitive) identified the text, hand-outs, and lectures as most helpful. On the other hand, those with strong "personal" styles (collaborative, participant, dependent) found review sessions, study questions, and learning from other students as most beneficial for their learning. Overall, findings from his study suggest that students with different learning styles find that different methods and different aspects of courses help them to learn.

Measuring the Grasha-Riechmann styles. A ninety-item scale is used to assess the degree to which students see themselves assuming the six roles we have described. Students' profiles are obtained from their scores on each of the six subscales covered by the instrument. A sample of some of the items for each subscale is presented in Table 5.6. The items shown are for the *general class version* of the instrument. Students are asked to judge themselves on a five-point rating scale in terms of how much they agree or disagree with the statements as they apply to *all of their classes.* Another version of the instrument, the *specific class version,* has the same items rewritten to give the scale a frame of reference appropriate to a specific class.

The general and specific class versions of the instrument are used in somewhat different ways. The general class version has been used by instructors to assess the learning styles of students at the beginning of a course. Based on this information, some of the instructional procedures are tailored to meet the styles of students in the course. This instrument has also been used to assess the presence of particular learning styles across disciplines and colleges. The profiles of students in such areas as psychology, education, physics, mathematics, chemistry, history, English, engineering, philosophy, and political science are not significantly different. Further-

---

Table 5.6. Samples of Items from the Grasha-Riechmann Student Learning Style Scale, General Class Version

---

Competitive

- To get ahead in class, I think sometimes you have to step on the toes of the other students.
- I feel that I must compete with the other students to get a grade.

Collaborative

- I think an important part of classes is to learn to get along with other people.
- I find the ideas of other students relatively useful for helping me to understand the course material.

Dependent

- I accept the structure a teacher sets for a course.
- Before working on a class project, I try to get the approval of the instructor.

Independent

- I study what is important to me and not necessarily what the instructor says is important.
- I work on class-related projects (for example, studying for exams, preparing term papers) by myself.

Participant

- I am eager to learn about areas covered in class.
- I do my assignments whether I think they are interesting or not.

Avoidant

- I seldom get excited about material covered in a course.
- I try to spend as little time as possible on a course outside of class.

---

more, norms for graduate and undergraduate courses at the University of Cincinnati are also quite similar. This finding has additional support in research by Mary Anne Dillon at Texas Women's University. *Such data suggest that the classroom roles students are encouraged to play are on the average quite similar across disciplines and in graduate and undergraduate courses.*

When we compare four- and two-year institutions, or consider the sex of students or their ages, several significant variations in the learning styles of students appear. Grasha has found that two-year students tend to adopt more dependent, less independent, more competitive, and more participant student roles than do students in four-year institutions. Robert Kraft finds that among physical education majors, males adopt competitive, avoidant, and independent roles to a higher degree than do females. Women, on the other hand, are slightly more dependent and much more participatory in their classroom roles. If we look at age, Kraft notes that students over twenty-five are much more independent and participatory in their learning styles. Those under twenty-five show higher levels of avoidance and competitiveness and are less willing to participate in the classroom. Findings similar to Kraft's have been reported by Jim Eison and Jane Moore among two-year college students, and these findings are much like those found by Fuhrmann and Jacobs using their inventory.

The specific class version of the Grasha-Riechmann scales has been used as an outcome measure. Instructors trying innovative procedures or purposely trying to encourage one of the styles, such as independent or collaborative, have used this version as a check on their success. The profiles from classes using a discussion group or an independent study format are quite different from those from a lecture-oriented classroom. As you might expect, the former classroom procedures tend to encourage collaborative and independent roles in students. It appears, however, that for this to occur, classes must make extensive use of such procedures. Occasionally using them does not seem to alter the roles students report using in class.

Instructional Preference Models

Instructional preference models are an emerging area in the study of student learning styles and their classroom applications. Workers in this area are interested in discovering the preferences that students have for study methods, instructional media, course format, and other dimensions of classroom-related learning. The instruments that are developed to discover these preferences are grounded directly in the classroom experiences of the students. Thus the questions refer to specific aspects of the classroom and do not have the general nature of the items found in Kolb's, Hill's, or Witkin's system. They are much more in line with the classroom-related items found in the Grasha-Riechmann and Fuhrmann-Jacobs systems. Some approaches, such as that of Agnes Rezler and Victor Rezmovic, give a specific classroom frame of reference to several common classroom dimensions. A description of the Rezler and Rezmovic model is found in Table 5.7. Other models, such as that of Charles Friedman and Frank Stritter, focus entirely on preferences for various types of instructional processes. A brief description of the dimensions measured by the Friedman and Stritter model appears in Table 5.8.

Because the student preferences are grounded directly in the classroom-related learning experiences of the students, the types of actions instructors can take to match or modify certain preferences are much clearer. At this time, these models suggest another direction that work on learning styles might take: Although they have undergone the test of being used in classroom settings, there is not much empirical evidence to verify their supposed advantages and disadvantages. This work needs to be done.

Table 5.7. Characteristics of the Learning Preference Inventory

The Learning Preference Inventory (Rezler and Rezmovic) has two parts. Part 1 asks students to rank order six sets of six words according to their learning preferences. Part 2 asks them to rank order sentences instead of words in terms of how the sentences match their preferences for learning. There are nine different sets of six sentences that students must rank order.

The dimensions assessed by the Learning Preference Inventory are the following:

1. *Abstract:* Preference for learning theories and generating hypotheses that focus on general principles and concepts.

2. *Concrete:* Preference for learning tangible, specific, practical tasks with a focus on skills.

3. *Individual:* Preference for learning or working alone with an emphasis on self-reliance and solitary tasks such as reading.

4. *Interpersonal:* Preference for learning or working with others.

5. *Student-structured:* Preference for learning via student-organized tasks with an emphasis on autonomy and self-direction.

6. *Teacher-structured:* Preference for learning in a well-organized, teacher-directed class with expectations, assignments, and goals clearly identified.

Sample Items

Word rankings

Rank order the following in terms of how how well they describe your preferred mode of learning: factual, teacher-directed, teamwork, reading, self-evaluation, theoretical.

Sentence rankings

Rank order the following sentence completions in terms of your preferred mode of learning: I prefer:

a. work that would require cooperation among team members.

b. work with specific and practical ways of handling things.

c. work that would let me do things on my own.

d. work that would permit me to deal with ideas rather than things.

e. work that I could plan and organize myself.

f. work that would be clearly defined and specified by my supervisor.

Teaching Styles

If we believe that teaching represents an interaction between the learner and the instructor, then some attention must be given to the styles that teachers use. The literature on teaching styles is even less complete than that on learning styles—in particular, it is much more descriptive and there is not as much empirical research available on the concepts presented.

Table 5.8. Characteristics of the Instructional Preference Questionnaire

The Instructional Preference Questionnaire (Friedman and Stritter) is a fifty-seven-item instrument that asks students to agree or disagree with certain items or to indicate how beneficial they would be to their learning.

The dimensions measured by the instrument are the following:

1. *Involvement in determining course content:* This dimension measures the extent to which a student prefers to have input into content decisions in the classroom.
   Sample item: "I would willingly spend some of my free time helping a faculty member decide on the topics to be taught in his or her course."

2. *Preferred instructional media:* The score on this factor indicates the degree to which a student prefers "high technology" media (such as computers and tapes) over live presentations of course content, augmented by more traditional media such as slides.
   Sample item: "Overall, I prefer sitting in a classroom learning from a good instructor over sitting at a carrel learning from high quality audio-visual materials prepared by that instructor."

3. *Formal course structure:* This dimension concerns the student's ability to work in courses with varying degrees of course structure (for example, regularly scheduled classes and exams versus independent study).
   Sample item: "I would learn a lot more in a course if I were able to progress through the subject matter at my own pace, rather than the pace of the instructor and/or my classmates."

4. *Discovery learning:* The score on this factor indicates the extent to which a student desires opportunities to discover personally the principles and determine their appropriate modes of application.
   Sample item: "I prefer to discover for myself how to do something without a lengthy explanation beforehand."

5. *Reality testing:* A score on this dimension indicates the degree to which a student is interested in obtaining feedback on his or her ideas and opinions.
   Sample item: "When I hand in an assignment, I always review carefully the comments and corrections I receive from faculty."

Nonetheless, there are several interesting and potentially useful aspects of teaching styles that have been observed.

Joseph Axelrod, in an extremely general overview, classifies teachers as those who rely primarily on didactic modes—that is, they pass information on to students—and those who rely on evocative modes—they draw information and meaning from students. Joseph Adelson analogously describes the teacher as either *shaman,* who keeps the focus on himself, *priest,* who focuses on the discipline and sees herself as a representative of it, or *mystic healer,* who focuses on the student and student development.

A more discriminating and very useful approach has been taken by Richard Mann. Like the Grasha-Riechmann learning styles, Mann's approach focuses on the roles that teachers typically play in the classroom. A description of the six roles he has identified appears in Table 5.9. We have asked faculty to identify what roles from the list that Richard Mann developed they typically play. One way to do this is to pick your favorite class and to evaluate your teaching style using the categories in Table 5.9. Assign a 1 to the style that is most like you and a 6 to the style that is least like you. Rank order the others in between. This will give you a profile for that class.

You might want to do two things with your profile. One is to check it against the profile for another class you teach. Is it different in any way? What is it about your favorite class that makes it different? Is there anything in your teaching style for your favorite class you could use in another course? A second thing you can do with your profile is to ask students to evaluate your teaching style as they perceive it using the same method. Obtain the class rank, and then share your perception of your style. Some-

---

Table 5.9. Teacher Styles Identified by Richard Mann

- *Expert:* Transmits information—the concepts and perspectives of the field. Leans toward scholarly preparation of classes and is most comfortable in the role of presenting material and answering questions. Students' need for achievement can increase with this style, and they may fear appearing stupid or being "snowed" by teachers with this style.

- *Formal authority:* Sets goals and procedures for reaching goals. Defines structure and standards of excellence for evaluation of student performance. Style helps create dependency in students, and students may fear failing or pursuing irrelevant activities.

- *Socializing agent:* Attempts to clarify goals and career paths for students beyond the course. Tries to help prepare students for the field. Acts as a guide and gatekeeper for the inner circle. With this style, students need to clarify their interests and fear being rejected by the field or having their options reduced.

- *Facilitator:* Attempts to promote growth and creativity in students' own terms. Wants the student to overcome obstacles to learning and tries to respond to student needs. With this style, students' self-discovery often increases, but they can fear not developing a clear and useful identity.

- *Ego ideal:* Wants to convey the excitement and value of intellectual inquiry in a given field of study. Acts as a model for students to follow once they enter the field. With this style, students tend to like having a model to follow, but there is a fear of being bored or unmoved.

- *Person:* Wants to convey that teachers are people with a full range of human needs and skills. Tries to be self-revealing in ways that clarify one's totality beyond the task at hand. Encourages students to be warm and open. With this style, students generally appreciate the desire of the teacher to be a person and to want to know them as more than a student. A potential source of fear is that the student may be ignored or treated as a product.

Source: Adapted from Richard Mann et al., *The College Classroom* (New York: John Wiley, 1970), pp. 293–332, by permission of John Wiley & Sons, Inc.

times discrepancies occur between the teacher's and the students' perceptions. Asking people in class to suggest reasons for the discrepancy makes for an interesting discussion. Comparing student and teacher observations of teaching style is also one way to evaluate a course. You may find, for example, that you are less of a facilitator than you thought. This might suggest the use of more student-centered classroom procedures in the future.

Another approach to assessing your teaching style is to use the version of the Learning Interactions Inventory that Barbara Schneider Fuhrmann and Ronne Jacobs have adapted for teachers. In this inventory, teacher experiences are categorized as independent, dependent, or collaborative modes just as student styles are. For example, "I had students critique each other" indicates one dimension of a collaborative style, "I presented most of the material in the course" represents a dependent style, and "I encouraged students to design their own experience" indicates an independent style.

Although it is possible to separate the styles teachers demonstrate from those of their students, there is no a priori reason teachers and students cannot be described in similar ways. *As instructors, we are also learners, and some of the ways we learn may influence how we teach.* Consider the styles described in the cognitive and social interaction models. It is possible to describe ourselves, for example, as field independent or dependent; divergers or assimilators; or dependent or collaborative learners. A preference for teaching using student-centered methods might reflect in part our styles as field dependent, divergent, or collaborative learners. A tendency toward instructor-centered classroom procedures might reflect in part our styles as field independent, assimilating, or dependent learners.

Implications of Information on Student and Teacher Styles

A major implication of knowledge about student and teacher styles is that it can help us become more effective in our classroom endeavors. In discussing the possible impact of cognitive models, Pat Cross notes the following:

- Teachers and students should be helped to gain some insight into teaching and learning styles.
- People will probably be . . . more productive if they are studying . . . via a method compatible with their style.
- No one method should be regarded as a panacea for all students in all subjects.
- We need to be knowledgeable in devising . . . strategies to teach [the subjects all students must learn].

- Educators need to be aware of the cognitive styles of students in order to provide the appropriate kinds of reinforcement.
- The learning program [should not be] biased in favor of a particular cognitive style.
- More attention needs to be given to the potential of cognitive style for educational and vocational guidance.
- Relatively greater attention should be given to [building] on the strengths of individuals.
- Educators should remain flexible and experimental in their use of the concept [of learning style] [1976, pp. 130–133].

To implement some of Pat Cross's suggestions using both cognitive and social learning styles, *we might consider matching classroom procedures to the styles of individual students.* This might be done by obtaining a class profile and trying to provide instructional procedures that are as compatible as possible with that profile. Or we might diagnose the styles of individual students and, to the extent possible, give them assignments and activities compatible with their styles. The latter suggestion would be easiest to do with a small class, but there is no reason it could not be implemented on a selective basis in a larger class.

On the other hand, *we might consider mismatching the instructional procedures to the styles of the students.* The rationale for doing this is that people need to experience new things in order to grow. A student who is comfortable in a dependent mode might benefit from having to work independently. Similarly, people who are comfortable withdrawing from class activities might learn useful social skills if they had to collaborate with other people. Emphasizing a particular learning style is another way to formulate classroom goals. Instead of just concentrating on our content goals, we might also want to focus on which specific cognitive or social learning styles we will emphasize.

To match or mismatch learning styles might demand that we modify our teaching style. To do one or the other could force us into new modes of teaching. As teachers, we also are likely, at least initially, to feel some discomfort with trying a new experience. Yet we might benefit by having to "stretch" ourselves in our classroom roles.

Another important implication of knowledge of teacher and student styles is that they can help us understand why our relationships with some students are better than others. This is particularly true of the social styles. They suggest that some teacher-student style combinations are likely to be facilitative or to produce conflict. Consider the following combinations for a moment. What are some likely effects on teacher-student interactions?

- Teacher (expert)–Student (dependent)
- Teacher (facilitator)–Student (independent)

- Teacher (formal authority)–Student (collaborative)
- Teacher (facilitator)–Student (competitive)
- Teacher (expert)–Student (avoidant)

A third implication of the teacher and student style information is that your personal ways of categorizing the classroom may be just as useful. As is clear from this chapter, there are many ideas for using student and teacher personality characteristics in the classroom. But none of the authors mentioned has a patent on the best approach to such styles. In fact, you could view what they suggest as only one set of metaphors for describing the characteristics of teachers, students, and the classroom. You might have a better metaphor. Jack Noonan,[1] for example, has used the Catholic Church as a basis for one of his metaphors. He acknowledges ways that some classrooms are similar to the old Latin Mass, in which the priest stood on an alter and spoke in a foreign language with his back to the congregation. In some instances, classrooms may resemble the English Mass, in which the priest faces the congregation and speaks in English, and the audience participates in the ritual by singing and responding to prayers. Other classrooms are analogous to a Folk Mass. The priest stands among the congregation, guitars play, people hold hands and sing, and much interaction takes place. Some instructors have problems, Noonan notes, because they think they have a "Folk Mass" in class, but in reality, they are celebrating the old "Latin Mass." Or some instructors may want to achieve the "Folk Mass" and, examining the metaphor, may be stimulated to try to liven up their current instructional procedures.

You might develop your own metaphor from some aspect of your discipline. You might imagine the teacher-student relationship as the relationship between Eliza Doolittle and Henry Higgins in *My Fair Lady*, as a set of electrons revolving around the nucleus of an atom, as the organization of the Senate and House of Representatives, or perhaps as a surgeon in charge of an operating room team.

Metaphors aside, you can also learn a great deal about student learning styles simply by observing students and noting their behaviors. Which students seem to appreciate a clearly detailed outline and lecture? Which respond enthusiastically to a group work setting? Which like to read and think on their own? Which demonstrate the concentration necessary to work through a lengthy laboratory procedure? Which plan their study activities most thoroughly? Which like the freedom of a creative assignment? Which learn best from films? Which seem to need active involvement? Which are motivated more by grades than by accomplishment?

---

[1] Personal communication, 1978.

Which are "turned on" to the same topics you are? Which relish a heated discussion of issues? Which prefer the generation of alternatives rather than the specification of one right solution?

Summary

In this chapter, we have explored the dimensions of both student and teacher learning styles and have suggested some of the vast implications these styles have for course and classroom design and for teaching behaviors. We have seen that among the many personality variables that ensure our individual uniqueness are certain characteristics that can be studied with an eye toward how they influence learning. Models of student learning styles based on cognitive, social interaction, and instructional preferences were presented. The cognitive models included Witkin's field independence and field dependence; Hill's cognitive mapping; and Kolb's learning clusters. Their uses in the classroom and ways to measure them were emphasized. The social interaction models, Fuhrmann-Jacobs and Grasha-Riechmann, emphasize the relative strengths of particular social needs and roles. Each helps to understand student motivation and provides a means for structuring learning experiences accordingly. Instructional preference models emphasize specific features of the instructional environment and suggest ways that teachers can structure the classroom based on a student's preferences for modes of learning. The Rezler and Rezmovic and Friedman and Stritter models were discussed. This last area is relatively new, but it holds great promise for helping instructors design learning environments.

References

Adelson, J. *The University Teacher as Artist.* San Francisco: Jossey-Bass, 1973.

Andrews, J.D. Teaching format and student style: Their interactive effects on learning. *Research in Higher Education,* 1981, *14,* 161–78.

Axelrod, J. The teacher as model. *The American Scholar,* 1961, *30,* 395–401.

Berquist, W.H. and Phillips, S.R. *A Handbook for Faculty Development.* Washington, D.C.: Council for the Advancement of Small Colleges, 1975.

Claxton, C.; Adams, D.; and Williams, D. Using student learning styles in teaching. *AAHE Bulletin,* 1982, *34,* 1–9.

Claxton, C., and Ralston, Y. *Learning Styles: Their Impact on Teaching and Administration.* Washington, D.C.: AAHE-ERIC/Higher Education Research Report No. 10, 1978.

Cross, K.P. *Accent on Learning.* San Francisco: Jossey-Bass, 1976.

DeNike, L., and Strother, S.D. A learner characteristic vital to instructional development: Educational cognitive style. *Educational Technology,* 1975, *15,* 58–59.

Dillon, M.A. An investigation of learning styles of occupational therapy students. Unpublished master's thesis, School of Occupational Therapy, Texas Woman's University, Denton, Tex., 1980.

Eison, J., and Moore, J. Learning styles and attitudes of traditional age and adult students. Paper presented at Professional Organization Development Network, Chicago Conference, October, 1979.

Erickson, S. *Motivation for Learning.* Ann Arbor: University of Michigan Press, 1974.

Friedman, C., and Stritter, F. An empirical inventory comparing instructional preferences of medical and other professional students. *Proceedings of the Annual Conference on Research in Medical Education,* Washington, D.C.: AAMC, 1977.

Friedman, C., and Stritter, F. *Instructional Preference Questionnaire.* Chapel Hill: Office of Medical Studies, University of North Carolina, 1981.

Fuhrmann, B.S., and Jacobs, R. *The Learning Interactions Inventory.* Richmond: Ronne Jacobs Associates, 1980.

Grasha, A.F. Observations on relating teaching goals to student response styles and classroom methods. *American Psychologist,* 1972, *27,* 144–47.

Harvey, O.J.; Hunt, D.E.; and Schroder, H.M. *Conceptual Systems and Personality Organization.* New York: John Wiley & Sons, 1961.

Hill, J. *The Educational Sciences.* Bloomfield Hills, Mich.: Oakland Community College Press, 1976.

Hill, J., and Nunney, D.N. Personalized educational programs. *Audio-Visual Instructor,* 1972, *14,* 25–30.

Holzman, P.S., and Klein, G.S. Cognitive system principles of leveling and sharpening: Individual differences in assimilation effects in visual time error. *Journal of Psychology,* 1965, *37,* 105–22.

Johnson, G. *Analyzing College Teaching.* Manchaca, Texas: Sterling Swift Publishing Co., 1976.

Kolb, D.A. *The Learning Style Inventory: Technical Manual and Self-Scoring Test and Interpretation Booklet.* Boston: McBer and Company, 1976.

Kraft, R.E. An analysis of student learning styles. *Physical Education,* 1976, *20,* 140–42.

Mann, R.D.; Arnold, S.M.; Binder, J.; Cytrunbaum, S.; Newman, B.M.; Ringwald, J.; and Rosenwein, R. *The College Classroom: Conflict, Change, and Learning.* New York: John Wiley & Sons, 1970.

Rezler, A.G., and Rezmovic, V. The Learning Preference Inventory. *Journal of Applied Health,* 1981, *10,* 28–34.

Riechmann, S., and Grasha, A. A rational approach to developing and assessing the construct validity of a student learning style scale instrument. *Journal of Psychology,* 87, 1974, 213–23.

Witkin, H.A. Cognitive styles in the educational setting. *New York University Education Quarterly,* 1977, *8,* 14–20.

Witkin, H.A.; Goodenough, D.R.; and Oltman, P.K. Role of field-dependent and field-independent cognitive styles in academic evolution: A longitudinal study. *Journal of Educational Psychology,* 1977, *69,* 197–211.

Witkin, H.A., and Moore, C.A. *Field-Dependent and Field-Independent Cognitive Styles and Their Educational Implications.* Princeton, N.J.: Educational Testing Service, 1975.

Chapter 6
Getting Students Involved
in the Classroom

I have a very interesting subject area. I just can't see why students don't get excited about it. It's fascinating information, yet all they do is just sit there and not ask questions.

Basically, I don't get lots of questions or much discussion because the students lack preparation. I would say that 80 percent of the class is just not ready for college.

I guess I am a bit sarcastic at times, but I don't think the students mind. I can't see how that might turn them off from asking questions.

I don't think I intimidate students more than any other teacher, yet I don't see some of my colleagues having trouble getting people involved.

Look, if I had to do things like have students write out questions in advance, use small groups, and other things like that, I'm not sure I would want to handle the types of responses such things generate. I want them to talk and ask questions because they want to do it and not in response to some gimmick that I use.

135

Do these statements sound familiar? Perhaps you or someone you know has said similar things. They are responses from people in our workshops, seminars, and consulting experiences who have difficulty getting students involved. We find such reactions typical, and if we read beyond the frustration inherent in them, we think they contain several clues about factors that hinder student involvement. *One is a personal unwillingness to use or to accept alternate ways of teaching and interacting with students.* Although it might be easy to dismiss an instructor's unwillingness as simply caused by rigid or old-fashioned beliefs about the classroom, we find that to understand it we have to look for other reasons as well. These include certain beliefs teachers have about who is responsible for a lack of involvement and what is possible to accomplish in a classroom, concerns over giving up control over classroom processes, and an insensitivity to feedback. *A second factor in students' remaining relatively uninvolved is the type of communication climate created in the classroom.* Generally speaking, the extent to which instructors are insensitive to the ways in which they create one-way communication climates affects their ability to get students involved. Finally, *an insensitivity to the group processes that operate in classrooms* is a third factor. Important considerations here are the types of norms instructors help create for interaction, the ability of classroom goals and activities to meet the personal needs of class members, the type of leadership style used by the teacher, and the specific activities and interaction patterns the teacher creates for encouraging interaction.

Based on what was said in the last paragraph, it is possible to examine the problem of student involvement (or lack of involvement) as related to three sets of factors. They are *personal constraints within the teacher* that contribute to the lack of use of alternative ways of involving students, the nature of the *classroom communication climate,* and the types of *group processes* associated with managing and running the class. In the following sections, we present in more detail the characteristics of each factor and suggestions for how to handle them effectively in your teaching.

Personal Constraints Within the Teacher

To some degree, each of us resists changing our teaching methods. Yet to increase student involvement we must explore new ideas and begin to use them. Unfortunately certain personal beliefs, perceptions, and behaviors tend to constrain our ability to and interest in exploring such things. Let us examine several of them in more detail.

Attribution Errors

Harold Kelley, Edward Jones, and Richard Nisbett have studied the ways we try to explain our behaviors and the actions of other people. Each author approaches this problem somewhat differently, but there is considerable overlap in the conclusions they reach. One is *our tendency to blame external things for our problems.* An instructor encountering a lack of interest or involvement in students typically blames the students, the classroom facilities, the time of day, the required nature of the course, or any other handy factor. What is usually ignored or overlooked is his or her personal responsibility for the lack of involvement. Questions like the following are seldom asked:

- In what ways am *I* boring the class?
- What am *I* doing that hinders communication and interaction?
- How does *my* relationship with the class interfere?

This does not mean that the tendency to "blame the victim" or the situation is entirely without merit. Classroom facilities and the time of day may dampen people's motivation for participation. Some students do not take responsibility for their learning and want to be spoon fed. Required courses are not always well received by students. *What attribution theory teaches us is that both personal factors and aspects of the situation are responsible for any behavior.* To ignore one in favor of the other is to make a judgment error. To overcome this problem we need to ask, "How are my behaviors *and* various aspects of the situation contributing to the problem?" Otherwise we may find it difficult to increase participation, interest, and involvement. When we fixate on the students or attributes of the situation, we may wait for such things to change without trying to intervene. This stance simply increases whatever amount of dissatisfaction we have with the amount or quality of student involvement.

Irrational Beliefs

Albert Ellis notes that what people say to themselves has a strong influence on their subsequent actions. If they say encouraging things about their self-concept, their skills and abilities, and the world around them, they tend to take charge and try to manage and adapt to the situations they face. When people give themselves discouraging messages about their self-concepts, their skills and abilities, and the world around them, their willingness to challenge their environments and their skill in adapting decrease. The nature and quality of our belief systems play an important role in our everday actions.

One of the important classes of beliefs that control our behaviors is irrational beliefs. According to Ellis, such beliefs are characterized by illogical and exaggerated thoughts. Clues to their presence are thoughts and verbal statements that present things in *extreme* and *absolute* ways and as a result keep us from exploring options or trying more adaptive behaviors. "Extreme" words include, among others, *all, every, always, awful, terrible, horrible, totally,* and *essential.* When they are used, we see ourselves and the world in ways that are worse than deserved. "Absolute" words in Ellis's system suggest that we have no choices. They include such words as *must, should, have to, need,* and *ought.* Absolute words direct our actions and prevent us from recognizing our choices in a situation. In our experience, it is not unusual to see irrational beliefs prevent teachers from exploring ideas for involvement. Consider the following statements for a moment. They represent several of the major categories of irrational beliefs that Ellis mentions. Each is taken from statements made by our consulting clients.

- *Overgeneralization:* "Oh, that idea will never work. I once tried small groups in a class and it was a disaster."

- *Arbitrary inference:* "Students just don't ask questions in my classes. I'm afraid that there is something wrong with them if they cannot get excited about the relevant and important things I cover in class."

- *Catastrophizing:* "I knock my brains out in the classroom trying to make things interesting for them. I get just about nothing from them in return. I'm beginning to seriously think that I'm a failure as a teacher."

- *Two-sided reasoning:* "From what I can see it is generally a matter of luck whether you get people involved. The material either turns them on or it doesn't. It's as simple as that. I don't think there are any gimmicks that will change this fact of life in the classroom."

- *Oversocialization:* "I learned to teach by watching some very good people. They never had any trouble turning students on to the information. If I just continue to do what I learned from them, things will break in my favor. I can't think of any good reason to change the things I learned earlier."

- *Negative thinking:* "I'm not that good a teacher. My skills are in the research area. I'm not comfortable in front of a class, and I'm sure that students pick this up. Let's face it, some people have what it takes and others don't. I just don't have it."

Irrational beliefs affect student involvement in several ways. They keep some instructors from exploring options or otherwise trying to make more adaptive responses in the classroom. It is difficult to change and adapt when irrational thoughts guide and direct our actions. A more likely response is to continue with past behaviors. Of course, this usually leads to more frustration, tension, and anger. Some instructors may then continue to berate themselves, or they may take their frustration out on people around them. This usually means that students or colleagues are affected. Relationships may sour, and a self-fulfilling prophecy begins to evolve. Responding to a deficiency in student involvement with the belief "I guess I'm not that good a teacher" eventually leads to behaving in maladaptive ways. Students continue to remain passive, and the negative beliefs continue to get reinforced.

To overcome irrational beliefs, Ellis argues, we must first recognize they exist and that they control many of our self-defeating emotions and behaviors. Once they are identified, we need to take actions that dispute them. In therapy situations, Ellis and other therapists work closely with people to help them learn verbal and motor responses that dispute irrational beliefs. In one case a businessman believed that "everyone watches me when I do things." Ellis asked him to wear a multicolored sport shirt over dress pants and sneakers when he came to work in the morning. He was told to observe the reactions of people as he walked through the streets and rode the subway. This individual was surprised by the lack of interest in what he was wearing. This and other activities led him to see that not *everyone* monitored his behavior.

In a similar manner, a faculty member who believes "there is not much I can really do to improve my teaching" might be surprised at the results obtained working with a colleague or instructional consultant. Such activities typically help dispute the irrational belief that there is very little that can be done to improve one's teaching.

Insensitivity to Feedback

Chris Argyris finds that people tend to be rather insensitive to feedback if it goes against their self-concepts. Instead of asking how the information applies to them, in what ways it is accurate, and what they can do about it, people may ignore it, distort it, or twist it to fit their own purposes. Teachers who believe they are doing a decent job may ignore examples of their actions that suggest otherwise. A lack of student interest may be shrugged off, or, as noted earlier, the student may be blamed. Argyris argues that this tendency helps people protect their self-images.

It is no surprise that we may believe certain things about ourselves and others, or even have certain thoughts about how we should behave, and then find that our beliefs are not supported by our actions. Most of us sometimes say one thing and do another, and Argyris finds this a rather prevalent part of human behavior. Yet he states that it is not the important problem. The more important issue is that *people are often not aware of the discrepancy*. The feedback from others that would make this discrepancy clear is, unfortunately, often ignored or distorted to fit the self-image of the individual.

The result of this problem is a restricted learning style. People ignore the bad and overemphasize the good things they do. Argyris finds that this has implications for our willingness to seek new experiences and redirect our lives in new directions. Basically, when this tendency operates, people continue with past habits rather than change actions they are not performing well. Teachers were included in Argyris's studies, so there is no reason to think we are different from individuals in other occupations.

Increasing student involvement means that the strengths and weaknesses of our current classroom methods need to be analyzed. Such analyses typically involve feedback from students, colleagues and consultants and whatever personal observations of the problem are available. The feedback problem identified by Argyris may interfere with such analyses.

For feedback to work properly, we must be open to it and willing to examine its relevance for our classroom problem. We are most likely to be open when the feedback is specific and deals with behaviors we can change. Thus it must focus on observed behaviors and not on inferences about our personalities. Suggestions based on personality inferences may help us benefit from whatever feedback is given, but they may not completely overcome the insensitivity to feedback Argyris discusses. A high personal commitment to change and a willingness to open oneself up to the suggestions of others are also needed for feedback to be effective.

Giving up Control

Carl Rogers observes that issues of control over the environment and the exercise of power play an important role in the design of classroom procedures. Teachers, like people in any other occupation, struggle to maintain their influence. One way they do so is through the classroom methods and processes used to design a class. Grading systems, rules for attendance, format requirements, topics for papers, various deadlines, and examination policies are prescribed by teachers. The same is true of the lecture method or any other process used to present information. Students typically have very little input into the design of the classroom.

Elizabeth Cohen reports that teachers are most comfortable with classroom processes that keep them clearly in charge. It is no accident that classroom interactions are dominated by the teacher. Some studies, Cohen reports, show that for more than 75 percent of the total time, classrooms are organized so that only a central communication group exists, with the teacher the most frequent emitter and target in the group. In the traditional classroom, teachers talk and attempts are made to discuss topics with the class as a whole. The result, as Cohen suggests and as most of us have observed, is that the instructor remains in control and relatively few students are able to participate.

One outcome of the instructor's controlling so much of the class time is that there is little opportunity or incentive for students to take more responsibility for their learning. From the students' point of view, the teacher will tell them what to do, how to do it, and what information is important for them to learn. A dependency relationship thus develops between teachers and students, and it is very easy under such conditions for the students to fall into a passive learning mode. To break this passive mode of learning, students must begin to feel more responsible for their content learning in class. Classroom procedures designed to modify this dependency relationship typically take some classroom time away from the instructor. For example, if students are asked to develop issues, solve problems, or form opinions in small group discussions, they begin to use time that formerly belonged to the teacher. During that time, the instructor does not have direct control over everything that occurs. As Mary Lynn Crow notes, an instructor must step into the background for a period of time or play other roles. She also states that, "To adopt interactive strategies, a teacher must make some changes with respect to his psychological position toward both his subject matter and his students" [1980, p. 42].

To gain participation, teachers must attempt to use classroom time somewhat differently. In particular, students need time allocated for their participation and instructional procedures that will help them use this time effectively. Specific suggestions for how to structure a classroom in this way are presented in the section of this chapter on group processes. For now, it is important to consider that an unwillingness to reorder the use of classroom time is a block to student participation. An instructor's concerns over giving up control, we believe, are one reason this reordering does not occur.

Communication Climate

The involvement of students is also related to the quality of the communication climate in class. Whether the communication climate is conducive or a hindrance to effective teacher-student interactions depends on several factors that are largely under the control of the instructor.

The Amount of One-Way versus Two-Way Communication

Classroom communications, like other interactions, vary in the number of ways that messages can be sent and received. Harold Leavitt found that the communication pattern used has important implications for how much people interact, the amount and accuracy of their work, and their satisfaction with their contributions to a task. He found that when communication moves from an open, unrestricted dialogue to more restrictive one-way patterns, errors increase, less work is accomplished, and people are less satisfied with their participation.

Leavitt's findings do not necessarily mean that a one-way pattern is always bad and a two-way interaction is always good. In any setting, including the classroom, each has particular strengths and weaknesses. Based on the research of Harold Leavitt, Fred Tesch, and others, the following characteristics of one- and two-way patterns and their relative strengths and weaknesses in the classroom are apparent.

- *One-way communication.* It is unlikely that a pure case of one-way communication exists in the classroom. The only exceptions might be televised instruction, extremely large lecture sections, and classes where the pace of instruction leaves no room for student input. There is generally some dialogue between students and teachers. However, as Elizabeth Cohen found, teachers account for 75 percent of the communications that occur in most classrooms. Thus the typical classroom has a relatively high amount of one-way communication.

  The major advantage of a one-way pattern is that it allows the teacher to control the amount, pace, and flow of the information. It typically allows a lot of information to be transmitted in a relatively short amount of time.

  There are several disadvantages to the use of a one-way pattern. Students have little or no opportunity to respond immediately and directly to the teacher's comments. Because feedback is low, a teacher must make assumptions about the listeners' skill levels, prior training, and understanding of the material communicated. Typically, this situation leads to students' getting less of an understanding of the information and the instructor's making the material too simple or too difficult for the level of the class. With little opportunity to respond, students can become frustrated with the class. Because the teacher models an interaction pattern of "I talk—you sit and take notes," students may not feel like taking initiative or responsibility in class. Thus they sit back, take notes, and become somewhat apathetic. The result is fewer student questions and less discussion.

- *Two-way communication.* With this pattern, there is a flow of information among and between individuals. Although few classes are characterized by completely open two-way communication patterns, there are times in most classes when the instructor plans group activities or discussions in which a large amount of two-way interaction occurs between students and the teacher.

The major disadvantage of a two-way pattern is that it takes longer for messages to get communicated. Furthermore, because both students and the teacher talk, the amount, pace, and flow of information in class is not exclusively under the instructor's control.

There are several advantages, however, of a two-way pattern. Because of the opportunity for immediate feedback, many of the assumptions teachers make about skill level, prior training, and understanding of the material get tested immediately. Thus it is more accurate than a one-way pattern. Furthermore, it encourages less dependence on the teacher, and students can thus take more initiative and responsibility. One result is that there is more involvement and interest on the part of students.

Based on this discussion, it appears that one-way patterns decrease the amount of student involvement. Apparently this occurs because the dependence this pattern encourages leads to a lack of initiative, to apathy, and to a generally low level of interest on the part of students in taking more responsibility for their learning. One way out of this dilemma is to use questioning procedures, discussion processes, and other classroom methods that encourage a dialogue. Specific suggestions for how to do this appear in the group processes section of this chapter.

The Instructor's Psychological Size

Two-way communication is sometimes difficult because there are status differences between the people communicating. A way to approach this problem in the classroom is to examine the concept of psychological size. Richard Wallen[1] suggests *psychological size* as a convenient label to describe the impact one person has on another. This impact is usually seen in terms of the potential that one person has for helping or hurting others. People who are perceived as psychologically big have a high potential for influencing and controlling other individuals. It interferes with an open dialogue between people when one party is seen as psychologically bigger than the other. Ronald Boyer and Charles Bolton note that this often happens in the classroom. Teachers generally have a greater psychological size than students.

Differences in psychological size have other consequences besides interfering with two-way communication. When someone is perceived as psychologically big, others expect that individual to solve problems, to see that all goes well, to take care of them, and to tell them what and how to do things. In the classroom, Boyer and Bolton imply, this dependence can easily lead to apathy and a lack of initiative. The result is that student interest and involvement decrease.

[1] The concept of *psychological size* is used by Richard Wallen in workshops on interpersonal interactions and has been passed down verbally.

There are several factors that contribute to an instructor's psychological size and consequently have implications for teacher-student interactions. As you read, try to think of which factors are issues for you.

- *Use of high status and titles.* Most of us forget the effects our status and titles can have on other people. Consistently using *Mister, Doctor, Professor,* or other titles for ourselves presents an image to someone else of a person who is more competent, somewhat distant, more intelligent, and certainly more powerful. This may cause students to feel less free and open in discussing or contributing their thoughts and ideas.

- *Inappropriate use of criticism, sarcasm, ridicule, and humor.* It is important to be sensitive to the way that we criticize another person's work, in writing or verbally. Our motivations may be constructive and positive, but students may well perceive the criticism as a form of ridicule. This is particularly true when we are negative about something without giving specific reasons. A similar point applies to the use of humor. Although we may wish to lighten a situation or introduce some fun into a relationship, we need to be careful of offending students in the process.

- *Use of terminal statements permitting no disagreement.* This often occurs when one-way communication is used. Sometimes we feel that our authority or expertise is challenged, and, consequently, we try to discourage disagreement. Such statements as "That's fine; let's move on," "I'd like you to think of it my way," and "There is nothing to be gained on this point by further discussion" have the effect of controlling and cutting off discussion.

- *Use of very formal manner.* Some teachers come across in a very formal fashion. Their body posture is not relaxed, they stand in front of a class and seldom move around, they look down with a hard stare at students, they talk with authority, and they are not afraid to interrupt students to interject their points of view. The impression they create is "I am the person in charge here." Students may label such instructors as rigid and tight. Given this portrait, it is safe to assume that students will have some hesitancy or difficulty in initiating discussions or being open and free in discussions.

- *Use of punishing remarks.* Saying things to students like "That's illogical," "That does not follow," and "How in the world could you do that?" may be perceived as very punishing. Such remarks may lead students to keep their ideas to themselves so as not to "get caught" again.

- *Display of a great amount of detailed knowledge.* As teachers, we do have a relatively large amount of information about our subject areas.

If we try to "one-up" students with our knowledge, or make sure that "students understand who has the information," we can decrease the chances of involvement. Students may not want to say something to a person with so much knowledge. They may not want to appear stupid or incompetent.

- *Use of language that is too complicated for the listener.* It is important to use good language and to have students learn the terms and concepts in our fields. Yet care must be taken to define those terms and not overuse highly complicated language. If at all possible, it is better to bring our words down to a level that we are sure students can tolerate. Otherwise we run the risk of "turning them off."

- *Failure to use the name of a student.* It is a good idea to know the names of people with whom you interact. This personalizes our interactions outside the classroom and has a similar effect on students. Students generally appreciate teachers who acknowledge them as individuals. Some teachers use mnemonic devices, take photographs of students, or use seating charts or name tags to help them learn names. This practice puts students at ease and tells them you think they are important. In the process, it helps break down some of the barriers to effective classroom communication.

- *Overemphasis on grades and grading.* Constantly stressing the importance of material for the midterm or final, the importance of a good grade in the course, and how much you appreciate good students may lead to a lack of involvement. Such actions put the teacher in an authority position and may make some students uneasy about their chances of succeeding in class. The resulting anxiety may hinder participation. Furthermore, such actions may lead students to resent attempts to control their behaviors. They may react to them by becoming less involved.

Whether large psychological size is good or bad depends on how people use it. Some teachers may intentionally or unintentionally use it to put students in their place or to distance themselves from students. Others may find it a helpful device to promote the growth and development of students. A teacher might employ his or her psychological size to influence students to learn new topics or learn to collaborate with each other.

If, however, you are one of the people for whom psychological size differences present problems in the classroom, there are several things you might consider doing. One is to *determine which of the factors outlined above produces a problem for you.* Taking actions to eliminate it probably will help the situation. Another possibility is to *consider increasing the psychological size of your students.* You can do this by exhibiting a genuine interest in what they have to say. Show some regard for their opinions, and give them a chance to talk. Let students see that they can influence you. Finally, *consider giving students more responsibility for what occurs in class.* Have them make reports, lead small groups, analyze problems in class, engage in role-playing activities, or make suggestions for topics to be covered. Acknowledge student contributions, and periodically state what you have learned from their input. One of the delightful surprises for students is that teachers often get new or expanded insights into issues through discussions with them.

The Physical Environment of the Classroom

According to Fred Steele, most of us are not as aware as we should be of the important role the physical environment plays in facilitating communication. We could, he argues, improve our interactions by becoming more environmentally competent. Steele uses *environmental competence* to refer to our ability to understand how the arrangement of people and objects (furniture, rooms, pictures, lights) influences our ability to communicate. Individuals who are environmentally competent are able to change physical settings to improve communications. They typically ask questions like "What am I trying to accomplish in terms of getting people to interact?" "Is the physical setting conducive to the type of interactions I want?" "What needs to be changed to make the setting better for my goals?" Answering such questions about the classrooms in which we teach may make the setting work for us instead of against us.

Physical settings affect our interactions by encouraging or discouraging social contact and by supplying symbolic meaning. Social contact is affected by the tendency of a setting to push people apart or together. Robert Sommer reports that chairs placed across a corner of a table are the most effective arrangement for encouraging seated conversations. Almost as good is a small circle with opposite chairs about 5 to 7 feet apart. The worst possible arrangement is to have people sit side by side in rows from front to back. One reason for the success of the circular and corner-table arrangements is that visual contact among all participants has a tendency to make people more responsive to each other.

The principle of maintaining visual contact is often violated in classroom situations. In many cases, the seats are placed in a front-to-back, side-by-side arrangement, with the teacher in the front of the room. Such an arrangement encourages one-way communication patterns, because the flow of conversation is directed toward the front of the room. Thus if the group is large, only a few people have the opportunity to speak. Another popular pattern is to have a rectangular table in a seminar room. Typically, one person is at each end, and the other participants sit along the sides. The tendency here is for the conversation to flow toward the leader (who usually sits at one end) and toward people sitting opposite each other.

People sitting adjacent to each other have fewer communications. The best physical arrangement for interpersonal communication is around a circular table or with chairs placed in circle.

The physical arrangement may produce problems in getting students involved, but Fred Steele finds that the belief that the physical setting is fixed and should be accepted as it appears also contributes. In reality, he argues, many objects in our environment are pseudo-fixed features of the physical space. They can be moved or changed if we want. The problem is that we have a bias to leave things as they are.

The amount of discussion in a classroom can be increased if the chairs or tables are rearranged to encourage visual contact. Even when the chairs are fixed, some instructors have students stand to discuss issues in small groups (the cocktail party model), sit on the floor in the open spaces in the room, or form clusters with those on either side of them or with a couple of people in the next row. Students may have to straddle a desk, sit sideways, or turn their bodies a bit, but visual contact is possible. To do any of these things, the bias about fixed features of the space must be overcome.

The location of objects in physical setting and their characteristics also convey symbolic messages that affect our interactions. Dirty floors, cracked plaster, old paint on the walls, poor lighting, and uncomfortable chairs do not create a very pleasant atmosphere. Such a classroom might convey the message "Get in and get out as fast as you can." Pleasant, clean, well-lit, and comfortable physical settings encourage interactions. Teachers faced with a poor room, when everything else failed, have resorted to fixing it up themselves. It is not unusual to find teachers enlisting the aid of students to make a classroom setting comfortable and pleasant.

It is also important to remember that physical settings seldom act alone to produce their effects. People occupy settings, and it is often their expectations and preferences for particular communication patterns that create and maintain the setting. A teacher's actions reinforce whatever implications a classroom environment has for encouraging or discouraging communication. Both must be examined when the contribution of the physical setting to classroom interactions is analyzed.

Group Processes

In the preceding sections of this chapter, the role of personal constraints within the teacher and the effects of the classroom communication climate on involvement were discussed. To these two factors we must add the types of processes that operate in classroom groups that inhibit participation. Any group, including one in the classroom, needs help to function effectively. We find four things important here: (a) meeting the needs of group members, (b) encouraging and supporting interactions by establishing appropriate norms for behavior, (c) selecting an appropriate classroom leadership style, and (d) designing group structures that facilitate interaction.

Meeting Members' Needs

Obviously, classroom groups exist to accomplish certain goals and objectives. What is not obvious and often overlooked is that the goals and objectives must relate to the personal needs of the group's members. A major problem with course design is that courses are typically planned with the instructor's needs and goals or the teacher's perceptions of student needs in mind. This may produce some overlap with the actual needs of the students, but many student needs may be overlooked. Students may want certain topics covered, they may prefer to have certain teaching methods used, or they may want to work on certain projects to help them learn. In some content areas, students also have skills, abilities, and information that would enhance the course's content.

To take such needs into account, students must play a more active role in course decision making. Frederick Richter and Dean Tjosvold identified a number of positive benefits when they did. These researchers noted that students who participated in classroom decisions developed more favorable attitudes toward school and subject matter, interacted more positively with peers, worked more consistently without supervision, and apparently achieved more content learning than students whose teachers made decisions. Along similar lines, Tony Grasha found that students given more influence in a course collaborated more and were less dependent and competitive.

There are several things you might try to involve students more in course decision making and, in the process, help meet other needs they have. Consider the following suggestions:

- Have students complete a questionnaire on the first day of class that asks them to specify content areas, teaching methods, and projects they prefer to have included in the course. Also ask them to indicate what special contributions they might make to the course given their backgrounds and experiences.

- At the beginning of the course, assess the learning styles of the students in the class. Discuss the results with the class, and ask them to help you think of classroom activities and procedures that you might try to help them use their preferred learning styles. The information on learning styles in Chapter 5 should be helpful to you in this task.

- Give students a detailed syllabus and briefly talk about the course to them on the first day. Then ask them individually to list two or three things they think they would like, dislike, or want to see added to the course. Have students meet in small groups of four to six to discuss their responses and develop a list of the major issues they raised. Post the major issues on the board, noting which ones are endorsed by more than one group. Commenting on the likes, dislikes, and preferred additions gives you a chance to clarify aspects of the course design and to consider adding student suggestions. *This process works best if students are told you want them to act as consultants and that the final decision must be yours.*

- Arrange to meet before the course begins with students you know will be part of the class. Such students can be identified through personal contact with those you already know, by advance class lists, or from the first class meeting. Use this group to plan refinements in the course design.

Will Schutz observes that people also have a tendency to want certain psychological needs satisfied in a group. These are the needs for inclusion, control, and affection. In the classroom, inclusion needs are shown in a student's preferences for interacting and associating with others. The need to influence the ideas, opinions, and actions of other members of the class indicates the need for control. Affection needs involve a person's desires to feel close to and accepted by other members of the class. Each of these needs has an expressed and a wanted component. To different degrees, people want various amounts of each need directed toward them and are able to express these needs in their interactions. That is, each of us wants others to include us in activities, show us affection, and try to influence us. Similarly, each of us needs an outlet to include others, show others affection, and try to influence people. Schutz finds that when people are able to have both parts of each need met, they are typically happier and better adjusted. Course designs that emphasize the provision of opportunities for students to interact, state their opinions, comment on one another's ideas, and participate in planning course activities stand the best chance of meeting such needs.

Providing Norms that Encourage and Support Interactions

A group norm is an idea shared by group members about how they should behave. Norms may be written as part of a group's operating procedures, or they may develop informally over time as the group interacts. Teachers and students share responsibility for establishing norms, but teacher behavior strongly influences whether the norms that eventually develop will facilitate or hinder involvement. Several of the things that create norms that hinder involvement (certain seating arrangements or perceptions of psychological size, for example) have been mentioned in previous sections of this chapter. In addition to trying to overcome these problems, you might consider initiating the following procedures:

- *Periodically get feedback on the nature and quality of the involvement in class.* Students might be asked to list the reasons they participate and the reasons they do not participate. Or a particular session, discussion, or group activity might be analyzed to gather information about what happened that encouraged or discouraged involvement and participation. Such comments can be written individually in a few minutes, discussed briefly in small groups, and shared with the class. Post the ideas on the board, and ask for suggestions about how things could be done better in the future. The purpose of the activity is to get students to begin to take more responsibility for what happens to them in class. By discussing behaviors that facilitate or hinder involvement, they begin to get ideas about things they can do differently. Taking twenty to thirty minutes three or four times a term to do this can have positive results, particularly if you and the students agree to try some of the ideas that emerge.

- *If the students are working or discussing issues in small groups, have them set fifteen minutes aside periodically to talk about what they liked and disliked about the discussion.* This is particularly helpful if the group will continue to interact over time. Talking about "how we worked together" may identify areas where improvements can be made. The form shown in Table 6.1 might be used by the group to facilitate such discussions. It would first be filled out by each member of the group. The first time this procedure is tried in class, one of the groups might be asked to do it in a fishbowl setting with the instructor faciltating the discussion. The target group and the instructor sit so that other members of the class can observe. This models the task and allows people to ask questions about the process.

- *Reward participation, and encourage other class members to do the same.* We are not necessarily suggesting that you assign grades based partly on participation. Although this is one option, there are other ways that rewards can be distributed. Thanking students for their comments and indicating their value are what students appreciate. Similarly, if people are working in small groups, encourage members to tell someone that they liked something he or she said or did. Finally, ask students to think periodically of the strong points of their

---

Table 6.1. What to Observe and Discuss Regarding Communication in a
          Discussion Group

One of the easiest aspects of group process to observe is the pattern of communication. Understanding it and taking actions to correct the problems in communication facilitate future discussions. Answer the following questions, and then share your responses with other members of your group. As a group, try to identify the major strengths and weaknesses of the communication in the discussion you just completed.

1. Who talked in the group?
2. Who seemed to talk the most and for how long did they talk? Was this helpful to the discussion, or did it leave some people out?
3. Did you want to say something but found you were unable to say it? What prevented you from speaking?
4. Did people interrupt one another a lot?
5. Did certain people seem to carry on a conversation with one another and to ignore other members of the group?
6. Did people look at each other when they discussed issues?
7. What style of communication was used (for example, assertions, questions, tone of voice, gestures)?
8. Did your discussion group have (a) leader(s)? What did the leader(s) do to facilitate the discussion? What did they do to hinder the discussion?
9. What could you do to improve the quality of the discussion the next time? What could other members of the group do?

---

participation on a given day. This might be done as a brief five-minute activity at the end of a few class sessions. Self-rewards are another form of reinforcement. The activity also sensitizes people to their behavior in class.

• *Model appropriate ways of leading interactive classrooms in your behaviors.* By doing this, you not only suggest norms that other members of the group might follow but you lessen the risk of having inappropriate personal behaviors interfere with student participation. Mary Lynn Crow suggests several things teachers might do that would help establish norms favorable to interactions. They are: (a) Clarify what people are trying to say when it is clear that a misunderstanding has occurred. Simply restate what that person said, and ask him or her to give an example or to elaborate. (b) Discourage members who try to monopolize conversations by avoiding eye contact with them, by asking what others think, or by asking how others react to what has been said. (c) Approach interactions with enthusiasm, responsiveness, and a genuine interest in the subject matter. Let students know why you think it is important to have such interactions and the goals you hope to accomplish. (d) Summarize what is being said at appropriate times, and encourage students to do the same. (e) Encourage students to question freely one another's ideas in a friendly manner and to resist being judgmental. A good way to do this is to ensure that you react to student ideas in the same way.

Generally speaking, norms that encourage the development of participation skills will enhance the quality of involvement in the classroom. Sometimes to develop these skills, it is necessary in effect to train a class to participate. Many students are not prepared or motivated to take an active part in classroom activities. They often need to be shown how and encouraged in their attempts.

Selecting an Appropriate Leadership Style

Paul Hersey and Kenneth Blanchard argue that leadership in classrooms, business organizations, committees, or any group must take into account *relationship issues, task concerns,* and the *maturity* of the members. Relationship issues revolve around the leader's concern for promoting good interpersonal relationships and communication among members. A major task concern is the extent to which the leader is interested in structuring the task for the group. How well group members are able to work independently and take initiative and reponsibility, and whether they possess the skills and knowledge to accomplish the task, reflect their maturity.

Of the three, the maturity of the group members is the key factor. It signals to the leader whether the group needs a high or low level of structure and whether group members need to focus on their interpersonal relationships. Depending on the maturity of the group, any leader has four potential leadership styles. They are:

- *Telling.* In an immature group of people, a task-oriented leader is perceived as the most effective. The leader will tell people what needs to be done and how to do it. Other than making sure people can communicate with the leader, the leader need not devote a lot of attention to developing interpersonal relationships. Relatively little collaboration is needed in such groups, and members will spend a lot of time just trying to get the job done.

- *Selling.* With a somewhat higher but still below-average level of group maturity, a leader is perceived as most effective if he or she is both task and relationship oriented. Group members at this level still need some structure, but they are also likely to need to collaborate more with each other or with the leader. Thus a concern for relationships and communication must be shown by the leader. With a relatively more mature group of people, a leader may find that he or she simply cannot tell people what to do. They will have some ideas on how to do things and expect that the ideas will get heard. A leader may find it necessary to "sell" the group on ideas.

- *Participating.* A group that is just better than average in maturity will perceive a leader as effective if he or she is less interested in telling them what to do but has an interest in interpersonal relationships. Members of such a group have the skill to set task goals, accept responsibility, take initiative, and complete a job. They need a leader off whom they can bounce ideas and who can help them collaborate better. They work best when the leader participates with them in the task but does not totally direct it.

- *Delegating.* A highly mature group will perceive a leader as effective if he or she can delegate assignments and responsibility. The group has the skills and knowledge to handle tasks and whatever relationship and communication issues arise. They will resent a leader who tries to tell them what to do and how to do it.

When applied to the classroom, the Hersey-Blanchard model places three demands on teachers. *They must know their students well enough to assess their level of maturity.* Then a teaching style appropriate to that level must be employed. In addition, *a teacher must show a certain amount of flexibility.* The relative level of student maturity will vary across undergraduate and graduate courses. Thus changes in teaching style must occur for an instructor to be perceived as effective by students. An instructor who is only comfortable using a "telling" style will have problems with a highly mature group of students. They will resent the dependency this style encourages. The same is true of an instructor who is only comfortable with a "delegating" style and has a very immature group. Such students will not be able to handle the independence and initiative demanded by this style. Finally, *a good teacher should be willing to work with students to help them develop their level of maturity.* To do this adequately, the Hersey-Blanchard model suggests, shifts in classroom leadership style must occur.

Paul Hersey, Arrigo Angelini, and Sofia Caracuhansky tested this last idea by trying purposely to increase the willingness of students to take responsibility and initiative, collaborate with each other, and work independently. To do this, they gradually shifted their teaching style over the course of a one-semester course. They began by using a "telling" style (teacher lecturing), then moved to "selling" (teacher and students discussing issues, with the instructor directing conversations), then to "participating" (the instructor participating in discussions but group members helping to determine topics and manage the discussions), and finally to "delegating" (the group discussing issues, with the teacher entering the discussion only when asked).

Over time they gradually decreased the teacher's role and increased the involvement of the students. Compared to a control group of students taught by a "telling" style, the experimental classes showed higher exam performance and higher levels of enthusiasm, morale, and motivation. They were also seldom late and cut classes less often.

Designing Group Structures

A basic principle we find helpful regarding classroom participation is "If you want students to act in a certain way, create a structure that specifically encourages appropriate behaviors." All too often, students are not specifically encouraged to share or have the option not to participate. Instructors ask the class at various times, "Do you have any comments or questions on what I have just said?" The blank stares and squirming are typically met with, "Fine, let's move on." A more appropriate structure would be "I'd like everyone to write down one question or comment they have on what I have just said." Having done this, students are called upon to report what they have written. This procedure generates many more questions and comments than does the traditional open-ended query, "Are there any questions?"

Such suggestions, unfortunately, are seen by instructors as manipulative and not really the same thing as eliciting spontaneous questions. As one workshop participant told us, "There is something second class about such questions and comments. Students aren't asking them because they want to." Of course, as we have argued in earlier parts of this chapter, there are many reasons participation may not come from the heart. We believe it is important to take actions to overcome such problems. One specific action is to establish procedures that encourage comments, questions, and discussion. Initially, this helps break down some of the barriers to sharing information. Because such actions increase the opportunity for student involvement, students learn the skills needed to contribute effectively. Many of the specific classroom processes mentioned in other chapters of this book create structures to facilitate interaction, but the following might be considered to supplement those discussed earlier.

1. *Presentation followed by question-and-answer period.* This is perhaps the most popular method used to increase student involvement. Its biggest advantage is that it allows some of the issues that are raised during the presentation to be addressed in more detail. Its biggest disadvantage is that the questions are usually directed solely at the discussion leader. Another limitation of this technique is that discussion is unlikely to occur among the participants if the group is any larger than six to nine persons. Furthermore, in a large group it is possible that not everyone's concerns will be addressed. Despite its

limitations, there are some things that can make this technique more effective.

a. Having finished your presentation (either verbal or written), ask students to take a few minutes to generate questions individually or in groups.

b. Post the questions where everyone can see them. This allows the entire range of issues and the overlap between concerns to be assessed fairly quickly. Once this is done, the following procedures can be used to answer the questions.

   (1) You can answer the questions in order of your interest.

   (2) You can quickly survey the class to determine which questions the group would like answered first. A rank ordering of priorities can be obtained by asking people to indicate by a show of hands those questions they feel are important.

   (3) After giving your opinion on the issue, ask if anyone has anything to add. Be careful to monitor the time fairly closely so you can get through the major questions along with comments from the students.

2. *Presentation followed by discussion.* As this technique is usually employed, the presenter lists issues for those in attendance to discuss. In large groups it is hard to get more than a few people involved, and often the flow of conversation is toward the presenter. The following can help in such discussions.

a. To increase the opportunities for discussion, arrange the chairs in a circle. Front-to-back seating arrangements make it difficult for people to discuss issues with one another.

b. For the first session, if the group is fifteen or fewer people, have people introduce themselves. Encourage people to use one another's names during discussions. No matter how many people are present, name tags can be useful, as can a seating chart placed where people can see others' names.

c. If you want people to discuss your issues, list them where everyone can see them. Then ask people if there are any issues they wish to add to the list. Have people rank order the issues, by their importance to them.

d. Before you begin, have the group set time limits on discussing each issue. In this way, you can address the major issues before time runs out. If you have materials that have to be covered, you might determine the time allotted to those issues.

e. To avoid domination of the conversation by a couple of people, ask people who are not speaking what they think of the issue. Take care to give everyone a chance to speak before a session ends.

f. Try to direct the discussions away from yourself. The best way to do this is to indicate to people that, although you have something to say, you are mostly interested in what they think of the issues.

3. *Group-generated agenda.* After the presentation, the intent here is for the teacher to act as a facilitator and to have the group develop the issues they want to deal with. Some ways to do this are the following.

    a. Ask people to list two of the most important issues that the presentation generated for them. This should be done individually, and the list posted where everyone can see it. No more than five to eight minutes should be spent on this activity.

    b. The group should then help you categorize the issues raised. Allow about ten minutes for this exercise. Note that time limits for each part of the discussion depend on how much total time you have available.

    c. Several options are then available for dealing with the issues generated.

        (1) Form small groups based on major categories. Have people form the groups themselves. Each group might deal with one to three issues in a category. Allow approximately twenty minutes at the end of the session for a brief report from each group on what was discussed. Major conclusions should be posted so that people can copy them if they wish.

        (2) Pick two to four major issues that the group generates. Form a fishbowl arrangement with an inner and an outer group. Have the inner group discuss the issue for eight to twelve minutes. Allow six to eight minutes at the end for those in the outer group to add comments. Switch the compositions of the inner and outer groups for each issue.

        (3) Pick three to five issues. Ask people to form pairs or trios. Have one pair or trio spend five to ten minutes outlining some of their thoughts on the issue. Have them present their thoughts to the group at large for comments and questions. Monitor the time closely. If enough people are present, it is all right to have more than one group present the same issue. In this way, a larger variety of responses can be assessed.

4. *No formal presentation.* If there is no formal presentation, but the teacher has issues that he or she wants people to discuss, the following might be helpful.

    a. Break the group into subgroups (three to six persons). Give each group a key issue or leading statement that is relevant to your area. Ask each group to develop a position on each issue or statement. Have a representative from each group report on the group's position. Both the teacher and students from other groups should be allowed to comment. Watch the time closely so that each of the issues can be addressed.

b. A variation of this is to give each small group one or more problems to solve that are related to the topic. Each group reports its position, and comments are encouraged. In an hour-and-a-half session, try to limit yourself to two or three such problems.

c. Give different groups different issues, leading statements, or problems. Allow them ten to fifteen minutes to prepare responses. Have them discuss their responses for five minutes each in front of the large group, and invite the group to make comments.

5. *Panel presentations and discussions.* There are several ways to involve students by using the panel discussion and presentation device.

   a. *Panel presentation with discussion.* Three to six students are assigned different aspects of the same topic to research and on which to prepare a five- to ten-minute presentation. After each presentation other members of the panel and the class are given several minutes to ask questions. Then the next speaker presents another aspect of the topic. To facilitate questions, panel members and several of the people in class might be assigned the task of listening and developing a question or two to ask. The instructor can act as a moderator for the question-and-answer periods and must work closely with students to develop topics and their presentations.

   b. *Panel discussion.* Three to six students are assigned a topic to research. The instructor prepares discussion questions, and the students present their responses. Once discussion is under way, other members of the class may question the panel.

   c. *Reaction panel.* Three to six students are assigned the task of reacting to the instructor's presentation. Twenty minutes should be put aside for this task. Five of those minutes are given to the students selected to develop questions based on the presentation.

   d. *Multiple panel presentation and discussion.* Students are asked to work in pairs or trios on a topic. Each group writes a paper on the topic. They also prepare a presentation with appropriate visual aids, handouts, and other devices that assist people in learning content. In class, three to five groups meet simultaneously to present their papers to small groups of students. The presentations should be twenty to thirty minutes in length, with five to ten of those minutes set aside for discussion. At the end of the time period, the students select another group to attend. Thus, during a class period, students get to hear two presentations. To give everyone in class a chance to participate, this device must be used over the course of several sessions. The sessions can be consecutive or spread over the term of the course.

6. *Role-playing activities.* Overall, role playing stimulates interest and encourages student participation. It is active learning. As Bill McKeachie points out, however, "the effectiveness of role playing depends to a large extent upon the confidence of the instructor in the procedure and the students' feelings (gained from the teacher's attitude) that it is going to be a successful and valuable aspect of the course" [1969, p. 118]. It is most effective when used as an integral part of the course and as a serious technique to enhance and complement content presentations. There are several types of role-playing techniques.

   a. *Define a problem situation that has no one correct answer.* The situation chosen could relate to the lives of the students, or it could be related to a real or fictitious event in your discipline. Situations should be related to the material that has been covered in class or to information that will be introduced into class in the immediate future. You should have a clear idea of the content goals for such a session before using this procedure. Here are several suggestions for how to run this type of role play:

      (1) *It's possible to simply give the assignment to students and let them shape the situation as they see fit.* A variation is for the instructor to assign roles and give some direction to the roles. In either case, depending on the topic, students can be given preparation time in class or the preparation time can be a take-home assignment.

      (2) *To begin things, ask students to volunteer for roles.* Students who volunteer will feel less on the spot than students who are chosen. Also, volunteers are likely to feel less inhibited about acting out the roles.

      (3) *Do not let the role play run too long.* Anywhere from five to fifteen minutes is usually sufficient. After the role play, let participants discuss it first. Have the observers then make comments about what they saw and what they learned from the situation. Sheets can be handed out with specific instructions to the observers, or responsibilities can be determined verbally.

      (4) *After discussing the role play, you may want to modify the situation and do it again or have other students play the roles.* Students in the class can also suggest modifications of the

situations and are an excellent source of ideas for situations to be role played.

(5) *A brief example:* A class on Treating the Delinquent Adolescent has been discussing drug abuse. The role-play situation chosen to illustrate the complexity of drug-related situations and parental effects on adolescents is the following: Two parents come to jail after being notified that their son has been picked up for possession of marijuana. The roles to be played are the parents, son, and arresting police officer. The role play can be varied by changing the sex of the adolescent, social class of the participants, and the number of times the adolescent had been arrested. Discussion of the role plays could focus on such issues as the following:

> How typical do you feel the response of these "parents" was?
>
> What stereotypes about police officers were exhibited in the role play?
>
> What could the "parents" have done to be of more help to their child?
>
> What do you think would have happened to the adolescent in this example?
>
> What can we as individuals do about situations such as those illustrated in class today?

b. *Student characterizations of real or fictitious persons.* In any field there are famous people, and in literary subjects one can often find an interesting character. Assign or ask students to volunteer to learn as much as they can about the life or a part of the life of such a person. Their task in class is to answer questions that the teacher or members of the class ask from the perspective of the person he or she is role playing.

(1) Preparation time is necessary to make this effective. The instructor can help by having a suggested list of reference works for the student.

(2) Students in the class should be assigned the task of writing one or two questions that they want to ask. Allow five to ten minutes for students to think of questions before starting the role play.

(3) If role playing is on a volunteer basis, you might consider giving the students extra credit for participation.

(4) Added interest can be obtained if students dress in costumes that are appropriate for that period.

c. *Instructor characterizations of real or fictitious persons.* You might want to role play an individual as well. Suggestions we have given about setting the stage are applicable here.

(1) One variation is to deliver a lecture to the class as you think that individual would have done it in his or her time. Having Sigmund Freud or Henry VIII talking to the students is often fun and can add to the content presentation.

(2) Students can ask questions, but additional information can be gained by having one character who represents a position debate another who represents a different conceptual position (for example, Skinner versus Rogers). This can be accomplished by your switching roles (changing chairs in the room helps separate the roles) or having a colleague or student play the other person. Dressing for the occasion often helps increase interest.

(3) Instructor and student characterization are best used for a fifteen- to thirty-minute block of time.

d. *Making role playing successful.* Consider the following suggestions to increase the chances that your role playing will have an impact on students.

(1) Role playing should be used as an integral and regular part of classroom instruction and not in isolated instances.

(2) The classroom environment should be open and nonthreatening so that students will feel free to experiment and explore.

(3) Role playing should never be graded.

(4) Role-playing situations should have some structure or limits to keep students focused on solving objectives, and to encourage serious attempts to solve the problem situation.

(5) Always use the role-playing situation as a stimulus for discussion and relate it to your objective for using the technique.

These suggestions should help encourage involvement, interest, and participation. It is important to keep in mind that any technique must fit the goals for the session, the maturity of the students, and the instructor's personal style. If you are uncomfortable with a technique, it is probably better not to use it. The effort is likely to appear forced, and students may not benefit as much. Whatever you decide to do, it is important to remember that participation is more likely if a specific structure is used to encourage it.

Personal Involvement Checklist

In this chapter we have discussed a number of issues related to student involvement. You might want to use the checklist in Table 6.2 to diagnose factors in your classes that tend to hinder student involvement and participation. The checklist was designed to help you consider how the factors discussed in this chapter apply to your teaching. (See pages 162–163).

Summary

Getting students involved in the classroom is a complicated issue. It is important first to diagnose the reasons the level of participation is inadequate and then to design strategies to overcome them. Generally, a lack of involvement appears related to personal constraints that inhibit the acceptance and use of new ideas, problems in the communication climate of the classroom, and the reliance on group processes that fail to facilitate interaction among students and teachers.

Personal constraints include attribution errors, irrational beliefs, insensitivity to feedback, and an unwillingness to give up control. In an *attribution error,* we blame students or other aspects of the classroom for the lack of involvement. In the process, we overlook or underestimate our responsibility. *Irrational beliefs* lead us to reject new ideas, put ourselves down, or make sweeping generalizations about why students are not participating. Unless we successfully dispute them, they are likely to hold back our attempts at facilitating involvement. A teacher's *insensitivity to feedback* might lead to overestimating how well things are going or ignoring specific suggestions for improving classroom interactions. Finally, an *unwillingness to give up control* blocks experimentation with alternative techniques that facilitate involvement. One reason is that many techniques that encourage involvement also shift some control over the content, how it is presented, and the specific learning that takes place.

The *communication climate* reflects the extent to which people are able to discuss issues and understand content presentations, and their satisfaction with their classroom interactions. The communication climate is often improved when two-way communication processes are encouraged. Unlike one-way patterns, they encourage less dependence on the teacher and more initiative and responsibility on the part of students. Similarly, by watching how their psychological size affects their interactions, teachers can enhance the communication climate of the classroom. To do this, instructors must monitor and change habits that distance them from students, and try to increase the relative psychological size of students. Finally, the physical environment plays an important role in determining the communication climate. How the setting is physically arranged may symbolically communicate that participation is not wanted or may keep people apart.

Certain *group processes* must also occur to encourage participation. Class members must find that the course meets certain content and psycho-

---

Table 6.2. Diagnosing Participation Problems in the Classroom

---

Think of a specific class and rate the extent to which each of the factors below hinders participation.

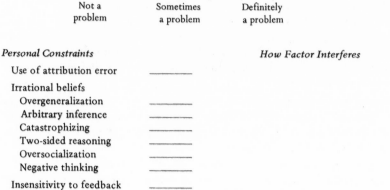

Personal Constraints   *How Factor Interferes*

   Use of attribution error   _____

   Irrational beliefs
      Overgeneralization   _____
      Arbitrary inference   _____
      Catastrophizing   _____
      Two-sided reasoning   _____
      Oversocialization   _____
      Negative thinking   _____

   Insensitivity to feedback   _____

   Unwillingness to give up
      control   _____

Communication Climate

   Extent of one-way com-
      munication pattern   _____

   Psychological size
      Use of high status and
         titles   _____

---

logical needs. Norms that encourage and support interactions must also exist. A teacher should select a leadership style that is appropriate for the maturity level of the class. Finally, care must be taken to ensure that specific structures are created in the classroom that actively support and encourage involvement and participation.

References

Argyris, C. Theories of action that inhibit individual learning. *American Psychologist,* 1976, *31,* 636–54.

Boyer, R.K., and Bolton, C. One and two way communication in the classroom. Cincinnati, Ohio: *Faculty Resource Center Monograph Series,* University of Cincinnati, 1971.

Cohen, E.G. Sociology and the classroom: Setting the conditions for teacher-student interaction. *Review of Educational Research,* 1972, *42,* 441–52.

Use of criticism and
  sarcasm   _____
Use of ridicule and
  humor   _____
Making terminal
  statements   _____
Making punishing remarks   _____
Display of detailed
  knowledge   _____
Use of complicated
  language   _____
Failure to use names   _____
Overemphasis on grades   _____

Physical Environment

Inappropriate physical arrangement and features   _____

Adherence to pseudo-
  fixed features   _____

Group Dynamics

No opportunities for stu-
  dent input in course
  design   _____

Students not able to meet
  inclusion, control, and
  affection needs   _____

Leadership style not appropriate for maturity of
  students   _____

No classroom structures
  that specifically encourage
  participation   _____

Crow, M.L. Teaching as an interactive process. In K. Eble, ed., *Improving Teaching Styles: New Directions for Teaching and Learning.* San Francisco: Jossey-Bass, 1980.

Ellis, A. *Humanistic Psychotherapy: The Rational-Emotive Approach.* New York: Julian Press, 1973.

Ellis, A. Rational-emotive therapy. In R. Corsini, ed., *Current Psychotherapies.* Itasca, Ill.: Peacock, 1973.

Grasha, A.F. Observations on relating teaching goals to student response styles and classroom methods. *American Psychologist*, 1972, 27, 144–47.

Hersey, P.; Angelini, A.; and Caracuhansky, S. Unpublished study. Reported in Hersey, P. and Blanchard, K.H., *Management of Organizational Behavior: Utilizing Human Resources.* Englewood Cliffs, N.J.: Prentice-Hall, 1977.

Hersey, P., and Blanchard, K.H. *Management of Organizational Behavior: Utilizing Human Resources.* Englewood Cliffs, N.J.: Prentice-Hall, 1977.

Jones, E.E. How do people perceive the causes of behavior? *American Scientist,* 1976, *64,* 300–305.

Kelley, H.H. *Attribution in Social Interaction.* Morristown, N.J.: General Learning Press, 1971.

Leavitt, H.J. Some effects of certain communication patterns on group performance. *Journal of Abnormal and Social Psychology,* 1951, *46,* 38–50.

Nisbett, R.E., and Valins, S. *Perceiving the Causes of One's Own Behavior.* Morristown, N.J.: General Learning Press, 1971.

Richter, F.D., and Tjosvold, D. Effects of student participation in classroom decision making on attitudes, peer interaction, motivation, and learning. *Journal of Applied Psychology,* 1980, *65,* 74–80.

Rogers, C. *Freedom to Learn.* Columbus, Ohio: Merrill, 1969.

Schutz, W. *Profound Simplicity.* New York: Bantam, 1979.

Smith, H.A. Nonverbal communication in teaching. *Review of Educational Research,* 1979, *49,* 631–72.

Sommer, R. *Personal Space.* Englewood Cliffs, N.J.: Prentice-Hall, 1969.

Steele, F.I. *Physical Settings and Organization Development.* Reading, Mass.: Addison-Wesley, 1973.

Tesch, F.; Lansky, L.M.; and Lundgren, D.C. The exchange of information: One-way versus two-way communication. *Journal of Applied Behavioral Science,* 1972, *8,* 90–95.

Chapter 7
Basic Principles
for Evaluating Students

Student Qualifying Test of Unknown Origin

Uses of Test: To identify highly capable and motivated students.

Time Limit: Four hours.

History

Describe the history of the papacy from its origin to the present day, concentrating especially, but not exclusively, on its social, political, economic, religious, and philosophical impact on Europe, Asia, America, and Africa. Be brief, concise, and specific.

Medicine

You have been provided with a razor blade, a piece of gauze, and a bottle of scotch. Remove your appendix. Do not suture until your work has been inspected. You have fifteen minutes.

Public Speaking

Twenty-five hundred riot-crazed savages are storming the classroom. Calm them. You may use any ancient language except Latin or Greek.

Biology

Create life. Estimate the differences in subsequent human culture if this life had developed 500 million years earlier, with special attention to its probable effect on the English parliamentary system. Prove your thesis.

Music

Write a piano concerto. Orchestrate and perform it with flute and drum. You will find a piano under your seat.

Psychology

Based on your knowledge of their works, evaluate the emotional stability, degree of adjustment, and repressed frustrations of each of the following: Alexander of Aphrodisias, Ramses II, Gregory of Nyssa, Hammurabi. Support your evaluation with quotations from each man's work.

Sociology

Estimate the sociological problems that might accompany the end of the world. Construct an experiment to test your theory.

Engineering

The disassembled parts of a high-powered rifle have been placed on your desk. You will find an instruction manual, printed in Swahili. In ten minutes a hungry Bengal tiger will be admitted to the room. Take whatever action you feel appropriate. Be prepared to justify your decision.

Economics

Develop a realistic plan for refinancing the national debt. Trace the possible effects of your plan in the following areas: Cubism, the Donatist controversy, the wave theory of light. Outline a method for preventing these effects. Criticize this method from all possible points of view. Point out the deficiencies in your point of view, as demonstrated in your answer to the last question.

Political Science

There is a red telephone on the desk beside you. Start World War III. Report at length on its sociopolitical effects, if any.

Epistemology

Take a position for or against truth. Prove the validity of your position.

Physics

Explain the nature of matter. Include in your answer an evaluation of the impact of the development of mathematics on science.

Philosophy

Sketch the development of human thought; estimate its significance. Compare it with the development of any other kind of thought.

Most people appreciate the humor in these exam items although several students have said, "You think that exam was difficult—you should have seen the final I just took." As teachers, we must evaluate our students and appropriately reward those who performed well in class. Highly motivated and capable students make the job of evaluation easier, but we also have students who are less motivated and capable within a diverse student body. Most of us struggle with being fair to everyone, setting reasonable standards for performance, and giving students feedback on their progress.

In this chapter, several principles for assessing students are presented to enhance your ability to evaluate them. We have divided the process of evaluation into three components: *gathering relevant information on students, giving students feedback on their progress,* and *assigning grades.* Considerations relevant to each component are presented in the remainder of this chapter.

Gathering Relevant Information

There are several types of data we might use to assess our students. Lunneborg describes the information used by seven hundred faculty members at a major state university. These data are presented in Table 7.1. As you can see, although people have access to different sources of data, exams and term papers account for 65 percent of the weight in assigning grades, and exams alone account for 54 percent.

It is no secret that exams are a very important part of our evaluation of students. But we need to be careful using them. Computer programmers have an expression: "Garbage in—garbage out." This metaphor reminds us that our evaluations of students are only as good as the information sources we use. With exams as the most important source of evaluation data, there is some cause for concern. They cannot give us all the information we might want or that students could use profitably. And, for reasons we will outline, flaws in their design often make them less than accurate and valid estimates of students' knowledge. Let us examine several problems with classroom exams and several ways to overcome them.

Improving the Construction of Exams

Determining what is being measured. After a review of the classroom exam literature, Richard Anderson concludes that *exams fail to meet the*

Table 7.1. Importance of Various Data Sources in Assigning Grades

---

Each source is listed with the weight assigned to it in parentheses. The weights were determined by distributing 100 points across the data sources. Sources are listed in order of importance.

- Objective exams (37 points)
- Essay exams (17 points)
- Term papers (11 points)
- Recitations/problem sets (7 points)
- Term projects (6 points)
- Class discussion (5 points)
- Laboratory performance (5 points)
- Other (4 points)
- Effort (3 points)
- Attendance (2 points)
- Laboratory reports (2 points)
- Ratings by teaching assistants (1 point)

Source: Adapted from Jim Eison, "Grades: What Do They Tell?" *Teaching-Learning Issues,* Spring, 1980, p. 3, by permission of the Learning Research Center, Knoxville, Tennessee.

first criterion for a system of measurement—providing a definition of what is being measured. Anderson's review concentrated on classroom exams used in educational research. One might expect that educational researchers would know better. Apparently, some do not. We have, however, in our experience noted similar instances of the problem that Anderson raises. It is a problem not only for those doing research on classroom processes.

The issue is that most faculty assume their tests assess "knowledge about course content." Of course, "knowledge about course content" can mean different things. It can refer to a student's ability to remember previously learned information, to grasp the meaning of new material, to apply the content in new and concrete situations, to analyze or synthesize the information, or to judge the value of the information. Benjamin Bloom labels these aspects of content or learning outcomes as *knowledge, comprehension, application, analysis and synthesis,* and *evaluation,* respectively. He argues that *it is important for teachers to define what learning outcomes they wish to measure and then to construct test items that assess them.*

There are three things you can do that will help you better define the content of your exams. When you do so, the major problem Anderson identifies with classroom tests begins to disappear.

- *Decide what aspects of the content you are interested in measuring.*
  To do this, you simply need to ask yourself how important Bloom's
  categories of knowledge, comprehension, application, analysis and
  synthesis, and evaluation are for the information covered. You might
  find yourself more interested in one than the others because of the
  nature of your course. Table 7.2 presents several ideas for how to define in Bloom's terms each aspect of the content of your course.
  These are presented in the center column of the table. On the right-
  hand side are words that you might consider using in exam questions
  that would help you to measure properly each of Bloom's categories.

- *Develop a blueprint for your exams based on what learning outcomes
  you want to cover.* A blueprint helps you decide what parts of the
  content you want students to apply, synthesize, comprehend, or use
  in other ways. Some of the content might be appropriate for all
  categories; other aspects might fit only one or two of them. Once
  you know, for example, that you want students to analyze and apply
  a certain theory, you can then write exam questions to achieve this.
  The blueprint also provides a record of how many of each type of
  question you write. This helps you check that you are in fact emphasizing what you want from the course on the exam. An example of a
  blueprint appears in Table 7.3, on pages 172–173, with test question
  ideas from several disciplines.

- *Let your students know what learning outcomes you have as goals for
  the course and the exams.* This is best done by taking care to plan
  your course from the beginning with the following sequence in mind.

  Course Objectives → Exam Objectives → Exam Items

  Students could be told what general learning outcomes you expect
  (for example, "In this course you will be asked to apply the theories
  covered in new situations I present"; "In this course you will be asked
  to analyze concepts and relate them to your daily experiences"). Or
  you could give students a study guide that lists major concepts to be
  covered and indicates the learning outcomes you expect (for example,
  "Hilgard's theory: Show how it predicts learning under conditions of
  frustration"). The important point is to keep your students informed
  about your course and exam objectives. Additional ideas for stating
  such objectives can be found in Chapter 5.

Paying attention to defining content and using a test blueprint will enhance the quality of your classroom exams. But there are several other
problems with such tests that need to be considered, such as inconsistent
scoring within and between graders, ambiguous questions, inappropriate
items, and, with multiple-choice or true-false items, identifiable patterns

Table 7.2. Bloom's Learning Outcomes

Learning Outcomes	Evidence of Outcome	Terms for Measuring Outcome in Test Questions
Knowledge	Knows common terms Knows specific facts Knows methods and procedures Knows basic concepts in course Knows principles	Define, describe, identify, label, list, match, name, outline, reproduce, select, state
Comprehension	Understands facts and principles Interprets verbal material Interprets charts and graphs Translates verbal material to mathematical formulas Estimates future consequences implied in data Justifies methods and procedures	Convert, defend, distinguish, estimate, explain, extend, generalize, give examples, infer, paraphrase, predict, rewrite, summarize
Application	Applies concepts and principles to new situations Applies laws and theories to practical situations Solves mathematical problems Constructs charts and graphs Demonstrates correct use of a method or procedure	Change, compute, demonstrate, discover, manipulate, modify, operate, predict, prepare, produce, relate, show, solve, use
Analysis	Recognizes unstated assumptions Recognizes logical fallacies in reasoning Distinguishes between facts and inferences Evaluates the relevance of data Analyzes the organizational structure of a work (art, music, writing)	Break down, diagram, differentiate, discriminate, distinguish, identify, illustrate, infer, outline, point out, relate, select, separate, subdivide
Synthesis	Writes a well-organized theme Writes a creative short story (or poem or piece of music) Proposes a plan for an experiment Integrates learning from different areas into a plan for solving a problem Formulates a new scheme for classifying objects (or events or ideas)	Categorize, combine, compile, compose, create, devise, design, explain, generate, modify, organize, plan, rearrange, reconstruct, relate, reorganize, revise, rewrite, summarize, tell, write
Evaluation	Judges the logical consistency of a written passage Judges the adequacy with which conclusions are supported by data Judges the value of a work (art, music, writing) by use of internal criteria Judges the value of a work (art, music, writing) by use of external standards of excellence	Appraise, compare, conclude, contrast, criticize, describe, discriminate, explain, justify, interpret, relate, summarize, support

Source: Adapted from *Taxonomy of Educational Objectives: Handbook I: Cognitive Domain* by Benjamin S. Bloom et al. Copyright © 1956 by Longman Inc. Reprinted by permission of Longman Inc., New York.

of correct responses. Such things also affect how accurately and validly our exams evaluate students. Fortunately, there are actions that can be taken to correct such problems. *Basically, we must be careful when writing exam items.* The following suggestions will improve the writing and scoring of multiple-choice, true-false, matching, essay, and short answer items.

Writing multiple-choice items. Some general considerations when writing multiple-choice items are the following: (a) Do not write all questions in one sitting. (b) Write stem first, correct response second, distractors third. (c) Write items on index cards.

Points about the stem. (a) Stems should indicate clearly to the student what he or she is to answer. (b) Direct questions are usually better than fill-in. (c) Stems should be stated without lengthy qualifications. (d) Stems should pose a unique problem that requires more than a one-word response. (e) Most items should require more than just recall to get the right answer. (f) Stems should be grammatical.

Guidelines to writing alternatives. (a) Write at least four alternatives. (b) Put alternatives at the end of the stem. (c) Arrange alternatives in a vertical column. (d) If there is a natural order among alternatives, use it. (e) Put as much of the item as possible in the stem. (f) Write alternatives in parallel form whenever possible. (g) Make sure each alternative completes a grammatical statement. (h) Use sparingly the alternatives "all of these" and "none of these." Make sure these are not always or usually the correct response to the questions for which they are used. (i) Make sure the distractors are plausible or attractive alternatives. (j) Do not use just two or three alternatives as your correct answer all the time. Divide your correct answers evenly over the a, b, c, d, and e alternatives. (k) Avoid making the correct answer the longest or the shortest response all the time. (l) All distractors (wrong answers) should be unequivocally wrong.

Writing matching items. (a) Direction must clearly state the basis on which items are to be matched. (b) The two sets of items should be homogeneous, for example, events and dates, not events combined with dates and names. (c) There must be several plausible choices but only one correct choice for each stem. (d) At least one set (stems or choices) should be single words or short phrases. (e) Arrange response alternatives in some order (numerical or alphabetical). (f) Have more response items than are required. (g) Sets of items should be on the same page. (h) Don't make sets too long. (i) Some choices may be used more than once, but this must be stated in the directions.

Writing true-false items. (a) Be sure statements are related to important objectives. (b) Write the statements clearly and precisely. (c) Write items

Table 7.3. A Test Blueprint for a Hypothetical Interdisciplinary Course

Course Content[a]	Type (level) of Question					Total No. of Items
	Knowledge	Comprehension	Application	Analysis/Synthesis	Evaluation	
Freud's theory of personality	Define id, ego, super-ego				Compare id, ego, superego, to conscious/un-conscious processes	
Paradigms in science		Give examples of two current paradigms		Point out major parts of physi-cal science model		
Helium	Describe its molecular structure		Show how it is used in avia-tion			

Friction	Define the term	Predict what will happen when oil is applied to a surface	Diagram how friction affects the ability of a car to stop	
Love	Define passionate and compassionate love	Give an example of brotherly love		Compare Rubin's use of *love* to Fromm's use
American Revolution		Predict what would have happened if American Revolution had failed	Determine the four major causes of the revolution	Justify why you think the colonists were right
Time		Explain how Einstein conceived of time	Describe how the concept of time is used in physics, psychology, and economics	

[a]The specific information of interest for each term can be converted into essay, multiple-choice, true-false, or matching exam items.

that require more than recall to get the right answer. (d) Be sure items require more than common sense or logic. (e) Watch for words such as *never* and *all* or *often* and *some*. These are cue words for the correct response. (f) Do not make false statements by just inserting *no* or *not* into true statements.

Writing essay items. (a) Items should be stated clearly. (b) Items should be sufficiently limited for the time allowed. (c) Items should challenge students with interesting and worthwhile problems. (d) Items should require more than just memory to respond.

Scoring essays: (a) Clearly state the questions. (b) Write out a model answer. (c) Score item by item rather than scoring all items for a given student. (d) Score questions anonymously—have students write their names on the back of the papers or use only ID numbers. (e) Don't ask pure opinion questions. (f) Shuffle papers before scoring next question.

Writing short answer items. (a) Make sure the facts asked for are important. (b) Do *not* take sentences directly from a book. (c) Have only one blank or require only one word or phrase as the answer. (d) If it is a fill-in-the-blank item, put the blank at the end of the sentence. (e) Be sure the question permits only one answer. (f) Be careful that the grammar of the sentence does not give the answer away. (g) Make sure the questions specify the knowledge required for a correct answer. (h) Beware of encouraging students to remember half-truths or superficial knowledge. (i) In completion items, be sure the student can determine the kind of word that is correct.

These suggestions are relevant to writing good items. A related concern about test items is how to place them on the exam. Should items follow a logical order (such as textbook chapters or schedule of topics covered in class), should easy ones get placed first to motivate students, or should an easy item get placed among harder items? A review of the research by Joshua Gerow indicates that *item placement does not affect exam performance.* Students do just as well on exams that have items randomly placed as they do with exam items set up in a particular order. Faye Dambrot's research suggests that these conclusions hold regardless of the academic ability level of the students.

Using Other Information Sources

Lunneborg's research mentioned at the beginning of this chapter suggests that instructors have a variety of information sources available to them, yet they tend to rely mostly on examinations and term papers in calculating student grades. One reason is that such measures are relatively easy to evaluate. Methods for writing and scoring them are well known. Behaviors like class discussion, effort, and unique contributions to the class are not as familiar. There are few commonly accepted or well-known means of evaluating such things. But such means do exist. In Chapter 11, we present several alternate ways to gather information about students that are compatible with various instructional goals. Several other suggestions are listed here:

Anecdotal records. These are simply written records of events that may be of importance in understanding or evaluating student behaviors. It is important to write a factual description of the behavior, keeping any interpretations separate from the behavioral account. Suggestions for improvement may also be kept as a separate part of the anecdotal record.

It is obvious that one cannot record all the behaviors that occur in the classroom, so the following limitations are suggested:

1. Record in this manner only behaviors that cannot be recorded by other means.
2. If you must observe all students, limit observations to a few types of behavior.
3. Record extensive observations only for those students who are most in need of help. The keeping of anecdotal records can be facilitated by one of the following methods:
   a. Keep a separate card for each observation.
   b. Keep a separate sheet in a notebook for each subject in order to keep a running account. (Watch out for being biased by a previous report.)

The anecdotal record is good, because it allows for descriptions of actual behaviors in the natural setting. It can serve as a check on other evaluation procedures (for example, a student may score high on the "good-neighbor test" but spend most of class kicking his classmates). Finally, it is useful for keeping a record of the exceptional but significant event.

The value of anecdotal records is limited by the difficulty of being objective when observing and reporting student behavior. One must guard against bias in deciding which behaviors are recorded and which are not.

Rating scales. Rating scales are a somewhat more systematic procedure for recording and evaluating educational change. The typical rating scale consists of a set of characteristics or qualities and a scale for indicating the degree to which each is present. There are two types of rating scales you might find useful.

A *numerical rating scale* consists of a question about a desired characteristic and a series of numbers (usually 1–5). The rater simply circles the number that indicates the degree to which the characteristic is present. Number 1 is usually the lowest rating, and 5 the highest.

Examples

1. To what extent does student participate in discussion?

1	2	3	4	5
Never		Occasionally		Always

2. To what extent are student's comments relevant to discussion?

1	2	3	4	5
Never		Occasionally		Always

A *descriptive rating scale* uses descriptive statements placed along the continuum. These descriptions are somewhat more helpful in deciding to what extent a characteristic is present. The descriptions help clarify to the teacher and student the different degrees of progress toward the desired goals.

Examples

1. To what extent are student's comments relevant to discussion?

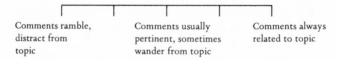

Comments ramble, distract from topic   Comments usually pertinent, sometimes wander from topic   Comments always related to topic

2. How well does student relate to other students?

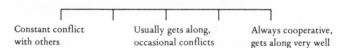

Constant conflict with others   Usually gets along, occasional conflicts   Always cooperative, gets along very well

3. To what extent does student have well-developed writing style?

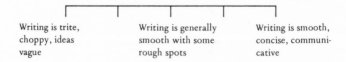

Writing is trite, choppy, ideas vague   Writing is generally smooth with some rough spots   Writing is smooth, concise, communicative

Checklists. The main difference between the checklist and the rating scale is that the rating scale is used when the *degree* of progress is to be noted, whereas the checklist is used when a yes-no or present-absent judgment is called for. Checklists are used in evaluating those performance skills that can be clearly defined as having been achieved or not.

The checklist is simply a list of the steps involved in a certain skill with a space for noting whether or not the student was able to perform each step.

Some behaviors that lend themselves to the checklist procedure are those with identifiable characteristics, such as laboratory technique, orchestra conducting, brush-stroke technique, hand-tool care, and proper grammar usage. These examples do not mean to exclude other, more affective behaviors. However, it does appear that other measures are more useful when trying to assess pupil characteristics like personality and adjustment.

Examples

_____Met with instructor to discuss term paper idea.

_____Able to define personality components measured by test.

_____Turned in draft of outline for paper.

_____Able to describe procedure for administering test.

_____Turned in revised outline.

_____Able to describe method for scoring test.

_____Wrote first draft and met with instructor for comments.

_____Can administer test to a client effectively.

_____Wrote acceptable final draft based on comments.

_____Able to write a satisfactory report based on test results.

Self-assessment. A source of information typically ignored in classrooms is students' own comments about their progress. In principle, there is no reason students cannot also respond to the rating scales and checklists we have described. Unfortunately, in a world where competition for grades may tempt students to be less than totally honest in their public self-evaluations, faculty have tended to mistrust and therefore not use this potentially powerful source of evaluation. When used in conjunction with other sources of information about students' progress, it may help fill in some of the gaps. In addition to having students respond to the rating scales and checklists you might use, consider the following idea.

Open-ended response to selected aspects of the course. Tell students that you may lack some information that could affect their grades in the course. Ask them to describe things that they did to help them learn the content of which you are unaware. You might ask them to describe how they prepared for exams, the amount of attention they gave to the textbook, how they prepared classroom assignments, and significant events that happened in the course that affected their thoughts, emotions, and lives in some way.

Using Alternative Testing Procedures

Students generally tire of the same type of exams. Most courses ask students to respond to exam questions that follow a predictable format.

Some variety in normal testing procedures would help maintain student interest and would give the instructor additional information on student capabilities. Several ideas for alternative ways to test students are:

- *Library search.* Students are given questions related to the course content but are required to use at least two sources in addition to the text and lectures to develop an answer. They are encouraged to use the library to do this.

- *Student-generated questions.* Students write exam items, and the instructor selects certain ones to be used on an in-class or take-home exam. Sometimes formulating a good question takes as much skill and knowledge as answering it.

- *Experiential test.* Students are given several concepts from class and told to observe or participate in some experience in which the concepts will be used. This might involve visiting a courtroom, a business organization, or a manufacturing plant. Students write reports on how the concepts played a role in the particular setting.

- *Open-ended exam format.* This type of exam gives students a chance to respond to very open-ended questions. In the process, they are encouraged to use their own ideas as well as ideas from the course. The questions should be fun items and not the standard "compare and contrast" or "develop the major issues" types of questions. One of our favorite open-ended exams appears in Table 7.4 on the following page. In many ways it is almost a universal exam.

Giving Students Feedback on Their Performance

We find that students appreciate knowing where they stand in a course. Quizzes and other exams are one of the ways they get this information. For some, however, this is not enough. They may want to know what you think about their performance in class discussions or on group projects, or the new ideas they have about content. Other students may wish to have additional and more detailed feedback about their exam or term paper scores. Or the nature of the course may demand that you give students much more timely and specific feedback. This is often necessary in courses that teach clinical, laboratory, or job-related skills. Depending upon how well it is done, giving feedback can enhance your relationships with students or act as a source of conflict. We now present ten suggestions for giving students feedback. We have presented them in a format that allows you to rate yourself on how well you already use these principles. Items given a rating of 4 or less represent areas you might want to develop further.

Table 7.4. Sample Open-Ended Exam

Facts, Insights, Values, and Uncertainties

1. *Facts* are an inescapable part of a _____ course, but they are not its chief reason for being. We have been exposed to many facts this term; it is good to have them in our possession, and they may even be useful. Select a fact from the term's work that seems to have some utility and discuss it briefly. If you mastered no useful facts during the term, skip this question.

2. *Insights* are more central to a study of _____ than are facts, though of necessity they are often based on facts. Sometimes an insight is entirely our own; sometimes it is an author's and we take it over because it has meaning for us. Whichever it is, its function is to illuminate a part of us. If you have had such an insight this term, describe it in context and explain its chief benefits. If you have had no insights during the term, skip this question.

3. *Values* are said by many to lie at the heart of human learning and to be the chief concern of _____. Through _____ we expand our consciousness by grappling with the values of others and come thereby to have a better understanding of our own values. Select a value or value-set of your own that has been tested or probed by the term's reading and describe the circumstances. If none of your personal values were involved in the work of the term, skip this question.

4. *Uncertainties* lie at the heart of the most profound human questions, and such questions cannot therefore be answered by rote or by formula; each of us must, according to his or her temperament and desire, find his or her own path out of the dark wood. Select a problem from the term's work that you consider to be of significant importance, recall briefly for your reader how the question was handled by the term's authors (whichever ones dealt with it), and discuss the ambiguities and paradoxes that prevent its satisfactory and complete resolution for you personally. If nothing struck you as ambiguous or paradoxical during the term, skip this question.

Ten Ideas for Giving Feedback

In the space next to each suggestion, rate yourself on the following scale in terms of how frequently you use the suggested behavior.

1. ____*I try to give feedback to students based on how well their performance met the objectives and standards of the course.* Unfortunately, this cannot be done unless you have a well-defined set of course objectives and performance standards given to students the first day of class or at timely intervals for particular assignments (term papers, laboratory assignments). Students need to know what content they must learn, how well they

should know it (rote memorization, application), and the deadlines for assignments. *This is best done in writing* with an opportunity for students to discuss the objectives and standards with you. Feedback can then be given using the objectives and standards as criteria against which their performance is judged. If the objectives are stated clearly enough, the student will understand why a particular test score, grade, or other form of feedback was given. *Teachers will be less likely to have students feel that the feedback merely represents the instructor's bias or personal opinion.*

Example: "You lost six points on the paper because it was a week late. Having an assignment in on time was one of the ground rules listed in the course syllabus, along with the penalties for a late paper."

2. ____*I try to be as specific as I can when giving feedback.* It is hard to correct performance when told in very general terms how well you did. Telling a student "You just did not cover the right amount of content" or "You earned a B on the exam" is unlikely to be helpful. *A better way is to describe the behavior you observed in very specific terms and, if applicable, suggest something the person could do to improve.*

Examples: Specific Feedback: "Your paper did not cover the theoretical developments in the field between 1945 and 1950." "Your coverage of the Jones theory was not complete—you left out her first three theorems." *Specific feedback plus suggestion for correction:* "Your right front wheel hit the sidewalk when you turned the car. Try to turn the steering wheel about a third of the way more to the left next time."

3. ____*I try to give feedback as soon as possible.* Feedback is not likely to have as much effect when it is directed toward behavior that occurred too far in the past.

Example: "Sally, three weeks ago you made a wrong response to my question in class. I've been meaning to tell you about it." Sally may have missed that question on yesterday's exam. A lot can change in three weeks, including one's memory of what occurred. It is best to give feedback as soon as possible after a behavior occurs.

4. ____*I try not to be evaluative when giving feedback.* "What a stupid thing to do." "I've never seen such poor performance." Statements like these are likely to make another person angry and inattentive. *Focus on the behavior of the student,* how it met objectives and standards and what can be done to improve.

Keep specific behaviors in mind and ignore tendencies to evaluate a performance negatively. The *overuse* of positive evaluations ("Great job"; "Best I've seen") has a similar effect. If overused, positive evaluations may lose their effectiveness and can place the teacher in a condescending role. Students may become resentful.

5. ____*I try to give positive feedback frequently.* No matter how thin you make a pancake, there are always two sides to it. In our culture we have a tendency to look at the negative side of things when giving feedback. A good idea is to think of things that people do well and let them know. Even when negative feedback is called for, you should consider preceding it with something positive.

    Example: "Your answer to question 5 had each of the five points that were covered in the book discussed well. In lecture, I suggested two other things that were important to know, and these were not included in your response. That was the reason for your losing four points in your answer."

6. ____*I try to give feedback only when I am sure a student wants it.* If someone is not ready to hear what you have to say, they are not likely to learn as much. Before giving feedback, check the other person's readiness for it.

    Examples: "Alice, I'd like to give you feedback on what you did. Can we discuss it now or should we meet later?" "Alice, would you like feedback on your performance?"

7. ____*I ask students what behaviors they would like feedback on.* Sometimes teachers are put in the position of having to guess what areas of performance a student really needs to hear about. Another aid to getting people to listen to you is to ask them what they would like to hear about. This does not mean that you cannot tell them about other things, but it helps ensure that some of the topics of concern to them will be discussed.

    Example: "Fred, what parts of your class presentation would you like me to comment on?"

    "Well, Dr. Jones, I would like to know how I handled the hypotheses in the theory."

    "I'm not sure what you want. What is it that you would specifically like to know about?"

    "How clearly did I point out the implications of each hypothesis?"

8. ____*I check my feedback to make sure that it was heard.* People really do not listen to one another as often as we think. A

helpful suggestion is to close a conversation on feedback by asking the student to summarize or paraphrase what he or she understood you to say. In this way you can check to see if the points you were trying to make were understood, and you can reinforce them if necessary.

Example: "Basically, Sam, you failed to discuss the attack on Pearl Harbor and the consequent hysteria that gripped our nation. Both of these points were asked for in part B of the question. In light of what I've said, do you see why you lost credit on that answer?"

"I guess I spent too much time on the first part of the question."

"But what about your answers to the second part?"

"I failed to include material on the bombing at Pearl Harbor and on the emotional reactions of people in this country to the bombing."

9. ____*I give feedback to the person who should get it.* Often teachers become angry or disappointed with a student's performance. They tell their office mates, the student's advisor, or the undergraduate or graduate studies director—anyone except the student. This often happens early in a term, and the student finds out after it's too late to rectify the situation. There may be tension or anxiety associated with giving feedback on certain issues, but it does not help to tell everyone except the student.

10. ____*I personally model giving and receiving feedback in my own behavior.* Make use of the principles presented here in your interactions with students. Furthermore, set a climate and develop norms for feedback by asking for feedback on your teaching and periodically holding conferences with students to discuss how they see things going in the course. The use of student assessment forms of teachers can be helpful. Students learn a lot from their teachers, including attitudes about feedback. If you are open and willing to receive it, this can help set a climate for your students.

Assigning Grades

Grading students is a rather complex business, and the practice has received a lot of criticism in recent years. *From one point of view, grades are a negative part of the educational process.* Robertson and Steele argue that the practice allows faculty to maintain a superior position and to exert unnecessary control and authority over students. They also believe that students eventually learn to assess their self-worth in terms of a grade and work for a grade rather than learning course content. This view has some empirical support in the research of Jim Eison. He found that students classified as "grade oriented"

- were less able to face reality with a mature attitude
- were less self-motivated and more wrapped up in inner urges
- had less confidence in their own capacity to deal with things
- were less trusting, self-sufficient, and relaxed
- were more competitive and less collaborative in academic settings
- suffered from higher levels of test anxiety
- had poorer study habits

.Grades also do not predict postgraduate performance or success very well. In a review of the research, Jim Eison notes there is at best a very weak relationship between course grades and later performance in life. One reason is that many factors influence a grade. These include the types of information presented in Table 7.1 and such things as the instructor's perceptions of student interest in the course and attitudes about course work. Another reason is that the types of skills and abilities needed in the world of work are different from the kinds of knowledge and information required on most classroom exams. Finally, personal traits vital to job success, including motivation or drive, creativity, persistence, and interpersonal and communication skills, are typically ignored by classroom tests and grading procedures.

These concerns led Robert Leeper to write: "To be discussing or writing about the efficiencies of grades—is incredible to me. For 50 years we have been discussing them and yet the solution seems obvious—to do away with them" [1971].

From another point of view, the practice of grading is a well-established and important part of our educational system. Many faculty and students perceive it as a valuable and important aspect of the educational process. It helps faculty to motivate students and reward them for their accomplishments, and provides at least general feedback on a student's progress. Students also tend to believe that grades serve a useful and important function. Polezynski and Shirland asked students to rate on a scale of 0 to 10 the "importance of attaining your expected GPA for a semester." A rating of 0 represented "no importance," and a rating of 10 represented "exceptionally important." The mean rating was 8.82. Zimmerman found that, when asked what motivated them, 75 percent of a sample of 287 college students listed grades among the important motivators.

The value of assigning grades is not clear cut. It is very easy to marshal evidence in the literature to support or not support the practice. Our purpose here is not to fan the flames of controversy. Apparently, grades are here to stay, at least in the foreseeable future. Given this fact, we want to suggest several principles that can enhance current practices in grading students.

Objectivity, reliability, mastery of content, and flexibility are desirable features of a grading system. Kyle Carter states that these four components should be a part of any classroom grading system. *Objectivity* refers to letting students know the criteria on which the grade is based. Our criteria are usually adaptations of the objectives or outcomes of the course. Using criteria and communicating them to students alleviates anxiety about what is expected and lets them know that the grades were not determined by throwing darts. *Reliability* or accuracy in grading is achieved when instructors have specific and unambiguous data on students and when both teachers and students understand what the data mean. For this reason, Carter argues, objective exams are probably the best input that can be used. We tend to disagree, because, as we show in the first section of this chapter, there are ways to make other input specific and relatively accurate. When exams largely determine the grade assigned, students should be expected to *master the content,* and the grade should reflect how much they did in fact master. Finally, it is necessary to maintain some *flexibility* in grading. The composition of student ability in class varies somewhat from term to term, and one's exams are not always equally difficult. Thus it is important to have a grading system that is flexible in the face of such variations.

Carter suggests a grading system based on Frank Costin's work that help to meet each of his four criteria. The steps in his procedure are as follows:

- Compute the total score (from exams, projects, and so forth) for each student.
- Construct a frequency distribution for the total scores for the class.
- Determine the upper 10 percent of the distribution.
- Compute the mean of the total scores for the upper 10 percent.
- Assign grades according to the following scale: A = 95 percent of the mean; B = 85 percent of the mean; C = 75 percent of the mean; D = 65 percent of the mean.

This system achieves objectivity because criteria for the grades are known in advance and can be applied uniformly. Reliability is achieved to the extent that relatively objective inputs are used to compute the total score. The system lets students know what "mastery of the content" means, because it is defined statistically. Finally, the system is flexible in that the grade distributions will vary as a function of changes in test difficulty.

This system is not flexible, however, with variations in student ability. In a high-ability class, the instructor may end up giving fewer A or B grades than are deserved. Modifications can be made, depending on the instructor's perceptions of student ability (based on test results, written work, classroom participation, and other factors). If the class is judged to be "superior in ability," the upper 15 percent or 20 percent of the exam scores could be used instead of the upper 10 percent in computing the mean. Or, for low-ability classes, the upper 5 percent to 8 percent of the distribution might be employed for A and B grades, but 10 percent to 12 percent could be applied for C, D, and F grades.

Carter's solution to achieving objectivity, reliability, mastery of content, and flexibility in a grading system obviously is not the only one possible. The contract grading approaches mentioned in Chapter 4 offer another method for achieving the same objectives. Carter's system, however, is much more consonant with the grading procedures used by most faculty. Consequently, with very little effort it could be adapted to a variety of courses. The important point is not that Carter's suggestions are the best to use. Rather, it is important that you ask yourself how whatever system you currently employ meets the criteria of objectivity, reliability, mastery of content, and flexibility. If necessary, adjustments can be made to bring it into line with the criteria.

Grading on the curve should be done cautiously. Students sometimes ask instructors whether they will "curve" the test scores to determine a final grade. More than a few teachers respond yes to the question. In our experience, people can mean several things by curving the test scores. Some consistently give as many A's as they do F's, and more C's than they do any other grade. Others scale the grades in proportion to the top score in the class, regardless of whether it was a high or low score. Thus, a score of 68 out of 100, if the best score in the class, could represent an A grade. Curving test scores acknowledges that tests are not perfect and that there is always subjective bias in assigning grades. The use of curves represents an instructor's attempt to be as fair as possible.

In most cases, curving procedures are indeed fair. One practice, however, that is questionable is the use of *"normal curve" procedures*, in which instructors assign just as many A's as F's and have more C's than any other grade. The assumption is that academic ability is normally distributed. This might be true of a large sample of students in the general population, but it is not necessarily true of students in a given class. *Students are selected because of certain abilities in most colleges. Their academic skills and abilities are not normally distributed.* Yet we have seen the assumption of a normal distribution of ability made on more than one occasion, and this was in colleges of pharmacy, engineering, and architecture where the assumption is questionable at best. Students in such colleges typically meet rather high admission standards.

Course grades typically reflect a student's knowledge and ability and the difficulty of the exams. Most instructors average test scores from two or more exams to determine a final test score distribution. From this distribution, grades are assigned. Most people assume that this practice will reflect the relative standing of students in class. Thus an A is awarded to those students who maintained a high performance relative to others. Their knowledge and ability are considered to be higher than those of other people in class. A similar assumption is made for people who are assigned B, C, D, and F grades. In most cases, this assumption is valid. Sometimes, however, a problem occurs when final grades are determined by averaging the scores from more than one exam. *The exam that had the most variability will contribute more to the student's average.* As a result, two students could have the same relative standing on the average but show different mean test scores. This situation is illustrated in the example in Table 7.5. Such a situation arises because the students' knowledge and ability varied across each exam, or the difficulty of the exams varied, or both.

One solution is to compute the standard deviation for each test using the formula:

$$\text{SD} = \sqrt{\frac{\Sigma(x - \overline{X})^2}{n - 1}}$$

To do this, we sum the squares of the deviation of each score from the mean, divide by the number of scores less one, and take the square root of the result. The standard deviation is a measure of how scattered or variable the exam scores are in a distribution. The larger the standard deviation, the greater the spread of the scores around the mean of the distribution. Dividing each student's exam score by the standard deviation and multiplying it by 10 to eliminate decimals will equalize the weight of the tests. You may then sum or average the corrected scores across exams, and the total or average scores for students will better reflect their relative standing. An example of this is presented in Table 7.6 on page 188. This correction is most appropriate when each exam has the same number of total points.

When the total number of points on each exam is significantly different, the exam with the larger number of points will contribute more to the final total or average even if corrected. To handle this situation, each exam score should be changed to a standard score. This correction is made using the formula:

$$\text{(standard score)} = \frac{\overline{X} - x}{\text{SD}}$$

or by dividing each score's deviation from the mean by the standard deviation. The standard scores can then be averaged or summed to determine a final grade.

Table 7.5. Variability in Student Exam Scores

	Test 1	Test 2	$\overline{X}$
Student 1	+1 SD	−1 SD	
Exam score	(25)	(10)	17.5
Student 2	−1 SD	+1 SD	
Exam score	(15)	(30)	22.5
$\overline{X}$	(20)	(20)	

Test 1   mean $(\overline{X}) = 20$
standard deviation (SD) = 5

Test 2   mean $(\overline{X}) = 20$
standard deviation (SD) = 10

Note: Student 1 is one standard deviation above the mean on test 1 and one standard deviation below the mean on test 2. Student 2 had a similar pattern but in the reverse direction. Thus, on the *first exam*, student 1 had a higher relative standing than did the second student. Just the opposite is true for the second exam. If we average their relative standing across the two exams, we find that both students have the same *average relative standing.* (Each was exactly at the mean when averaged across both exams.) Their mean scores across the two exams show that student 2 has a higher overall average. We might conclude based on the mean alone that student 2 had a higher relative standing. This obviously is not true. The problem is that the second exam has more scatter in the scores (a larger standard deviation), and thus it contributes more to the average of both students. The result is that the second student's average was increased more and the first student's was lowered more than would have occurred if the variability were equal.

Try to avoid certain judgment errors when assigning grades. Grades, like any other rating of performance, are subject to certain judgment errors. Listed here are four that tend to present problems for instructors.

- *Attribution errors.* As a general rule, research in how people perceive one another shows that a bias exists in making judgments. Instead of attributing the causes for someone's behavior to both environmental and personality factors, we tend to use one or the other. When factors in the situation are not salient or the situation is ambiguous, we tend to blame the person for a problem he or she has—that is, we look for defects within them. Thus students who perform poorly on exams are seen as "lazy," "stupid," "unmotivated," or any number of other things. Our grades reflect this judgment. Unless we have evidence

Table 7.6. Corrections of Exam Score Distributions: Dividing Each Score by the Standard Deviation

Student	Raw Score Exam 1	Corrected Score	Raw Score Exam 2	Corrected Score	Total Raw Score	Rank Based on Raw Score	Total Corrected Score	Rank Based on Correction
A.	95	78.2	89	42.6	184	1	120.8	1
[a]B.	75	61.7	70	33.5	145	4	95.2	5
C.	80	65.9	65	31.1	145	4	97.0	4
[a]D.	55	45.3	35	16.7	90	8	62.0	9
E.	90	74.1	75	35.9	165	3	110.0	3
F.	88	72.4	80	38.3	168	2	110.7	2
[a]G.	72	59.3	40	19.1	112	10	78.4	8
[a]H.	65	53.5	25	12.0	90	8	65.5	10
[a]I.	85	70.0	50	23.9	135	7	93.9	6
[a]J.	78	64.2	60	28.7	138	6	92.9	7
	SD = 12.1		SD = 20.8					

[a]Note how the ranks of these six students change when the raw scores instead of the corrected scores are used to compute their total exam scores. Variations at least as large as these are possible, and we are not unlikely to find larger differences in the ranks depending upon the relative standard deviations (SDs) of the exam scores.

that they are stupid, lazy, or unmotivated, we are making the fundamental attribution error.

It would be better to try to figure out what factors in the student's environment or the classroom environment are also contributing to the problem. In the former case, the student may have an illness, a full-time job, family problems, poor study habits, or other things that affect his or her performance. In the latter case, there may be things that *we* are doing in class that contribute. Poorly organized lectures, not enough time for discussion or questions, unavailability after class, and other things under our control could contribute. By looking for environmental factors we might find that we can improve study habits, or even refer the student to someone who can assist with a personal problem. In most cases, however, people find it much more convenient to blame the student.

- *Halo error.* Sometimes we form a very favorable or unfavorable impression of students based on physical appearance, comments in class, general reputation, or even the performance of someone else in the students' family we once taught. The result is that this impression guides our judgments of these individuals. Thus they are given higher or lower grades than they might obtain if we had no impression. Scoring tests blindly will help correct this problem, as will determining final grades in the same way if it is possible to do so. Furthermore, having objective criteria for scoring exams and grading students will lessen the chances that our overall impression of them will unduly influence their grades. Yet the best thing we can do is to be aware that the halo effect exists and not let it influence our judgments.

- *Leniency error.* This is a tendency to give people the benefit of the doubt. Unfortunately, we might do this to students who don't really deserve it. Leniency errors are more likely to occur when the criteria for grades are not well established. Establishing the criteria in advance will help attenuate this judgment error.

- *Logical error.* We often assume that certain traits go together. A person who is loyal and trustworthy must also be kind. An individual who is helpful and courteous must also be honest. A student who dresses neatly, is clean, and looks wide awake in class must also be intelligent. Of course, such traits may not go together. Yet each of us has an "implicit personality theory" that we carry around with us. It is a shortcut we use to try to know what people are like and to predict their future performance. To avoid the logical error, you need to ask yourself what evidence you have for the characteristics you attribute to students. In this way, you are unlikely to grade them based on what you assume they are like, but rather on evidence of their actual performance.

Remain open to other possibilities for assigning grades. The most prevalent model for assigning grades is to use information thoughtfully from the sources in Table 7.1 and then assign a letter grade. There are, however, other possibilities. Listed here are several ideas you might consider using in the future.

- *Contract grading.* The students and the instructor arrive at an agreement on what needs to be done for a certain grade. Procedures for establishing contracts were discussed in Chapter 4.

- *Student-assigned grades.* Students are asked to assign themselves a grade. However, they must justify in detail the reasons for the grade. The justification should relate to performance on exams, course projects, perceived grasp of material, time spent on course work, amount of reading completed, and participation and attendance in class.

  A variation on this procedure is to have students write a justification and for the instructor to read it after he or she has "tentatively" decided on what grade to give. The students may have convincing arguments that they should receive higher or lower grades than the teacher has contempleted giving.

- *Students grade each other.* Students are sometimes the best judges of how well they and other people in class are contributing to course work. This procedure tends to work best in classes where the instructor has small groups working on course-related topics and is willing to work with the groups on the grading task. Criteria are established for various letter grades, and the students rate each person in the group on the criteria. A colleague, Leonard Lansky, gives students criteria for a grade and then uses a sports analogy of first-, second-, or third-string players. A student's grade depends upon which team his or her peers think the student made.

- *Grades plus descriptive feedback.* Letter grades represent a rather general source of feedback. Some instructors write a note or put on an audio cassette and give a detailed rationale for the assigned grade. Students are then better able to make corrections in their future behavior.

Try not to overemphasize the importance of your grades to students. Regardless of the way you decide to assign grades to students, it is not a good idea to remind them constantly that their performance counts towards a grade. Students know they will be graded, and a good course syllabus will tell them what criteria will be used, and how. Continuing reminders throughout a term could have at least one undesirable effect:

They might undermine student's developing or expressing an intrinsic interest in the course material. Edward Deci and Chris Kleinke argue that people will often perform because of an intrinsic interest in a task. *When they perceive, however, that their behavior is guided by extrinsic rewards, they typically lose interest in the task.* Kleinke suggests that instructors are much better off if they praise students for good work and design learning tasks where students can feel successful. This will help students build mastery and competence over activities in class. Such suggestions also ensure that the development of intrinsic interest in course content will not be impeded.

Summary

Evaluating students and assigning grades is not an easy task. Most instructors spend a considerable amount of time developing and using evaluation procedures. Thinking about the evaluation process in terms of gathering relevant information on students, giving students feedback on their progress, and assigning grades suggests several ways to enhance the process.

Exams account for an average of 54 percent of the weight in assigning grades. They are an important part of the evaluation of students. A problem is that they cannot give us all the information we might want or that students could profitably use. Furthermore, flaws in their design often make them less than accurate and valid estimates of a student's knowledge. Exams can be improved by defining what learning outcomes one wishes to measure and then constructing test items that assess them. Communicating such outcomes to students before exams and developing a test blueprint ensure that learning outcomes are appropriately assessed. In addition, it is helpful to use a variety of information sources when assessing students. Anecdotal records, rating scales of classroom activity, checklists of appropriate student behaviors, and self-evaluations can help teachers form accurate judgments of students. Finally, using alternative testing procedures such as experiential tests and library searches increases student interest and provides an instructor with additional information on student capabilities.

Quiz and exam performance grades are only one way to provide feedback to students. A problem with them is that they are not always specific indicators of problem areas and they have little to say about performance in class discussions, group projects, and similar activities. Feedback from exams often needs to be supplemented with information about other aspects of a student's class performance. Such feedback should be specific, oriented toward behaviors the student can correct, related to criteria and standards for the course, and given often and on a timely basis.

Although there are positive and negative features of grading, the practice is likely to remain in higher education for the immediate future.

Current practices can be improved. One suggestion is to ensure that grading procedures are objective, reliable, based on mastery of content, and flexible in their usage. Another is to use grade curving procedures cautiously. In particular, normal curve grading practices are not recommended. Because a student's score on a test reflects his or her knowledge, academic ability, and the difficulty of the exam, such factors must also be taken into account when assigning grades. A problem is that the usual methods of averaging test scores may inadvertently lead to inaccurate evaluations of certain students. A third suggestion is to avoid attribution, halo, leniency, and logical errors when assessing students. Finally, it is important to consider other possibilities for assigning grades. Contract grading, peer grading, student-assigned grades, and the use of grades plus descriptive feedback provide several alternatives to current practices. Whatever system is used, it may help not to overemphasize the grading system and its importance to students. Constantly reminding students about grades may lower their ability to develop an intrinsic interest in the course content.

References

Anderson, R.C. How to construct achievement tests to assess comprehension. *Review of Educational Research*, 1972, *42*, 145-70.

Bloom, B.S. *Taxonomy of Educational Objectives*. New York: David McKay Company, 1956.

Carter, K.R. Student criteria grading: An attempt to reduce some common grading problems. *Teaching of Psychology*, 1977, *4*, 59-62.

Costin, F.; Dulany, D.E.; Greenough, W.T.; and Liberman, D. *Introduction to Psychology*, fall ed. Champaign, Ill.: Stipes Publishing Company, 1973.

Dambrot, F. Test item order and academic ability, or should you shuffle the test item deck? *Teaching of Psychology*, 1980, *7*, 94-95.

Deci, E. Intrinsic motivation, extrinsic reinforcement and inequity. *Journal of Personality and Social Psychology*, 1972, *22*, 113-20.

Eison J. Grades: What do they tell? *Teaching-Learning Issues*, 1980, *10* (43), 3-26.

Gerow, J.R. Performance on achievement tests as a function of the order of item difficulty. *Teaching of Psychology*, 1980, 7, 93-94.

Kleinke, C.L. *Self-perception: The Psychology of Personal Awareness*. San Francisco: W.H. Freeman and Company, 1978.

Leeper, R. "For Whom the Grades Toll," unpublished paper, 1971.

Lunneborg, P. College grades: What do professors intend to communicate to whom? *AAUP Bulletin*, 1978, *64*, 33-35.

Polezynski, J., and Shirland, L. Expectancy theory and contract grading combined as an effective motivational force for college students. *Journal of Educational Research*, 1977, *70*, 238-41.

Robertson, D., and Steele, M. To grade is to degrade: The case against the grading system. *The Halls of Yearning*. San Francisco: Canfield Colopian Books, 1971.

Zimmerman, J. What motivates students. *Journal of Higher Education*, 1956, *27*, 449-53.

Chapter 8
Assessing Your Teaching
for Instructional Improvement

Sometimes I think that I'm the only judge of how good my teaching really is. I'm not sure I can trust students or my colleagues to help me.

I would like to take a closer look at my teaching but I'm not sure how to go about it.

The college has a form they suggest, but, to be quite honest, I think the information it gives is too general.

I really wonder if I know enough about teaching to use well the information I could get.

For any assessment procedure to be really helpful, it would have to include information from people other than students.

I already assess my teaching informally and don't feel I need more information.

I can use all the help I can get to make my teaching better. I would welcome comments from students.

Who listens to student comments on how much they like a course, anyway?

I appreciate the comments my students make and try to take them into account when teaching.

The only people who care about evaluations around here are the administrators.

As you can see, a variety of opinions, biases, and feelings exist about the value of instructor evaluations and how to do them. The comments presented are those we hear most frequently. We hear them from people new to teaching as well as from more experienced instructors. In our experience, people are seldom totally negative about course evaluations, but they are often cautious about them. This is particularly true concerning procedures designed to provide data to be used in making decisions about faculty reappointments, promotions, tenure, or salaries. Michael Scriven and other authors label such procedures *summative evaluations*. They are generally used to make administrative decisions. Most teachers are introduced to formal systems for assessing teaching through their college or department's attempts at developing and implementing a summative system. Given the high degree of interest in faculty evaluation over the past several years, you are probably already familiar with such procedures.

What tends to get lost in discussions of teacher assessment is that it can lead to improved instruction. People lose sight of this because most of their experiences are with summative procedures, which by themselves seldom lead to instructional development. However, assessment procedures do exist that are designed to help you develop and enhance your teaching. These methods are called *formative evaluations* and are designed for the purpose of improving rather than judging teaching. In this chapter, we present several ideas for how to gather information to improve your instruction. They may be used simply to help you enhance your daily work, or, as has been the case in several institutions with which we are familiar, they may stimulate ideas on how to combine summative and formative procedures to make teaching evaluation more meaningful.

Formative Evaluation

Guidelines

If you are like most instructors, you already collect information on your teaching. Your department or college may have a required student or peer assessment procedure. Or perhaps you simply watch and listen to your students for their reactions to your teaching. In the latter case, you might do this informally, or ask for comments or ratings of your teaching. It is impossible to spend time with a group of students without getting at least a general idea about how you are doing. We would like you to assess your current procedures for gathering information on your instruction against several guidelines. Assessing what you already do should help you discover the advantages and disadvantages of your current practices. After you have done that, we hope you will consider some of the techniques we suggest later in this chapter that are compatible with our guidelines. If they allow you to overcome one or more of the disadvantages with your current assessment procedures, we hope you will consider using them. A variety of procedures is suggested to enable you to custom design an evaluation process for your course.

To begin to assess your current evaluation practices, read the guidelines below and answer the questions that follow them.

- *Evaluation must be continuous.* In order to improve, you need a clear record of both where you have been and how you are progressing. Change in teaching and other areas of our lives is often slow and painstaking. To justify the time and effort involved in modifying your behavior, continual progress checks are necessary. Through them, you can monitor how well you are doing and, if necessary, promptly modify the new things you are trying. Provisions for monitoring your progress must be built into any plans for changing your instruction.

- *Evaluation must be broadly based.* When assessing your teaching, information about various aspects of what you do is necessary. You need to assess such things as your lectures, your classroom discussions, your student evaluation tools, your meeting of student needs, and the usefulness of your classroom materials and activities. It is also wise to use a variety of input, including formal and informal feedback from students, general and specific perceptions of colleagues within and outside the classroom, and self-perceptions, feelings, and anecdotal records.

- *Evaluation must be descriptive and diagnostic.* To be useful, your evaluation activities must not label your teaching behaviors as good or bad. Rather, specific classroom behaviors and their effects should be described. Any classroom behavior has advantages and disadvantages for the instructor and the students. Such effects must be described in detail, using specific classroom incidents and behaviors as examples. Simply asking for feedback in terms of how "good" or "poor" things were is less helpful. For students to tell you your lectures were "poor" is not as helpful as their telling you that you mumbled, used too much technical language, and never asked questions.

- *Evaluation must reflect your personal goals.* As we noted in an earlier chapter, there is no standard of excellence for teaching. However, a tendency exists for people to want to compare "how they're doing" with their colleagues' performances. We do not believe that such comparisons are likely to help with your task of improving your teaching. Your classroom behaviors and activities must be judged against the personal goals and objectives that you set. You need to know how effective your teaching behaviors are given your personal style, your discipline, and the environment in which you teach. Comparing yourself to your colleagues is unlikely to help you accomplish the latter task.

Having read the guidelines listed above, respond to the following questions:

1. List the method(s) you currently use to assess your instruction.

2. Review each of the guidelines for formative evaluation. How is (are) your method(s) compatible or not compatible with each guideline? Based on this analysis, what do you see as the relative advantages and disadvantages of what you currently do?

3. Think about the disadvantage of your current procedures. What are three to five things you think you need to do to overcome the disadvantages of your current assessment methods?

4. As you read the remainder of this chapter, look for suggestions that will allow you to improve what you already do. As you discover suggestions, list them. We will ask you to return to them later.

Student Input

Our students are an extremely valuable source of information on our teaching. Most of us receive continuous feedback from our students unless we make a conscious effort to avoid it. The looks on their faces, the quality of a discussion, their questions, attendance in class, and test performance are all part of the network of informal feedback we receive. To use student information to improve our teaching, we must begin to gather it more systematically and formally. We now listed several ways that you might obtain student input.

Paper-and-pencil techniques: Open-ended question. Occasionally during your course, ask students to provide you with feedback on the aspect of the course that you wish to assess. *Open-ended sentence stems* can provide a great deal of information. For example:

The best part of this course for me is _____ .

The worst part of this course for me is _____ .

For me, the content of this course is _____ .

The thing I like best about you as an
instructor is_____ .

The thing I like least about you as an
instructor is_____ .

I would like you to do more_____ .

I would like you to do less _____ .

In this class I feel best when _____ .

If I could change one thing in this class
it would be _____ .

Open-ended sentence stems can also solicit information concerning specific goals. For example, if one of your goals is to help students become more independent, the following kinds of openers might be helpful:

When I am assigned to develop an independent project, I feel
_____ .

I feel most capable of working independently when _____
_____ .

You could help me become more independent by_____
_____ .

Following a unit in a course, statements like the following can be completed by students:

The most significant aspects of this unit for me were_____
_____ .

The least meaningful aspects of this unit for me were _____
_____ .

If I were teaching this unit, I would _____
_____ .

A variation on open-ended sentence stems is to ask students to respond to several open-ended questions. In this case the questions are more general, and care must be taken to ensure that both advantages and disadvantages are solicited. It also helps if students are told to respond by listing specific behaviors or incidents that occurred during the class session. One procedure to obtain this information is described in Table 8.1. Note that in addition to obtaining information about the instructor's performance, it also asks participants to respond with things the instructor could have done to make the presentation better.

Table 8.1. Open-ended Question Technique

On the scale below, place an X through your overall rating of the presentation. *Do not use a rating of 5.*

1. List two specific reasons (behaviors you observed) that you gave the presentation the rating you did.

2. List two specific things the presenter could have done to make it the best presentation you ever saw (a rating of 9).

3. Was there anything you as a participant could have done to make the presentation better? Yes ____ No ____. If yes, please list one or two things you could have done.

Paper-and-pencil techniques: Goal assessment. Students are obviously a good source of information about how well you accomplished your goals. We now describe a procedure for assessing the attainment of your goals. To use it, you need to have articulated several of your major goals and how your classroom methods are related to them. We find giving feedback on five to eight major goals and accompanying methods is a reasonable task for students. If you have more than eight major goals, consider assessing some one term and others during a second term or offering of the course.

My specific content goals were for you: (a) to know the principal author and five major aspects of each of the six theories in the book; and (b) to use concepts from the outside readings in your class discussions.

1. Were these goals made clear to you at the beginning of the course? Yes____ No____

   a. If *No*, which ones were not clear?

   b. Besides the instructor's not explaining these goals to you, what other factors might have led you not to understand what each of the content goals was?

2. Rank how hard it was for you to achieve each goal. Use the following scale: 1 = very easy; 2 = somewhat difficult; 3 = very difficult; 4 = could not achieve goal.

   Goal a _____ Goal b _____

3. If any of the goals were rated 3 or 4, indicate what factors were responsible for their being so difficult.

4. Indicate which one of the goals was the most important and which the least important to your education.

   Most important goal was _____.
   Least important goal was _____.

5. Should students be allowed to formulate goals for a course?
   Yes____ No____. If *No*, please give one reason for your answer.

6. Were the instructor's content goals adequate for a course of this type? Yes____ No____. If *No*, please give one reason for your answer.

7. What content goals would you have set if you were teaching this course? Please be as specific as possible.

8. Did these content goals seem better than, worse than, or about the same as the goals in your other classes? Please answer only for those goals that you feel overlap with goals in your other courses. If these goals seem worse than others, please specify the reason for your response.

When you assess the relationship between goals and methods, there are some important points to note.

1. With regard to each goal, rank the importance of the six methods listed that would allow you to achieve that goal. 1 = least important; 6 = most important. If you feel a method was not applicable, please so indicate by putting *NA* in the space provided.

	Goal a	Goal b
Lectures	_____	_____
In-class discussion	_____	_____
Textbook	_____	_____
Study guides	_____	_____
Outside readings	_____	_____
Exams	_____	_____

2. In the space provided, indicate whether these methods were generally adequate for allowing you to achieve the content goals. If *No*, give one reason you think they were inadequate and specify which goal the reason applies to:

	Adequate	Inadequate
Lectures	_____	_____
In-class discussions	_____	_____
Textbook	_____	_____
Study guides	_____	_____

Outside readings	_____	_____
Exams	_____	_____

3. What additional methods might have been used?

4. To what extent did the study guides help you organize and select the important material? Check an answer and give one reason you selected that response.

   a. Very little

   b. Some

   c. Very much

5. List below at least three goals and three methods that an instructor must use in order for you to learn adequately. Also indicate: (a) which factors were present in the current class, and (b) how well the factors were employed.

6. List three ways that you think the goals and methods of this course were interrelated.

7. List three ways that you think the goals and methods of this course were *not* interrelated.

Paper-and-pencil techniques: Student rating scales. You probably are already familiar with this technique. It is a widely used source of information on teaching in higher education today. Student rating scales are used best when they solicit a broad range of information on your teaching. One form that we have used and feel comfortable recommending is presented in Table 8.2. You might use all the items we suggest or pick those you want information on most. In addition to students' answering the questions, we suggest you ask them to do one other task. On a separate sheet of paper, have them pick the three items on which they gave you the lowest and highest ratings. Ask your students to list one or two specific behaviors or course incidents that made them give you the rating they did. Asking such questions will help overcome the tendency for rating scales to yield somewhat general information. Knowing that you need this information helps keep students objective in their assessments.

Paper-and-pencil techniques: Instructor and student skills. In Chapter 10 we identify several instructor and student skills that are used in various classroom procedures. If you have designed your course with such skills in mind, the extent to which students use the student skills and see the instructor skills in your behavior is helpful information. To use this procedure, students first rank order the importance of each of sixteen instructor and student skills for their learning in your class. They then rate the frequency with which they used each skill or saw it used by the instructor. Finally, they list one way each student and instructor skill helped them to

Table 8.2. Student Rating Form

This questionnaire is part of a special plan your instructor is following in an effort to improve his (her) teaching. This process has been initiated by your instructor; the results are used only as a guide to self-improvement.

The time and care you take in completing this form, and the sincerity with which you answer the questions, will benefit you and other students through improvement in your learning experiences.

In making ratings, use the other courses you have taken at UC with other instructors as a basis for comparison. Respond to each question on the attached IBM answer sheet by using the rating scale listed below. Please blacken the space that corresponds to your response for each item.

A. "Not at all" or "never" (low rating)
B. "Slightly" or "seldom"
C. "Moderately" or "usually" (average rating)
D. "Fairly well" or "often"
E. "Extremely well" or "almost always" (high rating)

IF ANY ITEM IS NOT APPLICABLE OR IS NOT IMPORTANT TO YOU, PLEASE LEAVE IT BLANK.

A. Rate the following teaching-learning methods in terms of how well you like them with regard to all the courses you have taken at U.C.

1. lecture method
2. discussion groups or seminars
3. lecture-discussion group combinations
4. small group activities
5. independent study

B. Rate the following for the course you are currently taking.

6. this course relates to my personal needs
7. this course ties in with my overall program of study
8. the day-to-day activities are consistent with the overall purpose of this course

C. Rate your satisfaction with the following in this class.

9. the content presented
10. the textbook(s) used
11. the quality of outside readings/handouts assigned
12. the quantity of outside readings/handouts assigned
13. the grading system used
14. your overall performance
15. the time of day the course is offered
16. the day(s) of the week the class meets
17. the classroom facilities - arrangements of seats, lighting, sound equipment, fresh air, etc.

D. Rate the following requirements of the course.

18. course requirements help me to achieve the course objectives
19. assignments (homework, papers, etc.) are at a reasonable level of difficulty
20. examinations are at a reasonable level of difficulty
21. the quality of work assigned in this course is reasonable

E. Rate your instructor's performance in this class.

22. I receive feedback in a reasonable amount of time
23. the instructor's evaluation of my work includes specific comments on its strengths and weaknesses

---

Table 8.2. *(Continued)*

---

24. the instructor uses a variety of learning methods, materials, and activities in the class
25. the instructor's way of presenting class materials is exciting, stimulating, and absorbing
26. the instructor uses humor, analogies, and examples in effective ways
27. the instructor shows personal involvement in the subject matter through examples from his own experiences
28. the instructor shows enthusiasm for this field of study through his teaching
29. the instructor sets standards which provide a clearly understood basis for grades in the course
30. the instructor spells out clearly the criteria for evaluation before the assignments are due
31. the criteria, standards, and grading system of the instructor tends to keep competition among students in the class within reasonable limits
32. the instructor informs me exactly when assignments are due and when tests will be given

F. Rate your instructor on the following general points.

33. discusses points of view other than his (her) own
34. contrasts implications of various theories
35. communicates clearly
36. evidences careful preparation for class
37. encourages class discussion
38. invites students to share their knowledge and experiences
39. shows a genuine interest in students
40. shows friendliness toward students
41. appears dynamic and energetic
42. encourages students to pursue further study in the field
43. demonstrates knowledge of subject matter
44. creates a friendly and open atmosphere in the class
45. organizes the course well
46. presents ideas which provoke careful thought and discussion
47. adapts course presentations and requirements to my level
48. challenges me to do my best
49. encourages students to learn from each other
50. helps me to build my interests in the field
51. presents issues as well as concepts and information
52. shows patience
53. receives questions and challenges openly
54. is available for individual help
55. is straightforward in working with students

G. Rate yourself in this class on the following general points.

56. Participating in class
57. Preparing for class
58. Sharing my knowledge & experience
59. Asking questions

H. Please list any other comments about the course or the instructor below:

---

learn or, if it impeded their learning, how it did this. Together, such information tells you how important each skill was to the students, how frequently they used it or saw it used by you, and some of the advantages and disadvantages of the skill. You might use this information to improve their use of a skill, to enhance how you use a skill, or to make sure that an important skill is not used infrequently.

To employ this procedure, you must determine which student and instructor skills you are interested in assessing. This can be determined by completing the activities in Chapter 10. You may have some interest in obtaining information on certain skills regardless of the analysis in Chapter 10. In either case, you are not obliged to use all the skills we have identified in your assessment. For example, Table 8.3 uses all the skills we identify in Chapter 10. This may not always be necessary for your purposes. Five or six of each type may be all that you need. Furthermore, we sometimes find that people are interested in skills that we have not covered in our analysis. If this meets your needs better, then all that is necessary is for you to label and define the skills you are most interested in. Your list is then given to students to evaluate.

Student lecture notes. People do a number of interesting things when they obtain information. They interpret it in terms of their personal attitudes, biases, and values. Furthermore, their attention drifts when listening to someone talk. They only get part of what is said and often use such bits and pieces to try to reconstruct the entire message. Finally, if they do not like what is said, they may even stop monitoring the message. Taken together, these tendencies often produce distortions in what people hear—and these distortions operate in the classroom. Thus, you might check the accuracy and completeness of your content presentations by asking a few student volunteers to let you see their class lecture notes. Or you might collect all of them to spot check what students wrote. In either case, a quick perusal will tell you whether students succeeded in highlighting the points you intended.

Student evaluation committee. You might consider requesting that a small group of students (three to five) form an evaluation committee for a course. You might want to substitute service on the committee for one or more class assignments. The committee should meet regularly outside of class time to discuss specifics of the course. It might consider clarity of objectives, progress toward objectives, work load, teaching style, clarity and appropriateness of assignments, student interest and attitude, and other dimensions you consider important. The rest of the class is encouraged to provide input to committee members. The committee might also solicit student input through formal and informal means. Although it is probably useful to have the committee meet alone sometimes to discuss

---

Table 8.3. Instructor and Student Skill Assessment

Listed below are instructor and student skills your instructor felt were important to this course. Please rank order from 1 to 16 the instructor and then the student skills according to those you thought were most and least important to your learning in this course. A ranking of 1 indicates *high importance* and a ranking of 16 *low importance*. Rank order the other skills between these two extremes.

Having made your ranking, use the following rating scale to indicate how frequently you used each skill or saw it used by the instructor.

1	2	3	4	5	6	7
Never			Sometimes			Always

For each skill, list one way that you think it helped you to learn in the course. If you think it did not help, list one way you saw it impeding your ability to learn.

Instructor Skills
Rank   Frequency

_____   _____   *Actor/Director.* Ability to direct or engage in role playing.

_____   _____   *Assigner.* Ability to assign relevant course materials to students.

_____   _____   *Coordinator.* Ability to coordinate multiple student projects and activities.

_____   _____   *Consultant.* Ability to act as a resource person for students who request additional information, resource material, or assignments. Must be able to fit interventions to the needs of the client (student).

_____   _____   *Content expert.* Knowledge and understanding of the essential concepts and facts of the course.

_____   _____   *Content transmitter.* Ability to transmit content to students orally or in writing.

_____   _____   *Evaluator.* Ability to provide timely feedback on an ongoing basis to students regarding specific strengths and weaknesses.

_____   _____   *Facilitator.* Ability to get students to maximize their potential and to demonstrate their skills and knowledge. Emphasis is on trying to get students to initiate such things rather than the instructor's telling them when and and how to do it.

_____   _____   *Grader.* Ability to assign a student to a general performance category.

_____   _____   *Goal setter.* Ability to set goals and specify procedures for obtaining them.

_____   _____   *Listener.* Ability to listen to and reflect upon student inputs regarding course issues.

_____   _____   *Materials designer.* Ability to design appropriate materials for students to use in the course.

<table>
<tr><td>____</td><td>____</td><td>*Manager.* Ability to view classroom as an organization where the instructor manages a variety of classroom inputs (teaching assistants, outside speakers, small student groups, multiple projects).</td></tr>
<tr><td>____</td><td>____</td><td>*Negotiator.* Ability to negotiate with students about standards to be achieved and assignments to be completed. This skill is most often used in contract teaching.</td></tr>
<tr><td>____</td><td>____</td><td>*Process observer.* Ability to watch the process of what is occurring in the classroom. Should be aware of issues related to communication, emerging norms, and leadership within the classroom.</td></tr>
<tr><td>____</td><td>____</td><td>*Speaker.* Ability to transmit orally content and instructions to others in ways that are clear and organized.</td></tr>
</table>

For each skill, list one way it helped your ability to learn in this course. If you think it did not help, list one way you saw it impeding your ability to learn. Do this by giving the name of each skill and your comments on the back of this sheet of paper.

Student Skills
Rank   *Frequency*

<table>
<tr><td>____</td><td>____</td><td>*Actor.* The ability to engage in role playing activity.</td></tr>
<tr><td>____</td><td>____</td><td>*Collaborator.* The ability to work with others on projects.</td></tr>
<tr><td>____</td><td>____</td><td>*Consultant.* The ability to act as a resource person for other students who may need additional information, resource material, or assignments. Must be able to fit the interventions to the needs of the client (other students).</td></tr>
<tr><td>____</td><td>____</td><td>*Content expert.* The ability to comprehend and understand the essential concepts and facts of the course.</td></tr>
<tr><td>____</td><td>____</td><td>*Content transmitter.* The ability to transmit essential content to other students.</td></tr>
<tr><td>____</td><td>____</td><td>*Explorer.* The ability to take initiative and search for the resources that are needed to learn.</td></tr>
<tr><td>____</td><td>____</td><td>*Exam taker.* The ability to transmit essential knowledge and understanding of the course content to the instructor.</td></tr>
<tr><td>____</td><td>____</td><td>*Independent learner.* The ability of the student to think through issues for himself, to work at his own pace, and to be able to demonstrate evidence of independent thinking.</td></tr>
<tr><td>____</td><td>____</td><td>*Listener.* The ability to listen to and reflect upon instructor inputs regarding course content. Through note taking or memory, information is stored for future reference.</td></tr>
<tr><td>____</td><td>____</td><td>*Negotiator.* The ability to negotiate with the instructor about standards to be achieved and assignments to be completed. This skill is most often used in contract teaching.</td></tr>
</table>

Table 8.3. *(Continued)*

——	——	*Process observer.* The ability to watch the process of what is occurring in the classroom. Should be aware of issues related to communication, emerging norms, and leadership within the classroom.
——	——	*Problem solver.* The ability to manage and complete a major project or problem within the context of the course. This can be done individually or with students working together.
——	——	*Reader.* The ability to read and understand textbook and other course reading materials.
——	——	*Researcher.* The ability to design and complete a laboratory type problem or major library research problem.
——	——	*Writer.* The ability to communicate in writing when the course demands such skills. This is in addition to taking exams.
——	——	*Speaker.* The ability to transmit orally content and instructions to others in ways that are clear and organized.

For each skill, list one way it helped your ability to learn in this course. If you think it did not help, list one way you saw it impeding your ability to learn. Do this by giving the name of each skill and your comments on the back of this sheet of paper.

---

the course, the committee should also meet with you periodically to present its findings and discuss the directions the course might take. It might also provide you with written summaries of its findings or written responses to questions you want to consider.

Adapting student input to your teaching. You have just read several ways to assess student reactions to your teaching. Each will provide you with information that should suggest ways to enhance your instruction. Perhaps you can see immediately how one or more of these methods might be helpful to you. On the other hand, it is possible that you are still not sure what to do with them. To assist you in thinking about ways to use student input, we suggest that you respond to the following questions:

1. Review your responses to the questions on page 196. There you listed several disadvantages of your current assessment procedures and several things you need to do to overcome those disadvantages. What procedures discussed in this section will help you improve what you currently do? Describe how they will assist you.

2. Assume that you want to get as many different kinds of student input about your teaching as you can. Answer the following questions.

- What are five open-ended sentence stems you could use?

- What are two open-ended questions you might ask?

- What are ten items you might give to students in a rating-scale format?

- What are five instructor and student skills you might want to assess in one of your courses?

- What would be a good day to collect student lecture notes? What are three things you would look for in the notes?

- What would be a good class session to have a student evaluation committee observe? What are four things you would want them to observe?

Using Peer Input

Your colleagues are another source of information about your teaching. Unlike your students, they present the advantage of also having to struggle with the demands of teaching. This experience may sensitize them to your concerns in ways that students are not able to identify. If they are from your discipline, they may assist you with questions and problems you face about what content to present. In this respect, they can go beyond helping you identify problems with your classroom methods. Because they are experts in teaching, or at least relatively experienced in it, they can assist you with suggestions for how to overcome any problems you may be facing. Unfortunately, your colleagues' relative expertise is a two-sided coin. The other side of the coin is that having them observe might threaten you. You might not be able to keep things from them that you could from your students. In spite of this problem, we feel that the advantages of using peers for formative evaluation overshadow any potential disadvantages. We describe several procedures in the following paragraphs that can make the use of your colleagues a positive experience.

Basic requirements. We do not suggest that you simply ask a colleague into your class to sit and passively observe. This method is often used, but we do not believe it is the best use of a colleague's time and expertise. There are at least four things you should do to help a colleague observe your teaching: (1) *Have a meeting before the class session.* Observers, and your colleagues are no exception, are likely to observe and judge what they see in terms of their personal values, attitudes, and biases. If they like to lecture, they may not see the value in or observe important aspects of your group discussion procedures. You need to discuss with them beforehand how you teach and why you teach a certain way. (2) *Give your observer specific things to watch for in class.* Observations work best if the observer has specific things to watch. You might tell your colleague what to look for, or you might design an observation scheme together. Examples of things colleagues might observe and how they can do so are presented in Table 8.4. (3) *Have a debriefing session immediately after the class session.* It is important to meet while the data are fresh in both your minds. You might want to give your colleague time to organize what was observed, however. Ask that positive as well as negative observations be included in the feedback. Then meet in a relaxed atmosphere (over lunch, at your home—anywhere but the office) to discuss what was observed. Try to summarize and paraphrase what is said, and avoid defending why you did certain things. The purpose is for you to get information that might help you. (4) *Jointly explore ways to improve.* You might want to make a list of things you need to improve. Discuss them with your colleague, and solicit suggestions and advice. You might ask your colleague to meet with you periodically to discuss any progress you are making and even to revisit your class at a later time. Research by Lawrence Aleamoni, Robert Menges, John Centra, Michael Sweeney, and Tony Grasha indicates that having someone with whom to discuss your teaching concerns and review feedback is an important aspect of improving what you do.

Forming a colleague support and observation team. There is no reason to work with just a single colleague. In fact, you might consider forming teams of two, three, or four people who observe and consult with each other on their teaching. In this way you are less likely to feel as if you are the only one with a teaching concern. You might discover that other people have similar problems. And you might discover that your ability to observe your own teaching and to think of ways to improve it is enhanced by helping others.

Forming a team offers you a chance to get a small group together that will support one anothers' attempts at enhancing teaching. The support aspect is especially important. When people experiment with alternative methods, they are likely to experience not only the loneliness of risk taking, but also some defeat. If a faculty member, for example, abandons a finely honed lecture style because it is inappropriate to a goal of increasing students' interactions and introduces discussion and interaction, student evaluations are likely to drop temporarily. Only after discussion-leader skills are developed and students become accustomed to the new style are the evaluations likely to rise. It would be much easier to maintain the old, proven style even though it may not satisfy all classroom goals for learners. This instructor needs the support group to provide a place to talk with others about issues in teaching and to get support for her efforts and risk taking. The support team becomes a safe place where it is acceptable to explore successes and failures, frustrations and joys, similarities and differ-

Table 8.4. Suggestions for Things to Be Observed During Peer Evaluation

A. *Types of Questions Teacher Asks*

Record the number of questions that occur in each of the following categories during a class session.

- *Giving information:* Such questions are often used to gain control or to get the attention of students. *Example:* Why are people in the back of the room talking to each other again?

- *Recall or knowledge:* Students are asked to repeat information asked for by the instructor. *Example:* Based on the presentation yesterday, how many elements do we now think exist in nature?

- *Basic comprehension:* Students are asked to use an idea but without seeing its fullest implications. *Example:* Based on the ideas in the textbook, what would you tell a friend who asked you to define a hidden agenda?

- *Application or analysis:* The student is asked to put an idea into practice or to identify or examine subideas so the relationship is clear. *Example:* How would you use Freud's ideas about ego-superego conflict to explain why some people are very rigid in their religious beliefs?

- *Synthesis:* The question is directed toward getting students to form an original idea from the pieces of information they have. *Example:* How would you use the information we just covered to redesign Bohr's model of the atom?

- *Evaluation:* The student is asked to make value judgments based on criteria. *Example:* Given the criteria for how to give feedback effectively, how well did John use them in the role play we witnessed?

An analysis of the number of questions asked in each category can help the instructor determine how deeply students are asked to think in class.

B. *Who Is Doing the Talking During a Conversation or Discussion Period?*

Set up a seating diagram of the class. Place a mark next to the name of the student who makes a comment, asks a question, or otherwise contributes. Each remark is recorded. Do the same for the teacher. *Example:*

		卌 卌 卌 卌		
		Teacher		
卌	II	I	卌 I	卌 卌 III
Sam	Sally	Dave	Tom	Ellen

C. *Who Responds to Whom?*

During a discussion, monitor how much people respond to one another that is, note the extent to which dialogue occurs between the teacher and individual students. The goal is to try to identify those people who typically receive comments and those who both receive and respond. *Example:*

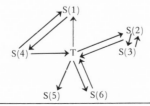

Table 8.4. *(Continued)*

D. *Potpourri*

The following ideas represent additional things to observe.

- Does the instructor have annoying mannerisms or other habits? They can be counted in blocks of five minutes. This will give the instructor a chance to notice any increases or decreases in such things.

- How long does it take for discussion groups to get started? How much time do they spend on the topics assigned?

- Are students given interesting and challenging topics to discuss? What occurred to suggest the topics were interesting and challenging? What occurred to suggest that they were not?

- Are the content presentations organized? Is this organization apparent to the student? How does the instructor let the student know about the organization for the session?

- Are students talking about class content while they are entering or leaving class?

- Do students take initiative in asking questions and trying to get issues discussed? What specific examples of behaviors suggest that this occurs?

- Are any demonstrations and role plays well integrated into the session, do they seem out of place? Is there an adequate discussion of such things?

- Does the instructor answer his or her own questions? If so, how often does this occur?

- Are new terms defined for the students? Which terms were defined and which ones were not defined?

- What are some of the things students are doing while the instructor is presenting or answering questions? Develop a list of them.

- Does the instructor walk around during class, or stay in one place? What effect does this have on the class?

- Does the instructor read his or her lectures or briefly refer to notes while talking? Or does the instructor simply talk without notes? What effect does this have on the class?

- Do students snicker or otherwise make fun of what the instructor says or does? What do they say or do? How often does this occur?

- What types of visual aids are used? Are they appropriate for the level of the course and the students in the classroom?

- Are visual aids well designed, or are they cluttered and hard to read?

- Does the instructor appear to talk down to students? List specific incidents of interactions where this occurred.

- Are students taking notes? Do their notes correspond to what is being discussed or presented in class?

---

ences. You can set goals and devise ways of providing one another with descriptive feedback on teaching.

Michael Sweeney and Tony Grasha have developed one procedure for using a colleague support team. Faculty members are assigned to working groups of three members. Each team works closely together for at least one academic term. Its goal is to help assess and develop members' instruction. The team follows a structured format that contains some of the same elements that were used in our description of having a single colleague visit your class.

Phase 1: Goal setting. The members attend a meeting where each team member is asked to specify the instructional goals he or she has for the class to be observed. Participants indicate only two to three of their major goals to avoid overloading the other team members. In addition, they are requested to show how such goals fit into two to three overall goals they have for the course. Each participant does this in writing, and for many, this is the first time they explicitly conceptualize their instructional goals.

Phase 2: First meeting of teams. Each team member shares his or her goal statements with the others. They are asked to spend about thirty minutes sharing and helping one another clarify their goals. This helps them note what similarities and differences exist among them and assists in building a collaborative relationship. They then establish the time and dates for the observations of each member's class.

Team members then concentrate on listing types of behaviors on which people want to receive feedback. These might include organization of the presentation, questioning procedures, the handling of a demonstration or lab experiment, and the extent to which students learned the information that was presented. It is important that people ask for feedback in particular areas that concern them. Team members are strongly encouraged to respect one another's desires and concentrate on only those areas for observation.

Having discussed what activities and behaviors will be observed, the team discusses what methods will be used. A variety of observational techniques appropriate to each individual's request for feedback is selected. These include standard classroom interactions, video- and audiotape, student input, and even custom-designed methods that team members are amazingly clever about devising. It is the responsibility of the two members making the observations to bring whatever they will need to that class session. Some of the suggestions in Table 8.4 are also helpful here.

Phase 3: Classroom observation. The instructor in charge of the class explains to the students that visitors will be present to help assess the class. If appropriate, students are informed that they may be asked to fill out some forms or to answer questions that the other team members may ask after class. They are requested to behave as they usually do in class and to try to ignore the presence of the visitors. The observers gather their data and schedule a meeting time afterward to review what they observed and discuss the feedback they will give to the teacher.

Phase 4: Team meets to discuss classroom visit. This occurs within a week of each classroom visit. The observers are asked to reconstruct the details of the session observed to establish a common ground for discussion. The positive aspects of the session are then pointed out, followed by any critical comments. Team members are encouraged to maintain a balance between positive and critical comments. All conversation is kept within the framework established earlier of what was observed. The person observed responds to the feedback and may ask additional questions, seek clarification of a point, or add other comments of what happened from his or her perspective. After discussing the feedback, the individual observed is asked to pick one to three things the feedback showed as problems and work on them before the next observation.

Phase 5: Next steps. Following the feedback, the team members critique how they worked together. The discussion includes how successful they felt, how helpful to the teacher they were, and whether any interpersonal or other barriers exist to their working together. Once the initial set of observations and feedback is carried out for each team member, members repeat the cycle beginning with Phase 1 for a second set of observations.

Adapting peer input to your teaching. Several procedures for using peer input about your teaching have been described. To consider whether or not they might help you enhance your teaching, answer the following questions. The questions are designed to sensitize you to possibilities for integrating peer inputs into your formative evaluations. They are also designed to help you assess how comfortable you might be with a colleague visiting your class.

1. Review your responses to the questions on page 196. There you listed several disadvantages of your current assessment procedures and several things you need to do to overcome those disadvantages. What procedures involving peer input will help you improve what you currently do? List them and briefly describe how you think they will assist you.

2. Have you ever asked a colleague to visit one of your classes? If not, why not?

3. For each of the reasons you identified in question 2, rate how likely you think you are to overcome it. Use a 5-point rating scale in which a 1 = unlikely to overcome the factor and a 5 = very likely to overcome the factor. Now that you have done this, does it look as if you can go beyond most of the reasons you have given in the past for not inviting a colleague?

4. Based on your responses, would you be more comfortable having a

colleague observe your class and discuss it with you or forming a team? What people are most likely to be helpful to you as observers and team members?

Using Self-Assessment

You alone are responsible for your growth as a teacher. Although you can collect data about yourself from your students and colleagues, your most important data source is your personal perceptions. Paying attention to your experiences and feelings and monitoring your progress toward the ideals you set for yourself is extremely important.

Richard Curwin, Barbara Fuhrmann, Melvin Weissburg, and Peter Seldin have shown that self-evaluation can be a valid and effective assessment tool. It is particularly helpful in altering behaviors toward specific goals, especially when the self-evaluation leads to a positive attitude towards growth. People who learn to understand and use self-evaluation techniques are likely to become more questioning, more analytical, more self-challenging, and more curious. These are all characteristics generally associated with effective teachers.

Self-evaluation is not something with which you are totally unfamiliar. Each of us monitors our classroom performance, and, when it deviates from a standard we hold for how to behave, we evaluate ourselves. This evaluation might lead to self-praise, admonishment, or correction of our performance. The data for this self-assessment come from our perceptions of our behaviors and the reactions students and others have. We might do this informally or through our interpretation of student and colleague data using procedures described earlier in this chapter.

There are two guidelines that we feel are important to the effective classroom use of self-evaluation procedures. First, attempts should be made to ensure that self-evaluation is done as objectively and systematically as possible. Casually thinking about what you are doing is not something we recommend. Taking a casual attitude may lead you to miss important pieces of information. Second, because we sometimes see only those things we want to see, we must take care to ensure that this tendency does not interfere with our self-assessments. It is best to have a procedure that will guide your thoughts and observations toward as many aspects of your teaching as possible. Furthermore, your self-assessment should be checked against the observations of other people to make sure that it is valid. Our experience suggests that people sometimes overestimate or underestimate how well they are doing. Your perceptions need to be checked with those of students, colleagues, or other people who have access to your teaching. You do not have to do this every time you follow a self-assessment procedure; however, you need to be careful that you do check your perceptions. Several suggestions for self-assessment in line with these guidelines appear in the following paragraphs.

Course activities questionnaire. This procedure requires you to think about your entire course and your role in it. If you use it, you might want to share your responses with your students. Ask them to add comments to yours and to give specific reasons they think your percpetions are accurate or inaccurate. An example of the process is presented in Table 8.5 beginning on the next page.

Audio- and videotape. Tape recording one or more class sessions using an audio cassette tape recorder or a videotape recorder is another valuable source of feedback. If you use television, a student, a colleague, or some-one from your media center can operate the camera for you. With video-tape, it is important that you also record student reactions to what you are doing. You do not have to record every minute of your class. There may be things you are especially interested in, or you might have a student or colleague operate the equipment to get a random sample of fifteen minutes of an hour session or twenty-five minutes of a one-and-a-half-hour session. Watching or listening to the tape afterward is thus not a lengthy process. We suggest that as you watch or listen to your performance, you answer the following questions in writing.

- What are the specific things I think I am doing well?
- What are the specific things I think I am not doing well?
- What do the students seem to enjoy most?
- What do the students seem to enjoy least?
- If I could do this session over again, what are three things I would change?
- What resources do I need to use in order to change?

Checking student and colleague perceptions. In the first two sections of this chapter, we described a number of devices for gathering student and peer input. If you use any of those devices in your teaching, you might also first answer the questions in ways you think your colleagues or students would. Check their responses against yours. Look for the areas where the largest discrepancies between your responses and those of students or colleagues exist. You might choose these areas of your teaching to begin working on.

Analyzing a specific classroom session. Tape recording a class and checking your perceptions of a given class with student or colleague data are helpful sources of information for a single session. The procedure illustrated in Table 8.6 on page 218 shows another way to view a specific session. In addition to having you assess how you think you handled the class, it provides a method for forming a self-contract to initiate changes.

Table 8.5. Self-evaluation Procedure

Course number and title: _____

Section I

1. In assessing your own strengths as the teacher of this course, what do you identify as being the five activities that you perform most effectively?

2. Which of these activities do you think are valued by the students taking this course? Which are not? Which of these activities are likely to be valued by your colleagues? Which are not?

3. What other activities would you like to be able to perform in an effective manner that you now either do not perform or perform in a mediocre manner?

4. What steps would have to be taken for you to acquire the necessary skills or resources to perform these activities?

5. In assessing your limitations as the teacher of this course, what do you identify as being the five activities that you perform least effectively?

6. Which of these activities do you think are valued by the students taking this course? Which are not? Which of these activities are likely to be valued by your colleagues? Which are not?

Section II

Please indicate by using the following scale the extent to which you think each of the following types of learning should occur in this course.

1 = This should be a major learning goal in this course.
2 = This should be a minor learning goal in this course.
3 = This should be a peripheral learning goal in this course.
4 = This should not be a learning goal in this course.
5 = Uncertain

_____ 1. Factual knowledge: New terms, methods, or information is acquired.

_____ 2. Skills training: Students learn how to perform specific tasks or how to fill particular professional roles.

_____ 3. Principles: New theories, generalizations, and ways of organizing information are learned.

_____ 4. Application: Students learn how to use new information, concepts, and methods to solve current problems.

_____ 5. Creativity: Students learn how to be more expressive in the use of a specific medium (words, paint, music) or how to approach and solve problems in a new way.

_____ 6. Appreciation: Greater sensitivity to specific intellectual, scientific, or artistic endeavors is learned.

_____ 7. Self-understanding: Students acquire a better sense of themselves or their relationships with other people.

_____ 8. Self-management: Students learn how to plan more effectively to control their personal or professional life.

Table 8.5. *(Continued)*

Section III

Following are four questions concerning the students' overall evaluation of this course. Please indicate for each item how you would rate yourself or the course, and how you think the students would rate you or the course (estimate of average student rating).

1. What is your overall impression of the quality of this course, given your objectives and expectations about the course?

Rating Scale	Your Rating	Estimated Average Student Rating
(1)	Outstanding	Outstanding
(2)	Good	Good
(3)	Satisfactory	Satisfactory
(4)	Poor	Poor
(0)	Uncertain	Uncertain

Actual average student rating (to be filled in after the estimate is made):

2. How would you compare the overall quality of this course with that of other courses of a similar nature at this college?

Rating Scale	Your Rating	Estimated Average Student Rating
(1)	One of the very best (upper 10 percent)	One of the very best (upper 10 percent)
(2)	Above average (upper 10 percent to 30 percent)	Above average (upper 10 percent to 30 percent)
(3)	Average (40 percent to 60 percent)	Average (40 percent to 60 percent)
(4)	Below average (lowest 40 percent)	Below average (lowest 40 percent)
(0)	Uncertain	Uncertain

Actual average student rating (to be filled in after the estimate is made):

3. Compared with other courses of a similar nature at this college, how would you rate the overall level of difficulty in this course?

Rating Scale	Your Rating	Estimated Average Student Rating
(1)	Very difficult	Very difficult
(2)	Somewhat difficult	Somewhat difficult
(3)	Average	Average
(4)	Somewhat easy	Somewhat easy
(5)	Very easy	Very easy
(0)	Uncertain	Uncertain

Actual average student rating (to be filled in after the estimate is made):

4. In comparison with other courses of a similar nature that are offered at this college, how would you rate the level of learning in this course?

Rating Scale	Your Rating	Estimated Average Student Rating
(1)	A great deal more was learned than usual.	"I learned a great deal more than I usually do."
(2)	More was learned than usual.	"I learned more than I usually do."
(3)	The usual amount was learned.	"I learned about as much as I usually do."
(4)	Less was learned than usual.	"I learned less than I usually do."
(5)	Considerably less was learned than usual.	"I learned considerably less than I usually do."
(0)	Uncertain	Uncertain

Actual average student rating (to be filled in after the estimate is made):

Note the basic reasons for any significant discrepancies between your ratings, your estimated student ratings, and the actual student ratings. If possible, share these reasons with your colleagues or students, or both, so that the reasons can be validated, clarified, or expanded.

You may use it alone, or your observations can be verified by another observer. You might complete it before watching or listening to a video- or audiotape of a session.

Adapting self-evaluation to your teaching. After reading about student and colleague input for assessing and developing your teaching, you were asked to begin to think about how they might be useful to you. We would like you to do the same thing with self-evaluations. The questions that follow are designed to help you develop ideas for how self-evaluation might help you and how comfortable you might be using it. Please note that the last question deals with selecting among student, colleague, and internal sources of information. Our intent is simply to get you to think about which one or more of the three data sources you might use. Ideally, we think that some combination of the three will yield the most comprehensive assessment. We also recognize, however, that you may not want to jump into this process without first getting your feet wet. This attitude is understandable, and, if you have not had much experience with assessment, it is preferable. You should select the assessment procedure(s) with which you are most comfortable and that you think you can handle competently.

1. Review your responses to the questions on page 196. There you listed several disadvantages of your current assessment procedures and several things you needed to do to overcome those disadvantages. What self-evaluation procedures will help you improve what you currently do? Describe how you think they will assist you.

Table 8.6. Classroom Session Analysis Questionnaire

As soon after a session as possible, complete the following worksheet.

1. Find the spot on the scale below that best describes your "gut-level" reaction to how this session went. A 1 means you feel terrible: the class went as badly as it possibly could have, you accomplished nothing, and you are extremely dissatisfied with the ways in which you responded. A 7 means you were superb: you accomplished a great deal and are extremely proud of how good your teaching was. Note that there is no 4 on the scale; you may not choose the middle of the scale, but must judge the class session to be better or worse than your concept of "the middle." In your rating, keep in mind your goals for this particular class and how successfully you accomplish them.

2. Having rated the class session, list all the factors that made it as good as it was. If you rated it a 6, why was it not a 5, or a 3? Make the list as complete as you can. Eight to ten factors are not too many for a reasonably competent class session.

3. Rank the items you listed in order of their importance to the goals of this session. The most important factor you listed should rate a 1, and so on.

4. List all the things you might do differently if you had another chance. To make sure that you can in fact do these things, write these factors in the form of sentences that begin with "I would . . ." You will then have a list of positive actions to work on rather than a list of past negative behaviors.

   I would _____
   I would _____
   I would _____

5. Translate into action your analysis of things you would do by writing three or four contracts with yourself either to maintain a positive behavior you identified in question 2 or to try a new behavior you listed in question 4. Begin each self-contract with "I will . . ."

   I will _____
   I will _____
   I will _____

6. Keep your responses to this analysis for future reference and to check your progress in meeting your self-contracts.

---

2. How accurate do you think your perceptions are about your teaching behaviors? In what ways might getting student, colleague, or other input help you enhance the accuracy of your perceptions?

3. Based on your responses to the other sets of questions in this chapter, what assessment procedures make sense for you to use at this time? Please list them. Having done so, what procedures are you

likely to be most comfortable with and competent to use? What procedures are you likely to be least comfortable with and competent to use?

4. Think about your responses to the last three questions. If you were to begin to evaluate your teaching starting with your next class, what would you do? If you were to begin the evaluation of your teaching beginning with your first class next term, what would you do?

5. What resources (time, energy, money, people, materials) do you need to initiate your assessment plans?

Summary

Assessment procedures can help us improve our teaching. In this chapter, several ideas for how to gather information to improve instruction were presented. They are based on the general guidelines that formative evaluation must be continuous, broadly based, descriptive, and oriented toward personal goals and objectives. The procedures discussed include:

- *Student input.* Examples included open-ended questions, paper-and-pencil techniques, student rating scales, student lecture notes, student evaluation committees, and a process of assessing instructor and student skills.

- *Peer input.* A process for using peer input on classroom effectiveness included forming a colleague support and observation team and working closely with a single colleague on classroom issues.

- *Self-assessment.* Several ideas for self-assessment were presented, including the use of course activities questionnaires and audio- and videotape, checking colleague and student perceptions, and analyzing a specific classroom session.

References

Aleamoni, L.M. The usefulness of student evaluations in improving college teaching. Research Report No. 356, Office of Instructional Resources. Chicago: University of Illinois, February 1974.

Bergquist, W.H., and Phillips, S.R. *A Handbook for Faculty Development.* Washington, D.C.: Council for the Advancement of Small Colleges, 1975.

Centra, J.A. *Determining Faculty Effectiveness: Assessing Teaching, Research and Service for Personnel Decisions and Improvement.* San Francisco: Jossey-Bass, 1980.

Curwin, R.L., and Fuhrmann, B.S. *Discovering Your Teaching Self: Humanistic Approaches to Effective Teaching.* Englewood Cliffs, N.J.: Prentice-Hall, 1975.

Fuhrmann, B.S., and Weissburg, M.J. *Self-assessment in Evaluating Clinical Competence in the Health Professions.* St. Louis, Mo.: Mosby, 1978.

Grasha, A.F. *Assessing and Developing Faculty Performance: Principles and Models.* Cincinnati, Ohio: Communication and Education Associates, 1977.

Menges, R.J. Teaching improvement strategies: How effective are they? *Current Issues in Higher Education,* 1980, *2,* 25-31.

Seldin, P. *Successful Faculty Evaluation Programs.* Crugers, N.Y.: Coventry Press, 1980.

Seldin, P. Self-assessment of college teaching. *Improving College and University Teaching.* 1982, *30,* 70-74.

Scriven, M. The methodology of evaluation. Washington, D.C.: American Educational Research Monograph Series on Curriculum Evaluation, no. 1, *Perspectives on Curriculum Evaluation,* 1967.

Sweeney, J.M., and Grasha, A.F. Improving teaching through faculty development triads. *Educational Technology,* 1979, *19,* 54-57.

Chapter 9
Using Media
in the Classroom

Media has become a household word, one that is often used rather imprecisely to refer to the many methods available today for transmitting information and delivering messages. *Media* in the broad use of the term refers to a variety of technologies and, if we might use the term, nontechnologies that communicate. Thus we can talk about print, electronic methods, and communication hardware such as radio, telephone, and cable, as well as the many face-to-face and other methods human beings use to communicate.

When we consider the use of these methods in the classroom, it is probably a good idea to maintain a broad perspective. Thus we prefer the broad use of the term *media* and have not organized this chapter exclusively in categories such as print and electronic and other types of hardware and software. Instead, we have sought a balance between offering guidelines for using media in the classroom and presenting some of the issues in using the more popular and readily available types of

221

media. Thus this chapter is organized around discussions of the reasons faculty have for using media in the classroom, guidelines for selecting and using classroom media, and the advantages and disadvantages of the most commonly used instructional media—textbooks, chalkboards, overhead transparencies, photographs and slides, audio recordings, filmstrips, films, simulations, and multimedia presentations. Other media formats, such as videodiscs, cable television, and interactive television, are not included, because their use is not yet extensive enough to make them available to the average teacher. Our concern is to present practical information about those classroom media that you would most likely encounter and have a chance to use given the rather limited budgets at most institutions.

Media and Teaching

Reasons for the Dramatic Rise in Media Use

If the second half of the twentieth century were to be characterized by historians of the future, its hallmark would likely be *dramatic change.* In every field, by any standard, rapid change is obvious. For our purposes, these changes can be categorized as changes in the nature and extent of knowledge, the nature and extent of available technology, the nature of society, and the nature of the students in our colleges. Each of them provides us with a rationale to consider developing competence in the use of audiovisual methods and technology in our teaching.

Changes in the nature and extent of knowledge. The "knowledge explosion" continues. We are in the 1980s faced with more information, and more rapidly developing new information, than anyone would have been capable of imagining. Old facts are shattered daily by new discoveries, and yesterday's knowledge is likely to become tomorrow's myths. In the face of such developments in knowledge, the teacher who drops pearls of wisdom into the eager minds of students may become as outdated a concept as the Pony Express. Students are exposed to a tremendous amount of new knowledge because of the rapid changes around them. Learners must acquire knowledge in new ways to keep pace. Modern, up-to-date media provides alternative means by which new knowledge can be transmitted, and teachers can improve effectiveness by learning to use them well.

Changes in the nature and extent of available technology. Many of us teaching in colleges today grew up during television's infancy and continue to think of television as a medium of entertainment only. But today's generation of college students has grown up with television, as well as computers and sophisticated electronics, as an important means by which the knowledge that continues to develop is communicated. With the vast array of new technology available, today's students are technology sophisticated and technology inundated. It becomes an increasing challenge for teachers to compete with these technological wonders for the attention and interest of the students. Students who have grown up vicariously experiencing world events ranging from war to space exploration are difficult to motivate with only the printed and spoken word. Under such circumstances, the task of knowing and selecting the most appropriate material and format for the classroom is indeed a formidable one.

Changes in the nature of society. The explosions in knowledge and technology have caused concomitant changes in the very nature of society. Children learn to spell with electronic games, television is the babysitter (as well as the primary mode of information dissemination), computers are commonplace in businesses, schools, and even homes, and people are exposed to a wide variety of choices very early in life. In an earlier time, young people had few choices to make and were relatively satisfied with whatever their circumstances of birth and opportunity had to offer. Today, however, the average college student has already considered a wide range of alternatives and been forced to make choices that seem overwhelming to others of us. The average college student of the 1980s has seen, via the mass media or lectures, consideration of abortion, ascetiscism, communal marriage, surrogate parenting, zero population growth, nuclear energy, equal rights, personal arms, legalization of marijuana, altered states of consciousness, organ transplants, and the potential for world annihilation. With these issues presented in living color and stereophonic sound, traditional teaching methods, no matter how inherently exciting the content (and we must admit that much necessary content is not inherently exciting), are difficult to attend to. Our society has progressively become multimedia oriented, instantaneous, and rapidly moving. Teaching methods must keep pace, or we face the possibility of losing the attention and interest of our students.

Changes in the nature of the student body. As noted in previous chapters, college campuses today are not inhabited by eighteen to twenty-two year olds, living away from comfortable, affluent homes for a four-year moratorium on the pressures and decisions of adult life. Today's college population is highly diverse, with a wide variety of backgrounds, interests, abilities, and learning styles. The traditional written and spoken word itself is probably not sufficient to meet the needs of these students. As teachers, we need to tap to a greater extent the vast array of instructional tools that are now available to us. An important tool is the effective use of educational media.

The Contribution of Media to Learning

Jerrold Kemp has noted the following as contributions that media can make to student learning:

- Media can transmit essential information.
- Media can be used as introductory motivation.
- Media can provide enrichment.
- Media can show relationships.
- Media can provide experiences that the teacher cannot.
- Media can assist individualization.
- Media can provide immediacy in the classroom.

At times you may wish to use methods other than the printed and spoken word to replace a more traditional means of presenting information; at others you may wish them to be a supplement. In either case, it is helpful to note the level of abstraction inherent in various forms of information dissemination. Direct experience with real objects is, of course, the most concrete, and verbal symbols are the most abstract. All other forms fall between these two extremes, as on this continuum:

Direct experiences	Games and simulations	Motion pictures	Still pictures	Verbal symbols

Concrete ⟵————————————————————⟶ Abstract

According to Jerrold Kemp, one basic principle of learning is that effective learning often begins with concrete experience. Media can often provide the concrete experiential component that verbalization lacks. Such experiences also provide motivation and interest, ingredients that contribute both to effective learning and to further creativity and productivity. Today's students are very interested in immediate relevance and applicability and settle for thoughtful hypothesizing less often. Yet concrete experience and abstract thinking are not independent; one can lead into the other. Thus a way for us to stimulate our students to an appreciation of the abstract, to an interest in exchanging and criticizing thoughts, to the enjoyment of sharing ideas, is to acknowledge and meet their more concrete needs for direct experience by our various substitutes for such experience.

Selecting Media

Jerrold Kemp provides an interesting and useful way to categorize media use and concomitant issues. He suggests that any material, be it a chart, film, text, drawing, photo, videotape, or total media package, can be used either to *inform*, in which case the audience remains passive, or to *instruct*, in which case participants are involved in planned overt or mental activities that ensure their active use of the material presented. In using media in the classroom, we suggest that Kemp's differentiation of function provides a practical starting point from which other questions about specific media selection and use can develop.

General Guidelines

In any consideration of using media, at least three issues need to be discussed. First is the *idea* that you wish to get across: the material must clearly present the idea or set of ideas better than you can without it. Second, you must match media to your *objectives*. A beautiful film on the topic you are considering may be a waste of educational time if it does not contribute to meeting the learning objectives you have established for the class. Finally, you must consider your *audience*: the material must be appropriate to their needs and interests.

Along these lines, James Brown outlines several other specific guidelines for media utilization:

- *No one medium is best for all purposes.* Whereas audiotape is an extremely useful tool in the language laboratory, it loses its effectiveness in analyzing the interactions occurring in a group, where videotape would provide a more comprehensive picture of the dynamics.

- *Media uses should be consistent with educational objectives.* If your purpose in using a film is to clarify a difficult concept, you must make sure that the film in fact *does* clarify and doesn't further cloud the issue. If your purpose in using an audiorecording is motivational and interest arousing, be sure not to use it to evaluate student responses.

- *Media users must familiarize themselves with the content of the media they choose.* More than one teacher has used a medium that he or she hasn't previewed, only to be embarrassed by its inappropriateness to the situation. Descriptions are written by commercial companies or media specialists who don't know you, your course, or your students.

- *Media must be appropriate for the instructional format.* Just because a film is colorful doesn't ensure its appropriateness. Remember that color, for example, is important only if color is in fact important to the instruction. So too with motion. Motion is important only if motion is significant to the learning: to demonstrate movement or to show spatial development or real movement. For some purposes, a black-and-white still photograph may be more appropriate than a technicolor movie.

- *Media must be appropriate for student capabilities and learning styles.* Media must meet students' cognitive capabilities, knowledge of and attitude toward the subject, and individual learning styles. For group presentation individual styles must sometimes be compromised, but you can arrange group presentations of varying types, thus meeting individual needs at least some of the time.

- *Media are neither good nor bad simply because they are either concrete or abstract.* At one time, you may wish to use media to provide concrete experiences; at other times, an abstract media presentation might be used to stimulate a variety of reactions and interpretations.

- *Media should be chosen objectively rather than on the basis of personal preference.* Each of us is tempted at times to use something just because we like it and want to share it with students, whether they like it or not. Further, it is tempting to stop using something when we tire of it, regardless of its positive value. In these times, we must remember that it is the effect on students, not the effect on us, that matters.

- *Physical conditions surrounding uses of media significantly affect the results obtained.* A long film shown in a too warm room late in the afternoon may be more effective in stimulating dozing than in presenting a fresh approach.[1]

Specific Media Selection

Selecting a particular medium is something that must be done with care, as Jerrold Kemp notes:

> Media decisions should be made not for a gross entity of learning as large as a *topic*, but rather for groups of objectives that collectively make up the topic. Within a given topic, carefully designed combinations of media, where each performs a particular function,

---

[1] Adapted from James Brown, *AV Instruction*, Fifth Edition, p. 71, by permission of McGraw-Hill Book Company.

based on its attributes, and reinforces the learning effects of the others, may be required to achieve the kind of instruction for group or individual that is most effective [1980, pp. 45-46].

Given the general guidelines, we must ask more specific questions about a particular item of media under consideration. James Brown notes the conditions of *purpose, content, appropriateness, cost,* and *circumstances of use.*

- *Purpose:* For what specific instructional or informational objective will the item be used?

- *Content:* Is the content significant? accurate? up to date?

- *Appropriateness:* Is the level of difficulty appropriate? Is the vehicle appropriate for the message? Has the item been appropriately tested?

- *Cost:* Is the item worth the cost?

- *Circumstances of use:* Is the item appropriate to the environment and the audience?

Most important to remember in selecting media is the tendency we all have to select that which is easiest or most comfortable or most convenient, rather than that which is most likely to serve the instructional objective most effectively. We hope that the guidelines and questions offered here will assist you in making your choices more objective than subjective.

Finally, it must be acknowledged that there will often be times when selection criteria reveal that there is no perfect media item for a particular purpose. It is then that our creativity comes into play—to use only a portion of something, to adapt what is available to our unique circumstances, or even to learn more production techniques to enable us to design exactly the media resource we need. You may not want to learn film-making, but other, simpler alternatives are not only available but may provide the means to create exactly what you need.

Using Media in the Classroom

Getting Started

Having adhered to basic guidelines, and having done a careful and comprehensive selection of an appropriate item, you are ready to use the media for instructional purposes. James Brown outlines the steps necessary:

- *Prepare yourself.* Once you have determined your purposes, preview whatever instructional medium you've selected as a dry run, note important points, develop a plan for introducing the item, and develop a context for student participation and study. (What will they do during it? How will it fit into the class context? How will it contribute to learning?)

- *Prepare the environment:* Arrange for equipment, provide for physical comfort, prepare handouts and other materials, and arrange any necessary assistance. Unfortunately, valuable class time is often wasted because an instructor has not arranged for and checked out media and equipment before the class begins.

- *Prepare the class:* Introduce the item, clarify its use, describe its content and what is to be learned, and tell students what will be expected of them during and after the use of the item. You might also introduce key words and develop pre-use questions as a study guide.

- *Use the item professionally:* If you have properly prepared both yourself and the environment, everything should run smoothly.

- *Follow-up:* Simply because you've used the item doesn't assure learning. Follow-up should clarify and assure learning through application. Structured questions, whether presented to the entire class or used as individual thought stimulators, help guide attention and discussion to the objectives you've already clarified. Study guides might be discussed, or students might be asked to write individual responses to specific questions before discussion. Portions of a film, slide show, or audiotape, for example, might be re-examined for clarification or a new perspective. Design additional related activities.

- *Evaluate:* Consider the extent to which the selected medium met the objective for which you chose it, the appeal of the item to students, the convenience of the item for both you and your students, and the costs involved in using the item. If you used the item again, what revisions in your use of it might you make?

Advantages and Disadvantages of Commonly Used Instructional Media

In the following pages, we will discuss advantages, disadvantages, and user tips for the most commonly available forms of media. These discussions are also summarized in Table 9.1, beginning on page 230, which you might consider using as a handy reference guide each time you are faced with a medium selection decision.

Teaching with textbooks. Not every reference on media use includes textbooks as a media form. We believe, however, that consideration of them belongs in this chapter, because they provide the most common and often most poorly selected and used form of media available to us, and the only one which students expect to pay for directly.

Judicious selection and use of textbooks can be a powerful contribution to the success of a course. If the content, format, level of difficulty, and so forth are appropriate and used creatively, students will likely value both the book and the course; if they've paid for what seems to be an inappropriate and badly used text, their resentment is likely to spill over to other aspects of the course. Well-selected and intelligently used textbooks provide economy of presentation, serve to organize instruction, help individualize instruction, reinforce course material, provide an introduction to class activity, and contribute to motivation, thinking, and understanding.

Unfortunately, some instructors use them in a way that encourages memorization rather than critical thinking. Too often the omniscient style in which many texts are written implies that what is written is in fact absolute truth, rather than just one interpretation of human observations. Also, because of the time it takes to publish a text, as well as the length of time the book must remain on the market for the publisher to justify the investment, many texts become outdated, and they certainly cannot reflect current innovations in the field. Finally, many instructors have a tendency to rely too heavily on the text, allowing it to serve as both the content and the organization for the course.

To minimize the disadvantages inherent in textbooks, James Brown suggests the following:

- *Use the textbook as a teaching assistant.* Adapt the text to your course and your course outline by changing the sequence of material presented, omitting some content, and using the text as only one source of classroom activity.

- *Add reality to text abstractions.* Sometimes you may want to have students read the text before a class presentation, discussion, or activity, but at other times the reading may prove more meaningful if it follows class activity.

- *Individualize through independent study assignments.* Some topics in the text might be read by only a few students, who then present those topics to others. Study guides that you prepare can also be used to individualize portions of the text that the whole class will not read.

- *Use the text as the basis for research assignments.* Many topics dealt with in the text may not be of general class interest, but they could be used as the germinal ideas for independent research.

- *Make use of any visual content included in the text.* Remember that

Table 9.1. Advantages and Disadvantages of Various Media

Medium	Advantages/Uses	Disadvantages/Limitations
Textbooks	• presents large quantity of information economically • can be used to individualize • can be used to organize course content • can contribute to motivation and thinking • can assist in course design and methodology (especially the manual and available notes)	• may be used as total course content • may encourage memorization rather than thought • may imply truth rather than observation • may not reflect current innovations • may become dated rapidly
Chalkboard	• is always on hand and readily accessible • is useful for spontaneous demonstrations and illustrations • can be used for mutual planning • is economical and easy to maintain • may provide a vehicle for recording progress	• is subject to misuse from careless lettering, improper maintenance, and by forcing instructor to face away from class • is difficult to see by large group
Overhead transparencies	• are always under instructor's control • allow creativity in preparation • are economical and reusable • provide clear focal point for class • are easily available and simple to use and maintain • can reinforce presentation • allow instructor to face class	• require some skill in preparation for most effective use • require relatively large projector

Medium	Advantages	Disadvantages
	• are economical, adaptable, and flexible • can be used for many purposes • can be prepared ahead of time or done spontaneously	• may get out of sequence or be projected backward or upside down • require some photographic skill
Photographs/slides and slide series	• are easy to prepare • are flexible and adaptable • are easy to handle, store, and use • may be used as part of programmed sequence • stimulate interest and aid memory • are economical and readily available or produced • may be easily produced locally to provide local application of general concepts • can be produced by students • can be combined with audio methods	
Audio recordings	• may be combined with slide series • lend themselves to individual and tutorial work • provide permanent record of visiting resource person • can be taken into the "field" • are economical, adaptable, flexible, and reusable	• may become boring with overuse • depend only upon learner's listening skill • may be of poor quality
Filmstrips	• are compact and easy to handle • are economical • can be used for both groups and individuals • provide structure and sequence	• require professional production • cannot be changed or adapted

Table 9.1. *(Continued)*

Medium	Advantages/Uses	Disadvantages/Limitations
Films	• can demonstrate motion • can show relationships • can include appropriate sound • can be used for both individuals and groups	• require expensive equipment • are expensive to produce • seldom show local application • become outdated quickly
Videotapes	• can record and play back the immediate moment • are available both commerically and through local production • can be used for both individuals and small groups • allow for creativity and experimentation • allow for immediate playback and critique • are highly portable, for both recording and monitoring	• require care in equipment handling • use expensive and sensitive equipment • susceptible to poor quality • are subject to incompatible systems • have limited image size
Games/simulations/role-playing exercises	• involve students as active participants • require interactions • involve affective as well as cognitive processes	• may be so enjoyable as to obscure the point • require more time than didactic presentations • cannot involve all students to the same degree
Multimedia presentations	• permit comparisons and show relationships • provide high interest level • provide for a variety of learning styles • allow for complete individualization through the use of total multimedia packages	• require considerable planning and preparation

authors and publishers include visuals only when they are convinced that their value is worth the additional cost of printing them.

Teaching with the chalkboard. Virtually every classroom has at least one chalkboard, but seldom is it used either creatively or to fullest advantage. The chalkboard, more than any other medium, provides an economical, easily accessible means of presenting new ideas, demonstrating or illustrating principles, recording individual or class progress, working out problems and group projects, and involving students in classroom planning activities. The handiness that provides the chalkboard's advantages also creates its potential for misuse. Because it is readily accessible, it's often used with little or no prior planning, with little or no attention to whether everyone in the group can see it, with poor lettering techniques, and with little concern by the instructor of the problem of the necessity of facing away from the class to write on the chalkboard. But with proper maintenance, attention to prior planning, good writing techniques, and thoughtful attention to its potential uses, the chalkboard can become an effective means of stimulating thinking.

Teaching with transparencies. The development of the overhead projector and the simplicity of both preparing and using transparencies have made this medium the most widely used technique of large group instruction. The advantages of teaching with transparencies far outweigh the disadvantages. In fact, we were hard pressed to come up with any disadvantages at all, as Table 9.1 shows.

Overhead transparencies have replaced the chalkboard in many classrooms, usually for very good reason. Whereas the chalkboard is often difficult to see, the overhead provides a large, bright focal point that can be placed for easy viewing by everyone. Student attention is held by both those transparencies that are prepared before class and those that you create during a presentation. Unlike a diagram on the chalkboard, the transparency can be kept and reused. Projectors, though somewhat bulky, are simple to operate and maintain and are widely available. In fact, many classrooms now have them as standard equipment. Most importantly, unlike other media, the teacher is in complete control of the materials used. You choose what to show, when to show it, and how to show it. Further, the transparencies afford you limitless creativity, both in your presentation and in your preparation of the materials. James Brown comments on the creative potential:

> Some teachers use the overhead projector chiefly as a substitute for the chalkboard. With a felt pen or other appropriate marker, they write on cellophane or other clear plastic material very much as they write on a chalkboard. But many other processes have been developed

for creating transparencies; to stop only with using a felt pen and a piece of plastic is to miss some of the most exciting experiences possible with the overhead projector. These other processes range from simple techniques needing no special skills at all to those requiring special equipment and considerable proficiency in using it [Brown, Lewis, and Harcleroad, 1977, p. 121].

You might find some commercially produced transparencies that relate to your class, and, if you do, the principles for media selection discussed earlier should be applied. More likely, though, you will have to create and produce your own transparencies. When you do, there are some important guidelines to follow:

- Always orient your transparencies horizontally rather than vertically; they won't become distorted when projected, and lower portions won't fall below eye level.

- Always use fine-tipped, water-based felt pens or wax-based A-V pencils (grease pencils).

- Place a clear plastic sheet on top of transparencies you will use repeatedly. Use this plastic sheet for marks you make to highlight or emphasize parts of the more permanent transparency.

- Use a roll of plastic over prepared transparencies, or use it alone instead of the chalkboard.

- Use several transparencies in overlays to build an idea or concept.

- Use a variety of colors to highlight related concepts.

- When typing on transparencies, use only boldface or primary type.

- Include only a few points or items. Too much information on a transparency inhibits its impact.

- Reveal only one item on a transparency at a time. Onion skin paper makes an especially good screen, because, although it is effective, *you* can see through it to the transparency underneath.

- The overhead projector can be used to project the shadow of an object, should the outline or shadow be a useful item in your class.

- Colored plastic can be used for permanent shapes—arrows, brackets, geometric shapes—that you might use repeatedly.

- In science, plastic dishes might be used with different colored chemicals to demonstrate mixing.

- A thermofax copier can be used to transfer original printed materials to transparencies.

- Other, more complex, methods for making transparencies are probably available through your media center. Use this valuable resource.

- Always mount your permanent transparencies in cardboard for easy handling and filing.

Teaching with photographs and slides. As with overhead transparencies, the advantages of using still photography in the classroom so far outweigh the disadvantages that its use has become widespread. You might think of the use of still pictures as providing a concrete context from which more abstract concepts can be drawn. They can provide a kind of contextual clue for finding the meaning of difficult or complex ideas.

Still pictures are inexpensive, readily available, easy to use, and flexible, require readily available and easy-to-use projection equipment, and lend themselves to self-instructional programs. Simple care in handling precludes the disadvantages that they can get out of sequence or be accidentally projected upside down or backward. In general, consider using slides when you want to:

- present local examples of general concepts
- stimulate interest
- aid memory
- demonstrate detailed steps of a process
- show relationships
- develop a series of materials that is readily adaptable to changing circumstances.

Slide series, with or without accompanying sound, are especially useful in a programmed sequence that is to be used by individuals rather than groups. When used in this way, the series must be self-sufficient, self-explanatory, and concise. Clear instructions, captions, and accompanying audiotape all enhance self-instructional slide series.

Teaching with audio recordings. The most often used learning skill is that of listening, and it has been documented that approximately 90 percent of a student's time in the classroom is spent in listening—primarily, of course, to the teacher (Brown, Lewis, and Harcleroad, 1977, p. 213). Listening is also one of the most important adult communication skills: about half our working time is devoted to listening. It stands to reason, then, that audio recordings, both records and audiotapes, can be used to enhance classroom learning and supplement skill building in listening.

High quality commercially available recordings include music, literature, foreign language, and documentaries, all of which lend themselves to both group and individual use. In addition, the simplicity and economy of tape recording make it especially useful for you in documenting and recording presentations by guests and students and interviews with local or visiting experts. You may also want to record class activities and role plays for possible future use.

Audio recordings are also receiving increased attention because of their usefulness in building specific skills. Autotutorial language tapes have proved their usefulness, as have tapes made to critique and evaluate such skills as interviewing, leading discussions, and making presentations. This unique capability of recording for immediate playback and evaluation makes audiotape especially useful for your personal evaluation of your teaching, allowing you to listen and critique either individually or with the assistance of one or more close colleagues. You may even find that someone on your campus responsible for faculty development activities would be available to record and critique tapes of your teaching with you.

Teaching with filmstrips. Although more filmstrips are used in elementary and secondary schools than in colleges, some commercially available filmstrips are highly useful at the college level, too. Filmstrips, as opposed to a slide series, offer the advantage of maintaining a fixed sequence that cannot be inadvertently rearranged, and are economical, compact, and easy to use. Their very advantage, however, is also their main disadvantage. Because they present photos in a fixed sequence, they are inflexible and unadaptable. Further, local production is limited. Filmstrips find their most potent use in higher education in individualized, programmed instruction, where in a tutorial carrel, a student need only push a button to start a filmstrip and synchronized audiotape presentation that he or she can view individually as often as necessary.

Teaching with film. Every college media center houses films, arranges for film loans and rentals, and makes films available to faculty and students. Film is perhaps the most widely used audiovisual medium available, for both educational and entertainment purposes. In a society in which students have been seeing extremely expensive entertainment films all their lives, it is necessary to teach them how to view film as an educational tool, but this teaching can have a high educational payoff. The concrete experience provides a common base on which you and your students can draw to give meaning to the more abstract concepts and understandings that may form the content of your course. In particular, films provide:

- common experience not otherwise available to students
- demonstrations of inherent motion
- the capacity to slow down or speed up motion
- demonstration of relationships

- dramatic impact
- re-creation of history
- viewing of processes that could not be seen by the unaided human eye.

Film, perhaps more so than any other medium so far discussed, is susceptible to misuse. Because we are so used to sitting down in a movie theater, seeing a film, and leaving, instructors are tempted merely to show a film with no preparation or follow-up and assume that students have gained whatever objective the film was used for. Unfortunately, when this is done students gain about as much as they do from a third-rate entertainment film. When using film, be sure to follow the guidelines for use in the earlier part of this chapter.

Although the subject and treatment are beyond your control, a film nevertheless can be used creatively. If only a portion of a film is appropriate for your objective, use just that portion. Set up the film before class, with the portion you want to use in place, and show just that portion at the appropriate time. A thirty-second film portrayal of a complex concept may be well worth the fifteen minutes of preparation time you spend. In another instance, you might consider showing a film without sound. We have found this effective in, for example, teaching students to interpret body language and facial expressions.

A particularly creative use of film is suggested by James Brown, who offers the following methods of using film to evaluate students:

- *In science:* Show a film of an experiement. Stop it at a crucial point and ask students to describe what would happen next. Or show the end of an experiment and have students describe what preceded it.
- *In social science:* (a) Show two films, both biased, on the same subject, and have students evaluate the positions; (b) stop a film about a social problem short of its resolution and have students defend their stands on the issue.
- *In literature or drama:* Have students create individual endings to a dramatic film.
- *For factual testing:* Show a film with no introduction by you; ask students factual questions on the film's content.

Teaching with videotape. Commercially available videotapes, both those purchased and those recorded from broadcasts, can be used in all the ways that film can be, with cautions concerning the disadvantages as outlined in Table 9.1. In particular, in comparison with film, the electronic systems are complex and expensive, the image size is highly limited, the picture quality is likely to be inferior, and the state of television technology is such that there is as yet insufficient uniformity among competing electronic systems.

In showing commercially available videotapes, follow the user guidelines outlined earlier in this chapter. Be sure that physical arrangements are appropriate, that the equipment is operating properly, and that you have prepared an appropriate lead-in and follow-up. Videotapes available for purchase are simply an alternative to film for most long-term use; film is probably preferable. The advantages of videotape are in the possibilities for more current coverage through broadcast television, and in the immediacy of being able to record and see what has just occurred. These two features differentiate videotape from all other visual media.

Concerning the use of broadcast television, James Brown notes:

> There is every reason for you to consider the valuable contributions television can make to your students and to remember that television is informing them and influencing them whether or not you make any effort to use their viewing experiences constructively. Thus, you are encouraged to look upon a television as a potential ally in your instructional program, and not as an enemy! What *you* do may make the difference [Brown, Lewis, and Harcleroad, 1977, p. 243].

To make use of broadcast television, you must become a discriminating viewer yourself, and knowledgeable about local and network programming.

Because developments in television are constantly occurring, and because current programming can often contribute to classroom learning, you might keep abreast of possibilities by keeping up with current literature under a variety of appropriate headings: cable television, closed-circuit television, educational television, instructional television, and public broadcasting.

Finally, recognize copyright limitations on commercial broadcasting. Some programming is available to you to re-record; some is not. With the vast array of recording equipment available, copyrights are flagrantly violated, but the holders of copyright do in fact have legal rights that the rest of us are obliged to honor. Check with your media specialists to determine your rights and obligations.

The other quality of video recordings that makes them uniquely applicable in the classroom is their immediate playback characteristic. With this feature you can record and immediately evaluate your own teaching, as well as student performance in public speaking, drama, music, sports, presentations, laboratory experiments, role playing, interviewing, and any other behavior you wish to record. You can record a visiting speaker and use the tape in subsequent classes; you can record aspects of community life in lieu of field trips; you can record student presentations for playback in other classes. Should you wish to become involved in television teaching, you might even record, evaluate, and polish lectures and demonstrations for use by students to review or catch up on material they may have missed. It is even possible to record all your presentations and demonstrations, saving your usual class time for personal contact and small group work of a more spontaneous and personal nature. If you should want to try television teaching, see your media specialists. There are specific, highly detailed ways in which to plan, prepare, rehearse, and record a television presentation. You will need to be well versed and well prepared in these techniques to make them effective. There is a significant time commitment involved in television teaching, but one that may be well worth your while in the long run, especially if you can have available specific modules or demonstrations that will aid you in individualizing instruction.

Finally, students can use videotape to record ideas and analyze events. Because they can record, erase, and re-record, students are given the freedom to be creative, to experiment, to try a variety of approaches as they attempt to put ideas on tape.

Teaching with games and simulations. Games and simulations, whether commercially prepared or designed and produced by you, supply an active, experiential component to the classroom that is not possible through other means. The previously discussed instructional media all require at least some passivity on the part of students; games and simulations, however, require their active participation and interaction, including mutual cooperation and insight into interactive and social problems. Simulations are working models of some part of reality. Thus they can be used to teach concepts and to demonstrate social relationships and conflicts. Several examples of the types of games that are available appear in Table 9.2. To avoid their potential for misuse (see Table 9.1), consider the following guidelines:

- Make sure the game can meet your objective(s) for it.
- Change the game to suit your needs.
- Prepare students for the game.
- Decide how many will participate, and the role of the others.
- Give the simulation a chance to work to produce student learning.
- Follow up with discussion.
- Evaluate the effectiveness of the game.

Sometimes it may be necessary to devise your own simulation games because those commercially available are not suited to your needs. The simulation may be conducted as a board game, or it may involve people playing various roles and trying to react to situations expected of people

Table 9.2. Several Examples of Simulation Games

Title	Time to Play	Number of Students
Anticipation	30–90 minutes	5–30

Teachers and teacher-trainees experience a variety of learning disabilities.

Artificial Society	a full semester	up to 500 and more

This semester-long game focuses on principles of organization and management. Students work in teams to solve societal problems.

Economic System	2–4 hours	7–13

This game is used to teach the concepts of profit and living standard. Students work in teams to buy, sell, produce, and consume goods. The team that makes the best use of its productive potential wins.

Family	20 minutes–1 hour	1–50

This game provides an experience in competitive and cooperative family situations. Students learn the benefits and rewards of cooperative problem solving.

Polyominoes	variable	1–2

Students manipulate wooden shapes to demonstrate a variety of geometric and topological principles.

Tuf	up to an entire semester	1–4

This is an equation and algebra game that can be used to teach an entire algebra course.

Source: Selected and summarized at random from Robert E. Horn, *The Guide to Simulations/Games for Education and Training*, 3d ed. (Lexington, Mass: Information Resources, Inc., 1977).

in those roles. To design a good simulation takes time, but it is not an impossible task. David Zuckerman and Robert Horn suggest several things to consider.

- *Define the problem to be simulated.* To begin, it is important to assess the interests you have. This might be with social systems, an organization, particular problems you encounter in your work, or a task that needs to be accomplished. You might ask yourself one or more of the following questions to get started:

  Examples: What areas of society do I want students to understand (family, economics, international relations, business, government, the penal system)?

  What problems do I want to understand (pollution and other environmental questions, nations deciding to go to war, labor negotiations, how a nuclear power plant handles an accident, the effects of inflation on consumer purchasing, the building of a skyscraper, how company mergers occur)?

- *State the objectives and scope of the simulation.* Write several statements that define clearly the purpose of the simulation and scope of the simulation.

  Examples: Deciding how to spend money is a complex issue for the state legislature. The interaction among the legislatures, the governor, special interest groups, citizens of the state, and other groups is important in such decisions. How this is done and the ethical and unethical practices that play a role in such decisions will be simulated.

  The functioning of nuclear power plants is a major area of interest of utility companies, local communities, and various state and government regulatory agencies. The role each plays in facilitating and constraining the operation of such plants and how a plant functions and interacts with various groups after an accident will be examined to illustrate the effects of each group on the plant.

- *List the key actors for the simulation.*

  Examples: Governor of the state, heads of the major political parties in the state, key legislators, lobbyists, prominent citizens, news media reporters, and legislative staff.

  Manager of the nuclear plant, key workers at the plant, news media personnel, mayor and city council members, concerned parents, federal officials concerned with atomic power, state regulatory agency officials.

- *Define the motives and purposes of each key actor.* Of interest here are the major motives, purposes, or goals that each role player has.

  Examples: The governor is facing re-election and wants to hold down state spending. Lobbyists for highway construction companies and building construction industries want to get additional money. Prominent citizens are lobbying for additional money for the school systems in the state. Some lawmakers are accused of accepting bribes, and news media reporters are trying to uncover this activity. Several of the key legislators are friends of the governor, and guilt by association is something the governor wants to avoid in an election year.

  The manager of the nuclear plant makes mistakes in supervising people and ignores their complaints. An accident occurs and the manager wants to pin the blame on subordinates. A key supervisor wants to let the media know what occurred. Concerned parents want to evacuate the area and to hold the company responsible for the costs of doing so. Regulatory agencies want to get the plant back to normal operations and not focus a lot of attention on the accident. The agencies are concerned about the effects of the accident on the industry.

- *Determine the sequence of the transactions to be simulated, the amount of playing time, and how decisions will be made.* It is important to have an idea of the sequence of the transactions among the players. These should be checked against the learning objectives for the simulation. Another important consideration is whether the game should be played in a single class session or over several sessions. Decisions might be made by verbal agreements negotiated among the players, by the use at critical points in the game of special cards with decisions on them, or by the roll of dice.

  Examples: A fifty-minute session might be devoted to the role that lobbyists play in trying to enact legislation. How lobbyists interact with the governor and key legislators would also be considered. This might be followed by a session that examines several of the illegal tactics used by special interest groups and how the news media operate to uncover and report such activity. Decisions are made by negotiations among the game players.

  An initial session might examine how a nuclear plant runs when everything is going well and the interactions that occur among key personnel. This could be followed by two class sessions that examine how the relationships change when an "accident" occurs and people try to protect themselves. The influence of community members and regulatory agencies in determining responsibility for the accident will be a part of this process. Key actors will make decisions based on negotiating with other players and on their own. They will be given roles that define whether they will make decisions to protect the company, the community, or themselves. Since different actors will use different decision rules, the conflict this generates will become a part of the simulation.

- *Formulate the evaluation method that will determine who wins or loses, or how one can tell when the game is over, or what the good or bad effects of some processes are.*

  Examples: Whether the governor or the lobbyists are successful might be determined by who gathers the most points by getting others to make decisions in their favor. Such points are awarded to the successful negotiators.

  How much money the company saves or loses might be one way to measure outcome. The amount of damage to the environment and to people forced to leave their homes is another. The amount of satisfaction players have with how things were handled is a third way to determine outcome.

- *Develop a simulation prototype.* Field test the initial plan for a simulation and work the bugs out of it.

If you are unfamilar with simulation games, you might check your local media center or library to obtain a commercially available game. Studying it will give you a better idea of how to implement the suggestions we have presented.

Teaching with multimedia. A combination of media resources may be used both in the classroom and in individualized instruction, with the major use in multimedia packages designed for individual learning. For our purposes, *multimedia* are a sequence of a variety of instructional materials, each appropriate for a different instructional objective or designed to meet a different student learning style or need. A typical classroom example is the use of an overhead transparency to outline and describe a particular concept, followed by a commercially available videotape that deals with the concept on a universal level, in turn followed by a series of audiotaped local interviews concerned with the concept on the local level. Within an individual learning packet might be printed worksheets, audiotapes, and filmstrips used in a specified order to present, demonstrate, and apply the concept being taught. One word of caution, however, is in order. Avoid the use of multimedia just for the apparent novelty. Multimedia presentations require multimedia skills and careful and extensive coordination, and they should be used only when a single medium technique is clearly unsatisfactory or inappropriate. Multimedia packages, usually commercially prepared, are currently most frequently used in mathematics and languages, where they contribute effectively to students' attainment of specific skill objectives in the most efficient manner possible.

Analyzing Your Use of Media

To analyze your own use of the media forms described in this chapter, use Table 9.3. You might want to duplicate the table to provide one for each course that you currently teach.

Student Media Production

So far in this chapter we have concentrated on your use of media, both commercial and self-produced, to enhance and supplement your teaching. A word needs to be said concerning student-produced materials. Through media production activities, students can contribute to your subject area and course by providing local applications of otherwise general concepts. They can engage in meaningful problem-solving activities, either individually or in groups, and they can be stimulated to think creatively and originally. Students can also learn through productive experience to

---

Table 9.3. Media Use Checklist

The following checklist is designed to let you analyze your current use of the various forms of media and to speculate on those you might like to use in the future.

Course _____

	Current Use			Potential Use		
	Used now	% of class time spent on it	Purpose for which used	Ideal % of class time spent on it	Might use in future	Purpose for which it might be used
Textbooks						
Chalkboard						
Overhead						
Photographs/ slides						
Audio recordings						
Filmstrips						
Film						
Videotape						
Games/ simulations/ role playing						
Multimedia						

be better media consumers and critics, and they can gain experience in teamwork, meeting deadlines, and the satisfaction of a job well done. Student production of audiovisual materials, from transparencies through videotape, may provide just the real world application and exciting stimulation your course needs. Don't overlook its possibilities.

The Future of Media in Higher Education

With the rapid development of increasingly sophisticated media over the past twenty years, it may be foolish to attempt to predict the future, but even a conservative estimate of the future impact of media on higher education would have to include the following:

- Media centers will continue to expand, with both materials and services increasing to serve ever-growing needs.
- Communication through media technology is likely to expand considerably faster than communication via the printed word.
- Both students and faculty will become increasingly sophisticated media consumers, media users, and media producers.
- Computer technology will have an increasing impact on teaching and learning, both in data storage and retrieval and in instructional programming itself.
- Media equipment will continue to improve and to be made simpler to use.
- Media packages for individualized instruction will continue to increase.
- Media will continue to provide the variety whereby individualization of instruction becomes possible.

Summary

In this chapter we have explored the vast changes in (1) the nature and extent of knowledge, (2) the nature and extent of available communication, (3) the nature of society itself, and (4) the nature of students in colleges, changes that have made it necessary for us to keep pace by developing competence in the use of audiovisual methods and technology in our teaching. Media contributes to learning not only by assisting in transmitting information, but also by providing motivation, enrichment, immediacy, and direct experience to enhance memory and understanding. We have also reviewed the issues to be considered in using media: the appropriateness of the content, the relationship to your objectives, and the audience with whom you will be working. The preparations for media use were presented, with the bulk of the chapter devoted to an examination of the advantages and disadvantages of various forms of media, including textbooks, the chalkboard, overhead transparencies, photographs, slides and slide series, audio recordings, filmstrips, film, videotape, games, simulations, and multimedia presentations and packages. With the vast advances in media technology that we are likely to continue to experience, our competence as teachers may rely on our familiarity with and ability to take advantage of the media resources that will be available to us.

References

Anderson, R.H. *Selecting and Developing Media for Instruction.* New York: Van Nostrand Reinhold, 1976.

Brown, J.W.; Lewis, R.B.; and Harcleroad, F.F. *Av Instruction: Technology, Media and Methods,* 5th ed. New York: McGraw-Hill, 1977.

Gerlach, V.S., and Ely, D.P. *Teaching and Media, a Systematic Approach.* Englewood Cliffs, N.J.: Prentice-Hall, 1980.

Kemp, Jerrold E. *Planning and Producing Audiovisual Materials,* 4th ed. New York: Harper & Row, 1980.

McKeachie, W. *Teaching Tips: A Guide for the Beginning College Teacher.* Lexington, Mass: D.C. Heath, 1978.

Wittich, W.A., and Schuller, C.F. *Audiovisual Materials, Their Nature and Use.* New York: Harper & Row, 1967.

Zuckerman, D.W., and Horn, R.E. *The Guide to Simulation/Games for Education and Training.* Lexington, Mass: Information Resources, 1973.

Chapter 10
Considering Alternative Course Designs

Do you need to examine the way your currently teach or think about teaching? Are you really sure that your current plans and procedures are the best thing for you and your students? How would you go about the task of course redesign? We are not assuming that you need to change. Regardless of whether you are just starting out, are satisfied with your current classroom procedures, are thinking you might want to change, or are absolutely sure you need to change, you should find the suggestions in this chapter helpful.

Considering what to change in one's teaching and how to do so is facilitated if a framework for such consideration is followed. In this chapter we present three planning processes for thinking about course redesign. They are *a process based on an analysis of student and instructor skills, a process based on ideas in the creative thinking literature, and a process that employs knowledge about human development.* Each makes somewhat different assumptions about what you need to do in order to redesign

247

your classes. Yet together they provide an integration of the types of issues you should consider when planning a course. Each of them has been
field tested in our work with faculty, and the versions presented here reflect modifications based on such experiences.

A Design Based on an Analysis of Instructor and Student Skills

The process presented in this section assumes that three kinds of information are needed to design a course. They are the content and noncontent
goals you have, the instructor and student skills needed to achieve such
goals, and a knowledge of various course designs and the different instructor and student skills each demands. Our process helps you obtain this
information for a course you want to consider changing. Once you establish
the goals and the instructor and student skills they require, this procedure
helps you map the skills into those required by various classroom procedures. All solutions to this process are unique and have as their foundation *the goals you have as an instructor.*

The Process

Each of the five phases of this process gives you some of the pieces of the
jigsaw puzzle that is your course design. In the first place, you identify
several general content and noncontent goals for a course you select. Our
intent is initially to help you think quite generally about what you wish to
accomplish. The second phase presents several criteria to assist you in re-
fining your general goals. We ask you to become more specific in your goals
so that in the third phase you easily can identify important instructor and
student skills required by each goal. Our fourth phase identifies several
alternative course procedures and the instructor and student skills needed
by each. In the last phase, you can match the student and teacher skills
you identified earlier to those required by various course designs. Before
beginning, you might want to skim quickly the remainder of this section
to familiarize yourself with the process.

Phase 1: General goals. This is perhaps the most difficult part of the
whole process. Most of us seldom stop to articulate why we are doing
things, yet this is necessary to establish specific goals for ourselves. Consequently, the initial step is for you to list the general goals you have for a
class. Goals can be categorized as either substantially content related or
substantially noncontent related. In the latter case, such goals are processes,
attitudes, and values you want students to achieve. They include goals that

belong to the affective domain and goals that deal with process considerations. Examples might include wanting students to collaborate, to think positively about the scientific method, or to value certain literary styles. Most courses contain a mix of content and noncontent goals. In many cases neither are specified or articulated well. Our intent is simply to have you explicitly state some things you probably already implicitly do.

To accomplish this, *pick two or three each of the major content and noncontent course goals you have.* Our experience with this process suggests that two or three of each type are generally sufficient to help begin the process of assessing your current methods and to permit you to locate others that might enhance your instruction. Later you might want to develop other goals to complete the details of your planning. For now, however, two or three each of the major content and noncontent goals are needed. There are two ways to decide on them. One is to pick a current course and state your goals in terms of what happened the last time you taught it or how you expect to teach it in an upcoming term. On the other hand, you may find it useful to break out of current thinking patterns, especially if you are already sure that you need to change. In this case, select the course you most enjoy and state content and noncontent goals for that course two to five years from now. Try to imagine what the course's potential is. Be creative and imaginative in your thinking. Examples of content and noncontent goals are the following:

A. Content goals

    1. I want the students to understand the content of the course.

    2. I want the students to use the content in creative ways.

B. Noncontent goals

    1. I want the students to become good team members.

    2. I want the students to learn at their own pace.

Phase 2: Goal refinement. A problem with general goal statements is that they are easily misunderstood and misinterpreted by others. A good content or noncontent goal must describe:

- what you expect from students
- the behavior that you will accept as evidence that the goal was achieved
- the level or extent of the acceptable performance.

At all times, the emphasis should be on observable behaviors. With a noncontent goal particularly (such as individual research or collaborative behaviors), the expected and criterial behaviors should be checked with at least one other person to ensure that they are adequately related to the goal. Such agreement would help increase the likelihood of validity of the relationship you see between the behavior and the goal.

How specific you wish to be is really a matter of personal bias and whether or not your goals are explicitly shared with others (students in the course, colleagues). From our point of view, you should be as specific as you can, so that the instructor and student skills needed to accomplish each goal are accurately determined. The three guidelines for description that we have just outlined will normally allow you to make the transition from the general goal to the specific version(s) of that goal. Read the examples that follow and then write specific versions of your general goals.

A. Content goals

General goal 1: I want the students to understand the content of the course.

Specific versions

1. For each theory presented and discussed in the course, students must know the principal author and five major aspects of the theory. Students will be expected to list the author and five major aspects of each theory on the examinations.

2. Students are expected to read each assigned outside reading before class. Students must use three or four concepts from each reading as part of what they write on the examinations.

General goal 2: I want the students to use the content in creative ways.

Specific versions

1. Given any theory presented, each student must be able to write a hypothesis (original) that follows from that theory.

2. Given a hypothesis from one of the theories, each student must be able to design an original experiment to test the hypothesis.

B. Noncontent goals

General goal 1: I want the students to become good team members.

Specific versions

1. Students will work in groups of three. There will be two assigned out-of-class projects. Each group will collect relevant material and write a joint report for each project.

2. Students will be expected to discuss content topics or the group's solution to problems with other members of the class.

General goal 2: I want the students to learn at their own pace.

Specific versions

1. For all activities in the course, students will be allowed to complete assignments, with the exception of exams, whenever they are ready. The only restriction is that all assignments must be completed no later than one week before the course ends.

Phase 3: Skill identification. The assumption underlying the identification of instructor and student skills is that both share responsibility for achieving classroom goals: although the goal may be for the student to learn and list specifics of content, you, as the instructor, need to understand what student and instructor skills are needed to ensure that the goal is accomplished. The course design that maximizes the opportunity for the instructor and student skills appropriate to the stated goals to be used is the one that you should consider employing. Tables 10.1 and 10.2 list and briefly describe several common instructor and student skills that different course designs and methods typically demand.[1] Please read the tables before proceeding.

The best way to generate the necessary skills is to review each of your general and *specific content goals*. Then for each one list the instructor and student skills that appear necessary to accomplish the goal. You should select only those skills that you feel are extremely important and absolutely necessary. Your goal is to identify only the major skills that are needed. It is often helpful to add a reason that skill is really needed to accomplish a particular goal. Read our examples of instructor and student skills that follow and then develop a similar list for your content goals.

Instructor Skills

- Content expert.
- Speaker. Presentations will have to be made on the theories.
- Content transmitter.
- Grader. Students will have to be assessed for course performance.
- Evaluator. Students will need feedback on how they are doing, particularly for how well they use the concepts in the readings, develop hypotheses, and design experiments.

Student Skills

- Content expert.
- Reader.
- Writer.

---

[1] The skills were identified by a content analysis of a variety of classroom designs used in higher education.

Table 10.1. Major Student Skill Demands That Occur Across Different
          Course Designs

- *Actor:* The ability to engage in role-playing activity.
- *Collaborator:* The ability to work with others on projects.
- *Consultant:* The ability to act as a resource person for other students who may need additional information, resource material, or assignments. Must be able to fit the interventions to the needs of the clients (other students).
- *Content expert:* The ability to comprehend the essential concepts and facts of the course.
- *Content transmitter:* The ability to transmit essential content to other students.
- *Explorer:* The ability to take initiative and search for the resources that are needed for the student to learn.
- *Exam taker:* The ability to transmit essential knowledge and understanding of the course content to the instructor.
- *Independent learner:* The ability of the student to think through issues for himself, work at his own pace, and be able to demonstrate evidence of independent thinking.
- *Listener:* The ability to listen to and reflect upon instructor input about course content. Through note taking or memory, information is stored for future reference.
- *Negotiator:* The ability to negotiate with the instructor about standards to be achieved and assignments to be completed. This skill is most often used in contract teaching.
- *Process observer:* The ability to watch the process of what is occurring in the classroom. Should be aware of issues of communication, emerging norms, and leadership within the classroom.
- *Problem solver:* The ability to manage and complete a major project or problem within the context of the course. This can be done individually or with students working together.
- *Reader:* The ability to read and understand textbook and other course reading materials.
- *Researcher:* The ability to design and complete a laboratory-type problem or major library research problem.
- *Writer:* The ability to communicate in writing when the course demands such skills. This is in addition to taking exams.
- *Speaker:* The ability to transmit orally content and instructions to others in ways that are clear and organized.

Source: Anthony F. Grasha, "A Planning Sequence to Assist Faculty in Selecting Alternative Course Designs." *Educational Technology,* Vol. XV (September, 1975) p. 11. Reprinted by permission.

Table 10.2. Major Instructor Skill Demands That Occur Across Different
Course Designs

The name of each skill is followed by the ability that characterizes it.

- *Actor/Director:* The ability to direct or engage in role playing.
- *Assigner:* The ability to assign relevant course materials to students.
- *Coordinator:* The ability to coordinate multiple student projects and activities.
- *Consultant:* The ability to act as a resource person for students who request additional information, resource material, or assignments. Must be able to fit interventions to the needs of the client (student).
- *Content expert:* Knowledge and understanding of the essential concepts and facts of the course.
- *Content transmitter:* The ability to transmit content to students orally or in writing.
- *Evaluator:* The ability to provide timely feedback on an ongoing basis to students about specific strengths and weaknesses.
- *Facilitator:* The ability to get students to maximize their potential and to demonstrate their skills and knowledge. Emphasis is on trying to get students to initiate such things, rather than on the instructor's telling them when and how to do them.
- *Grader:* The ability to assign a student to a general performance category.
- *Goal setter:* The ability to set goals and specify procedures for obtaining them.
- *Listener:* The ability to listen and to reflect upon student input about course issues.
- *Materials designer:* The ability to design appropriate materials for students to use in the course.
- *Manager:* The ability to view the classroom as an organization where the instructor manages a variety of classroom inputs (e.g., teaching assistants, outside speakers, small student groups, multiple projects).
- *Negotiator:* The ability to negotiate with students about standards to be achieved and assignments to be completed. This skill is most often used in contract teaching.
- *Process observer:* The ability to watch the process of what is occurring in the classroom. Should be aware of issues of communication, emerging norms, and leadership within the classroom.
- *Speaker:* The ability to transmit orally content and instructions to others in ways that are clear and organized.

Source: Anthony F. Grasha, "A Planning Sequence to Assist Faculty in Selecting Alternative Course Designs." *Educational Technology*, Vol. XV (September, 1975), p. 12. Reprinted by permission.

- Exam taker.
- Listener. Theory presentation will place a premium on this skill.
- Problem solver.
- Independent learner.

Another facet of skill identification relates to your *noncontent goals*. Here we employ the same process. An important point to remember is that most noncontent goals are not accomplished with passive instructor and student skills. For example, if you are interested in teaching students new attitudes, values, or interpersonal skills, you cannot expect your goal to be accomplished by passive students. They will learn such things only to the extent that they are able to practice and use them. Read the examples that follow of skills needed for noncontent goals and develop the instructor and student skills for the noncontent goals you identified earlier.

Instructor Skills

- Assigner. Specific assignments will have to be made to the small groups.
- Process observer. Groups might benefit from analysis of their work together.
- Facilitator.

Student Skills

- Collaborator.
- Independent learner. Learning at their own pace will require independence on the part of students.
- Process observer. In any group work, it would be helpful for the student to be in tune with the process of how the group is working together and make suggestions for improving the process.

Review your list of instructor and student skills for the content and noncontent goals. Do you see some overlap in the types of skills you identified? There is nothing wrong with some overlap; many of the skills are similar for the two types of goals. Before proceeding to the next phase, you need to summarize the skills for your content and noncontent goals into a single list. The summary list should reflect the fact that some skills overlap, and once again you should make sure that any skill you place on that list is highly important. Read the sample summary list that follows and summarize your skills.

Instructor Skills

- Content expert
- Speaker
- Evaluator
- Assigner

- Content transmitter
- Grader

- Process observer
- Facilitator

Student Skills

- Content expert
- Reader
- Writer
- Exam taker
- Listener

- Problem solver
- Process observer
- Independent learner
- Collaborator

Phase 4: Selecting an instructional design. Now that you have generated both your course goals and the instructor and student skills that are needed to accomplish those goals, you are ready to select the instructional design that best meets your needs. There are numerous course designs and methods applicable at the college level. Each can be used either alone, as the only design for the course, or in combination with other designs to provide a varied design. Before outlining the process we suggest for matching course designs to goals and skills, let us first briefly review characteristics of nine useful course designs for college teaching.

Lecture is, of course, the oldest and most common form of teaching in higher education. It probably needs little further explanation except to note the many variations of the process. In an attempt to operationalize the design, let us use a most common lecture approach. In this design, the instructor spends the majority of the time sharing information with students in what is essentially a one-way communication process—that is, the flow of communication is from the instructor to the student, with the student most often placed in a listener role. Student questions and comments are usually welcome, and an occasional discussion occurs between the students and instructor. Depending on the size of the group, students may be asked to write term papers or do other outside projects in addition to taking scheduled exams and unscheduled quizzes.

Small group designs share the goals of actively involving students in the learning process and increasing students' interpersonal and group problem-solving skills. Examples of such designs include:

1. *Group discussion designs.* Small groups of students are given a series of questions, topics, or problems to discuss and work on. Each small group is asked to resolve a given question, topic, or problem. Students may be asked to come up with a solution in one class period or over several. In either case, the small groups are usually asked to report to the larger class. At this time, comments and discussion from other students are welcomed. The groups are often required to write up the results of their discussion activity. Student panel discussions or

presentations can also be used to discuss and present information in the context of such a design.

2. *Group-designed courses.* Small groups of students are asked to design a course of their own for a given period of time (two weeks, one quarter). The students are responsible for teaching themselves or for obtaining adequate resources for teaching certain topics. Faculty participation varies with the needs of the students and teacher. The faculty member is often helpful in making suggestions to the students. This design is particularly effective if students have had some previous exposure to the material. It is best to have students initially design for relatively small amounts of course time. Once they have gained some experience at course design, the amount of course time they design can be gradually increased.

Self-paced instruction, also known as the Keller Plan or IPI (individually paced instruction), is an individual student-paced, student-tutored, and mastery-oriented instructional design that has been used in a variety of disciplines (Keller, 1968; Kulik, Kulik, and Carmichael, 1974; Johnston, 1975). Printed study guides are used for communication, and a few lectures may be given for motivational purposes.

A student entering a self-paced course finds that the course work is divided into clearly defined topics or units. In a simple case, the content of a unit may correspond to a chapter in the text. Study guides are used to direct the student's work on each unit. Such a study guide introduces the unit, states student objectives for the unit, suggests study procedures, and lists study questions. The student may work anywhere to achieve the objectives outlined in the study guide.

Before moving on to the second unit, the student must demonstrate mastery of the first unit by perfect or near-perfect performance on a short examination. The student requests the exam when he or she feels prepared. Each unit must be passed before the subsequent unit can be attempted. Students are allowed to complete all course objectives before the end of the term, or they may require more than a term for completing the course. How much time is allowed is usually at the instructor's discretion.

The staff needed for implementing such a plan usually includes the instructor and one or more tutors. The instructor selects and organizes material used in the course, writes study guides, and constructs the examinations for the course. A few lectures or demonstrations may be given during the course. The lectures are usually not compulsory, and no examinations are based on them. They are used to stimulate the students, or, in some cases, to motivate students to do well. In the latter cases, students can be motivated by your making attendance at a lecture dependent on the student's successfully completing and passing unit(s) that the lecture covers. Obviously, when these lectures are given, they must be special and entertaining.

The tutors are usually advanced majors in the field or people who have done well in the course recently. Tutors evaluate readiness tests as satisfactory or unsatisfactory. They also prescribe remedial steps for students who encounter difficulties with the course material and offer support and encouragement for new students. In large courses where graduate assistants are available, the graduate assistants are often used to supervise the tutors and to deal with issues that the tutors cannot handle. In smaller courses, the instructor performs these functions.

Simulations involve the use of devices that attempt to mimic the real world (Boobcok and Child, 1968; Maier, Solem, and Maier, 1975; Werner and Werner, 1969). These devices can include a mock jury, a complex criminal justice organization, an economic system, a social environment, and other simulations of real life. Students are asked to play various roles, and problems that are typical to the situation are introduced for the students to solve. The emphasis is on the student's using the content learned in reading and studying by applying it in controlled situations in the classroom. Simulation techniques are available commercially, or they can be custom designed by the instructor. (See Chapter 9 for guidelines for designing simulations.)

Modular instruction is based on the offering of individual units that cover major content areas of a course (Novak and Murray, 1969; Johnston, 1975; McKeachie, 1978). Each module is a curriculum package designed for self-study. A set of modules may be completed in some particular sequence, or students may choose from various modules at any particular time. Time limits may be set for completion of modules, or students may be allowed to complete them at their own pace. The modules are usually large, with each requiring several hours of the student's time. The instructor's role is limited to developing the modules and to monitoring their use. Audiovisual tutorial aids may be used, but they are not essential. Some modules may be set up for groups of students to complete together.

The following steps are used in developing modules (these same steps apply to the units of study described in the more highly structured self-paced instructional units): (a) A minimum number of objectives are stated, preferably in observable, behavioral terms. (b) A hierarchy of these objectives, which determines the sequence of instruction, is constructed. (c) A pretest is constructed to determine what competencies each student possesses when beginning the module. (d) A rationale for the module is stated. This includes the value of a particular unit and explains to the students why it is beneficial for them to achieve the stated objectives. (e) Instructional activities are designed to help students acquire the competencies stated in the objectives. Important here is the use of options so that the student may choose among different learning modes. These options might include having the student choose between reading books or articles and taking field trips to learn the necessary information. (f) A posttest is given to assess the student's learning from the module.

Peer teaching refers to techniques in which students help one another learn. Two examples of peer teaching follow. You may design other variations.

1. *Teacher of the day.* Students are divided into several small groups, usually with between five and eight students in each group. The instructor designs a schedule for the course, with a clearly defined topic scheduled for one or two class periods (Grasha, 1972). Responsibility for teaching that topic rests with a designated student in each of the groups. Each small group on a given day has the same topic being taught by one of the group members. After a topic is completed, one session is spent in having each small group leader summarize for the entire class how he or she taught the topic and share the major points presented in that group.

   The instructor may sit in on the groups or may answer particularly hard questions that the student teachers cannot. To ensure that quality instruction takes place, the instructor must monitor closely the work of the students. They should receive feedback on their performance and be given tips on how to improve the next time they are assigned a topic to teach. During a course, students may expect to teach two or three times. Part of their grade is based on their teaching performance. Usually both the instructor and the student teachers write questions for the exams.

2. *The learning cell.* Students are divided into pairs and each pair is given the same, specific assignment for each classroom period (cf. Goldsmidt, 1971). The students then read the assignment on their own. Each student prepares questions relating to the assignment before the next class meeting. Questions should deal with the substantive content of the assignment, applications of the content, or deduction of new ideas from the material. The instructor collects copies of the questions and gives students feedback about the adequacy of the types of questions they are asking. Exams are given in the usual manner, but students should be allowed to submit exam items. To help maintain interest, and to avoid interpersonal difficulties, pairs should be rotated frequently.

   A variation of this design is for each student to have read a different assignment. Part of the time is spent with one student explaining what he or she read and then asking the other student questions. The roles are then reversed, with the other student explaining and then questioning.

Contract teaching consists of students contracting or forming agreements with the instructor on how much work they will do in the course (Rogers, 1968; Chapter 4 of this book). This contract or agreement is usually written. It should have a clearly understood set of specific responsibilities for both the student and the teacher to fulfill. Each student may have a different contract (e.g., planned set of projects to complete, number of classes to attend, number of exams to take, exam performance), or there may be one class contract. The contract may be designed in a joint effort by the students and the teacher, or the teacher may present a contract for acceptance on the first day of class. A contract presented by the teacher can be constructed by specifying clearly the amount of work and types of activities that are expected for different grades. Each student is asked to indicate within a week what grade he or she wants to work for in the course.

In *tutorial teaching* the instructor meets with students individually or in small groups of four to six. The topics chosen for study are jointly agreed on by the instructor and the students. The amount of faculty guidance and faculty-student interaction varies, depending on the needs of the particular faculty member and students involved. Students usually share with the instructor the responsibility for presenting and discussing ideas. The instructor shares ideas but usually spends a good deal of time helping students sharpen their thinking. Students are usually required to do an integrative writing or research project as part of the tutorial.

In all these course designs, the instructor assumes most, if not all, of the responsibility for defining objectives and determining both what should be taught and how it should be taught. In a *self-directed course design*, however, the learners take the initiative, diagnose their own learning needs, define objectives, identify resources, implement learning strategies, and evaluate outcomes (Knowles, 1975; Tough, 1979).

In a class designed by self-directed learners, students determine the questions they want to answer, the data they need to answer them, the most likely data sources, the best means of obtaining such information, the most reasonable approach to using the information, and the best ways to report and evaluate their answers. Often the teacher and learners use a contract approach, but with the students rather than the teacher assuming major responsibility for all the steps of the contract. Table 10.3 presents a self-directed contract for a learning project on self-directed learning.

Table 10.3. Learning Contract

Name: John Doe

Learning Project: Self-directed learning

1 Learning Objectives	2 Learning Resources and Strategies	3 Evidence of Accomplishment	4 Criteria and Means of Validating Evidence
1. To develop an understanding of the theory and practical implications of teacher-directed learning and self-directed learning.	Inquiry Projects 1, 2, & 3. Read Born, Eble, Houe, and Tough. Learning Resource A.	A written or oral presentation of the definitions, rationales, assumptions, and required skills of each.	Make presentation to a high school student, college student, teacher, and adult friend, and have them rate it on a three-point scale as to clarity, comprehensiveness, and usefullness to them.
2. To enhance my self-concept as a self-directing person.	Learning Resource D. Inquiry Project 4.	Creation of a satisfying learning contract.	Rating of the contract by two peers and a teacher as to degree of self-directedness it demonstrates.
3. To gain skill in relating to peers collaboratively.	Learning Resource E.	Performance as a helper and as a receiver of help in a learning project with two or more peers.	Rating by the peers on my effectiveness as a helper and my openness to feedback as a receiver of help.
4. To increase my ability to assess learning needs.	Inquiry Projects 3 & 4. Learning Resource B. Learning Resource G.	Self-assessment per Learning Resource G.	Rating by an expert on adequacy of model and accuracy of assessment.
5. To increase my ability to translate learning needs into learning objectives.	Inquiry Projects 3 & 4. Learning Resource I.	Inquiry Project 4.	Rating by two peers and a teacher of objectives in contract as to their measurability.
6. To gain skill in making use of teachers as helpers and re-sources	Inquiry Project 4.	Utilization of a teacher as a consultant and information source.	Rating by teacher used in Inquiry Project 4 of my skill in getting help and information.

Phase 5: Matching instructor and student skills. Having identified the major skill demands for both yourself and your students, you should consider and select alternative course designs that will best assure achievement of your content and noncontent goals. Table 10.4 presents the type of instructor and student skill demands made by each of the nine course designs presented. The left-hand column in each course design outlines the major instructor skills needed. The right-hand column indicates the major student skills needed.

To use this table, take the instructor and student skills you summarized earlier. Circle each of your instructor and student skills in the columns at the far left and far right of the table, respectively. These are the skills you need for your course goals. Then for each instructor and student skill, *place a circle around the X in each course design column* that corresponds to a skill you identified as needed for your goals. This tells you which course designs utilize skills you thought were necessary.

There are three methods you can use to help determine which design or combination of features from different designs are best for your goals: (1) *Prioritize* the top five or six instructor and student skills you listed for your course goals. (2) *Select a single design* that best allows you to meet the requirements of these skills. (3) *Select two or three course designs* that overlap the important instructor and student skills you identified. Your course design should include relevant aspects of these alternative course designs. Sum the number of your instructor and student skills each course design seems to match. The design that allows you to match the highest number of such skills may be best for you. The assumption underlying this suggestion is that you may be trying to accomplish too much—or at least this is a possibility. Finally, if a match is still not possible, you may need to reconsider or rework your goals. Often the addition of new goals or the modification of existing goals allows a match to occur.

A final point should be remembered. The procedures outlined here will assist you in identifying designs that are appropriate for your needs. However, it is important that the design you select is one that you will be comfortable with. It should be one that will enhance your values as a teacher. In many cases, alternatives will emerge using this process. The final selection must make sense both in terms of the goal-skill analysis you completed and for you as an individual. You should make sure you really see and can accept the advantages an alternative appears to have. Otherwise, you may not want to give up your current practices or plans. An alternative must also make sense to your students, especially if it places them in an unfamiliar or uncomfortable position. It is therefore advisable to share with your students both the content and noncontent goals you have for the course, and to explain and discuss with them how the course design itself will enable these goals to be met.

Table 10.4. Instructor and Student Skill Demands Associated with Nine Common Course Designs

Designs

Instructor Skills (IS)	Lecture IS	Lecture SS	SGL[a] IS	SGL SS	SPI[b] IS	SPI SS	Siml[c] IS	Siml SS	Modular IS	Modular SS	Peer IS	Peer SS	Contract IS	Contract SS	Tutorial IS	Tutorial SS	SDL[d] IS	SDL SS	Student Skills (SS)
Actor	X						X	X											Actor
Assigner[e]	X		X	X	X			X	X		X	X				X		X	Collaborator[e]
Coordinator			X		X				X		X	X	X		X	X	X	X	Consultant
Consultant			X	X	X	X	X		X	X	X	X	X	X	X	X	X		Content expert[e]
Content expert[e]	X		X		X		X	X	X		X	X	X		X	X		X	Content transmitter
Content transmitter	X			X		X		X		X		X		X	X	X		X	Explorer
Evaluator[e]		X	X		X		X	X	X		X	X		X		X			Exam taker[e]
Facilitator[e]					X		X		X		X			X	X	X	X	X	Independent learner[e]
Grader[e]	X	X	X	X			X	X	X		X	X	X	X	X	X		X	Listener[e]
Goal setter					X			X	X			X	X	X				X	Negotiator
Listener			X	X	X	X	X	X				X	X		X		X	X	Process observer[e]
Materials designer			X		X	X	X	X	X	X	X		X			X		X	Problem solver[e]
Manager	X		X		X	X	X			X	X			X		X		X	Reader[e]
Negotiator													X	X		X	X	X	Researcher
Process observer[e]	X		X		X			X			X			X		X		X	Writer[e]
Speaker[e]	X		X		X		X		X		X							X	Speaker

[a]Small-group learning. [b]Self-paced instruction. [c]Simulation. [d]Self-directed learning. [e]These are the skills associated with the goals identified in this chapter. You might circle the skills associated with your goals to see what instructional designs are possible.

Source: Anthony F. Grasha, "A Planning Sequence to Assist Faculty in Selecting Alternative Course Designs." *Educational Technology,* Vol. XV (September, 1975), p. 15. Reprinted by permission.

A Design Based on a Creative Thinking Technique

Attribute Listing

Creative problem-solving techniques generally suggest that solutions are best selected after considering a range of alternative ideas. One method for considering alternatives is a technique called *attribute listing*. Robert Crawford has noted that new ideas are actually the improvement of characteristics or attributes of existing things or the tranference of such attributes from one situation to another. By breaking some problems into their component attributes, it is possible to generate ideas for solutions. Crawford shows that this process is implicitly or explicitly used by automobile designers, television show producers, toy and game manufacturers, and others interested in entering the market place with a "new" product likely to sell. Automobile designers, for example, might break the characteristics of an automobile into the attributes of body size, color, shape, horsepower, seating capacity, fuel consumption, and decoration. They then make improvements in each of these characteristics from one model year to the next. Creating a television series often involves the transfer of characteristics from one show to another. Rival television producers use the characteristics of a hit show to form a "new" series. Although such things solve manufacturing and production problems, they leave a number of cars, and many police, western, and comedy shows, looking quite similar.

Robert Crawford suggests that attribute listing is used best when the various characteristics of the problem are combined to produce novel solutions. For example, using the attributes of a credit card—its shape, the materials used, the type of lettering, and its color—one might invent a circular rubber card, with printed numbers and a polka-dot pattern. The application of the attribute-listing process to course design is suggested by William Bergquist and Steven Phillips in their "clock program for course design" and by Tony Grasha in *Practical Applications of Psychology*. To use it the following steps are employed:

- *List the major attributes of the course that you currently teach or would like to teach.* These might be such things as teaching format, student-teacher interaction, testing procedures, student learning styles, teacher styles, study materials, time of day for class, and location of class.

- *Generate alternatives to each attribute.* One way to do this is to use a format similar to the one shown in Table 10.5. Try not to censor yourself as you list alternative ideas.

- *Pick various combinations of alternatives across the attributes you listed.* This can be done randomly to give you an initial impression of the wild and wonderful things that are possible. Having done

Table 10.5. Example of the Attribute-Listing Process

			Attributes				
Teaching Format	Student-Teacher Interaction	Testing Procedure	Student Style	Teacher Style	Study Materials	Time of Day	Location
Lecture	None	None	Dependent	Expert	Text	8 A.M.	Classroom
Lecture-discussion	One to one	Objective exams	Competitive	Facilitator	Outside readings	10 A.M.	Office
Television	Small groups	Essay exams	Collaborative	Formal authority	Films	1 P.M.	Home
Film	Telephone	Applications of concepts	Avoidant	Very personal	Video-tapes	3 P.M.	Hospital
Simulations	Audio cassette	Standardized exam	Field-independent		Position papers	7 P.M.	Laboratory
Role plays	Videotape	Oral exam	Field-dependent		Slide-tape	9 P.M.	Park
Field trips						1 A.M.	Bus
Guest presentations						3 A.M.	Boat

Combining alternatives: Various combinations of the list you generated might be tried to see what they suggest about your course. *Would you believe:* a course in chemistry that uses lectures and field trips with telephone interactions between students and teachers, that has oral exams over the phone, that encourages a collaborative student style with a formal authority teacher, that meets at 1 A.M. in a laboratory? If not, what might you see as other alternatives that are more reasonable?

this, you might then want to evaluate various combinations to obtain something you can work on further.

As you can see, this process does not give you all the details of a complete design. It provides a broad structure which you can use to begin to think about the various details.

A Design Based on Theories of Human Development

Each individual "becomes the kind of person he is as a result of continuing and continuous interaction between a growing, changing biological organism and its physical, psychological, and social environment" (Conger, 1973, p. 33). The students we face in class may range in age from eighteen to eighty and are different from one another physically, cognitively, psychologically, and morally. Furthermore, in a program of study lasting several years, we can expect our students to continue to develop in various ways in each of these four areas. An important issue for teachers is how to design instructional processes that not only complement students' current developmental stages but facilitate their growth and development. Several implications for course design based on current views of cognitive, personality, and moral development are presented.

Cognitive Development: The Views of Jean Piaget

As people mature, Jean Piaget argued, their thinking processes change dramatically. As adults, they think not only quantitatively differently but qualitatively differently from children. Piaget's theory includes a series of invariant stages through which people pass. The stages are thought to be universal, and although they can be influenced by teaching, everyone of normal intelligence achieves them. Of particular interest to teachers of young adults and adults are the stages. Piaget labels *concrete operational thinking* and *formal operational thinking.*

Between the ages of seven and eleven, people tend to think in terms of concrete operations. Concrete operational thinkers attend to reality and to the present. They like the tangible, the real, and the provable. They are able to use rules to solve problems and have acquired considerable sophistication in the use of concepts and categories. They realize, for example, that "all the pets that are cats" plus "all the pets that are not cats" make up a category called "all pets." They also realize that objects or attributes belong to more than one concept—that is, that all animals can be tame or wild, furry or feathered. Individuals in the stage of concrete operations show an ability to reason logically about objects and to apply rules. But they seem to reason more effectively about objects that they can see or feel than about more abstract concepts. They may not be able to answer the question "If A is the same size as B, but B is smaller than C, which is bigger, A or C?"

According to Piaget's theory, people after age eleven begin to develop what he terms formal operational thinking. Individuals who think in formal operational terms are capable of reasoning beyond the present and forming "theories about everything, delighting especially in consideration of that which is not" (Piaget, 1947, p. 148). Guy Manaster describes formal operational thinking in the following way:

> The concrete, clear, tangible basis for thinking about an issue is still available and used, as in the concrete-operations stage. However, as formal operations develop, the adolescent finds that new perspectives open as thought operates from the base of possibilities, hypotheses, and propositions. This may be immensely exciting, but may also be somewhat frightening. It sometimes has the feeling of whole new worlds opening, and as with all adventures, new cognitive adventures have their pitfalls [1977, p. 397].

Three specific thinking processes characterize the formal operational stage. Instead of being locked into the tangible, the formal operational thinker begins to think instead about possibilities and is therefore able to entertain realistically improbable ideas. Second, the formal operational thinker is able to use the hypothetico-deductive method to deduce from hypotheses (which may or may not be true) the logical consequence of the hypotheses as if they were true. Third, the formal operational thinker can manipulate ideas, juggling intellectual relationships among thoughts that have no basis in fact. These new skills allow the individual who achieves them the ability to think in the abstract, to weigh alternatives, and to imagine a variety of possibilities.

In theory, people are supposed to move beyond the stage of concrete operations after age eleven. In practice, this is not always the case. Many individuals never progress into formal operations. Certainly those with limited intelligence do not. Based on intelligence, family and social environment, and direct teaching, most of us acquire the characteristics of the formal operations stage. But it is not unusual to find college students who are much more comfortable and skillful at the level of concrete operational reasoning.

The fact that formal operational thinking skills are not necessarily well developed in college students is a challenge to any instructor. Processes in the college classroom should in part foster the development of operational thinking or enhance the current level of such skills in students. Deficiencies in skills such as applying, analyzing, synthesizing, and evaluating information are important clues to the absence of formal operational thinking in students. Thus students need practice in such skills as part of their training. The emphasis should be placed on applying, analyzing, synthesizing, and evaluating, not on mere memory. For some students, this might even mean that they are exposed to such things in gradual steps to facilitate their development of higher-order skills. Group discussions, debates, peer teaching, problem solving, and application projects are all more likely to stimulate critical thinking than is the lecture alone. See Table 10.6 on the next page for examples of the kinds of operations that would typify these developmental levels in the classroom.

With the vast increase in the "new student" population (older adults, minorities), classrooms may have to become somewhat more concrete and active. Many of these people have not achieved formal operational thinking and are looking for specific vocational advancement. They are usually holding jobs and raising families and are less flexible than traditional college students. They tend to make more practical demands of their course work. Some may even need remediation in basic skills, and this should be supplied in a helpful, nonjudgmental manner.

Personality Development: The Views of Erik Erikson

According to Erikson, personality develops in an invariant sequence of stages that he calls *normative crises*. Unlike traumatic crises, these are normative in that they are normal, healthy tasks of development that everyone must experience and master. As we mature, we have a series of eight tasks to accomplish, and although we approach these tasks largely in sequence, all eight are really present at all times. We may even regress to an earlier stage when a life crisis occurs. Each task has both a positive and a negative outcome. Healthy development occurs when we integrate the positive and negative so as to achieve a preponderance of the positive. Table 10.7 on pages 270–271 describes each of the eight stages.

Erikson was especially interested in the psychology of adolescence, including the years that the traditional student spends in college. He viewed youth as an adaptive time for the individual, both personally and socially. Recognizing the importance of these years to future psychological health, society, said Erikson, grants youth a "psychosocial moratorium." This is a kind of halfway house or temporary reprieve from social responsibility and an encouragement to experiment in the attempt to discover an identity. What used to be the typical four-year, on-campus experience epitomized society's granting of the psychosocial moratorium to late adolescents. Guy Manaster comments:

> The adolescent may be forced face-to-face with himself, his identity. Very consciously, he attempts to piece it together to make some

Table 10.6. Examples of Concrete and Formal Operations in Two Content Areas

Course	Concrete Operations	Formal Operations
History	• Recall historical dates • Recall important facts • Identify historical patterns • Make comparisons among historical periods • Show how various historical events developed • Show relationships between two events in history • Understand the major concepts presented in class	• Analyze competing hypotheses about why events occurred • Evaluate the motivations of important historical figures • Form hypotheses about why particular events occurred • Bring together ideas from different sources to draw conclusions • Identify the assumptions that historical figures made in taking actions
Mathematics	• Recall important formulas • Use rules to factor equations • Demonstrate ability to solve algebraic equations • Show understanding of major concepts covered in class	• Theorize about mathematical relationships • Develop hypotheses to solve difficult problems • Create new problems to solve • Manipulate abstract mathematical concepts and ideas to gain an integration

sense, that is consistent and integrated, of who he is. This total sense of integrated, consistent self or ego identity is what must be gained by the end of adolescence. [1977, p. 118].

In order for the individual to be introspective, to come face-to-face with self, and to develop this sense of uniqueness, at least two preconditions seem necessary. First is the mental ability to weigh alternatives, to evaluate strengths and weaknesses, and to perceive both self and environment accurately. In other words, the ability to think in formal operations may be a necessary precondition for experiencing an "identity crisis." Second, the society must grant the psychosocial moratorium necessary for such personal and intense self-confrontation.

The implications of these preconditions are significant in understanding the learner. If a person does not achieve formal operations, he or she will probably not have an identity crisis as Erikson described it. Because some adults apparently have not achieved formal operational thinking to a high degree, they may lack the introspective character necessary for the identity-gaining task. In addition, the longer the psychosocial moratorium, the longer the identity crisis. But regardless of when an identity crisis occurs, if one occurs at all, adolescents and many young adults must wrestle with difficult questions: Who am I? What will I become? How do I want to spend my life? How will I earn a living?

For such students, the classroom becomes one arena where they begin to work on the issues of "who I am." The opportunities for them to reflect on course content as it applies to their lives are perhaps very important to this development. Again, the need for more interactive course designs that allow instructors and students to share, reflect, and openly discuss the implications of course content for their lives is apparent.

For the increasing number of "new students" we see in college, a change in identity may be the real motivator behind college attendance. Whether the motivation is to escape a background that is perceived as unsuitable, to "retool" for another career, or to develop a professional commitment that earlier was shelved to accommodate family needs, the "new" student can be viewed as psychologically, if not chronologically, adolescent. At the same time, it is necessary for faculty to be aware that these students, most of whom hold jobs or have family responsibilities, or both, have not been granted the psychosocial moratorium that allows them the freedom of endless rap sessions of idle thought. They are rather more likely than the typical eighteeen to twenty-two year old to have clear vocational goals, accompanied by a strong need to have all their work "count" in a very tangible sense. With their previous schooling frequently in the distant past or less than totally successful, their needs for competence (the stages of initiative and industry) may be as strong

---

Table 10.7. Summary of Erikson's Personality Development Stages

---

Trust versus Mistrust (Birth to 1 year)

Whether we trust ourselves and other people is related to our early experiences. If our basic physical needs were met as infants and we were shown affection, then we began to develop a sense of the world as safe and dependable. If our early care was chaotic and rejecting, then we probably began to approach the world with fear and suspicion.

Autonomy versus Shame and Doubt (2 to 3 Years)

On a daily basis, each of us decides whether and how much to assert ourselves. Our ability to see ourselves as independent is important to our becoming competent. Parents who were patient and encouraged us to do things helped us become independent. If we were overprotected and not allowed freedom early in our lives, we began to develop a sense of shame and doubt about our skills and abilities. We may come to believe that we lack self-control and confidence.

Initiative versus Guilt (4 to 5 Years)

Each of us plans the things we want to do. How much initiative we take is related to the freedom we had as children to play the games we wanted, to seek our own friends, and to develop various motor and mental abilities. Parents who allowed us to do this encouraged the development of initiative. Parents who curtailed this freedom probably led us to see ourselves as nuisances and inept intruders in an adult world. This led to feelings of guilt for wanting to do things and not being able to accomplish them. This early sense of being able to take initiative or feeling of guilt for our efforts continues as we develop.

Industry versus Inferiority (6 to 11 Years)

An ability to be productive and to achieve success at what we do is important. Our early achievements in school and other areas of our lives were important to gaining a sense of industry. The recognition we obtained helped most of us to continue productive activities and to complete tasks successfully. Most of us meet some rebuff and failures and failures along the way, but an excessive amount leads to a negative self-concept, feelings of inferiority, and an unwillingness to try new things.

Identity versus Role Confusion (12 to 18 Years)

"Who am I?" Erikson believes this question is most important during our

---

as those for identity and generativity. If they do not experience success, they are likely to give up very quickly.

The complexity of the problem in dealing with "new students" is perhaps best seen in the examination of the "reentry woman." A reentry woman is commonly thought of as a middle-class woman who has remained out of higher education and the labor market to raise her children. She has typically spent from ten to fifteen years as a homemaker. Although these women are highly motivated and mature, they also reenter the classroom feeling inadequate, out of touch, and afraid to take risks.

adolescence. The roles we play, the jobs we seek, the friends we associate with, and our assessment of our personal qualities help us develop an integrated and coherent sense of self. When we fail to see our identity, we become trapped in either role confusion or a "negative identity" (delinquent, drug addict).

Intimacy versus Isolation (Young Adulthood)

Most of us have a capacity to reach out and make contact with other people. Intimacy finds expression in the deep friendships we form. We need to share and care about another person without losing ourselves in the process. Sometimes close involvement may also result in people rejecting us. This fear makes some people choose shallow relationships or withdraw and isolate themselves from others.

Generativity versus Stagnation (Middle Adulthood)

At this time in our lives, most of us are well on our way in our careers. We notice that younger people are facing the same challenges we did and we become more aware of shortcomings in society. Many of us decide that we want to do something to help. We might become a mentor or guide to another person or we might take an active interest in the welfare of society. Running for political office, contributing to charity, or volunteering time for social causes may increase. To do this we must become somewhat selfless. However, for some, a preoccupation with material possessions and self occurs. Little interest is shown toward others. This results in stagnation and even bitterness toward other people.

Integrity versus Despair (Old Age)

We become increasingly aware of our age. Relationships with other people begin to decline. Friends and close associates die more frequently. We cannot do some of the things we did earlier. These are the twilight years of our lives. People spend a good bit of time taking stock of their lives and reviewing what they have accomplished. This review may lead to thoughts and feelings that suggest we have done a good job. On the other hand, it is possible to conclude that we have failed, and that it is too late to find alternative paths to accomplishing things. Depending on the outcome, we might find ourselves pleased at our accomplishments or angry that we could not achieve much. A sense of integrity accompanies a positive review—despair accompanies a negative review.

Source: From Anthony F. Grasha and Daniel S. Kirschenbaum, *Psychology of Adjustment and Competence: An Applied Approach.* Copyright © 1980 by Little, Brown and Company (Inc.). Reprinted by permission.

They may even feel somewhat intimidated by the younger students. It takes a wise and sensitive faculty member to nurture their development from dependence to participation and autonomy. A reentry woman herself, Kathy Feeney comments:

I needed no further proof that the experience can be frightening and confusing, as well as exciting and stimulating. In talking with other reentry students and in reading professional journals, it became clear to me that many reentry students share a large number of concerns, such as

- confusion about procedural matters, such as admissions and financial aid
- reluctance to ask for help
- isolation from other adult women students in many instances, leading to loneliness and lack of support and information
- dealing with faculty and staff used to working mainly with young undergraduates
- family and work responsibilities, leaving little opportunity to establish contacts and to develop networks with other adult students
- changes in roles within the family as a result of the new role as student [1980, p. 14].[2]

Clearly course procedures designed to give students the best chance to succeed will help develop a healthy self-concept in both the traditional student and the "new student." Some individualization of the instructional process along the lines suggested in other chapters of this book may prove helpful in this process. The ability to appreciate the uniqueness of students and to bring their knowledge and experiences into the classroom will facilitate their learning.

Moral Development: The Views of Lawrence Kohlberg

As we mature physically, cognitively, and psychologically, we are faced with questions of right and wrong, good and evil. How we respond to ethical and moral issues seems to change over time. Lawrence Kohlberg has argued that six stages appear to define the relevant dynamics of moral reasoning. They are described in Table 10.8.

Kohlberg's research demonstrates that any one individual generally reasons more than half the time at one level, with the rest of his or her reasoning at adjacent levels. Furthermore, Kohlberg notes that people generally do not regress, but tend to remain where they are or to move slowly to the next higher stage. In a moral discussion, people understand arguments from the levels below their own but do not accept them. They also understand arguments one stage above their own, but they do not understand arguments more than one level higher. It is futile, therefore, to use stage 5 reasoning ("I have the right to engage in peaceful protest") with a person whose moral reasoning is at stage 1 ("Take down that protest sign or I'll knock your block off"). Most important, people prefer the reasoning at the highest level they can understand. Finally, moral reasoning is dependent on intellectual development. The concrete opera-

---

[2]Kathy Feeney, "A Program to Assist Re-Entry Students," unpublished manuscript (Richmond, VA: 1980), p. 8. Reprinted by permission of the author.

Table 10.8. Kohlberg's Stages of Moral Development

Preconventional (premoral): Based on meeting personal needs

 Stage 1: *Punishment and obedience orientation:* "I'll do it if I don't get punished."

 Stage 2: *Instrumental-relativist orientation:* "I'll do it if you do something for me."

Conventional: Based on meeting group norms

 Stage 3: *Good-boy, nice-girl orientation:* "I'll do it to please you."

 Stage 4: *Law and order orientation:* "I'll do it because it's my duty."

Postconventional (autonomous): Based on moral principles

 Stage 5: *Social-contract orientation:* "I'll do it because it's best for the majority."

 Stage 6: *Universal-ethical orientation:* "I'll do it because my conscience tells me it's right."

tional thinker is capable of moral reasoning up through stage 4, but formal operations are required for stages 5 and 6. Cognitive development sets limits on moral development, but it is not sufficient for it. Most people are at a cognitive level that is higher than their level of moral reasoning.

In order to develop mature moral judgment and behavior, people do not need to be told what to do. Instead, they must experience an environment that gives them freedom and power to wrestle with moral and ethical issues, argue positions, make decisions, and assume responsibility for the consequences of those decisions. In the classroom this kind of environment can be provided through the extensive and intensive discussion of moral and ethical issues where views are freely exchanged. People need to be consistently exposed to moral reasoning that leads them to reevaluate their own thought processes and advance up the moral reasoning ladder. Providing moral and ethical real-life problems to which there are no single correct answers is one means of exploring such issues. Although the social sciences and the humanities may appear best at providing a forum for such discussions, all disciplines possess their own unique ethical problems. Students should be encouraged to explore and debate such issues.

One way to encourage moral development is through the use of what Lawrence Kohlberg calls *moral dilemmas*. A dilemma is a choice situation with no one clearly right answer. Students are encouraged to commit themselves to a course of action and to argue their reason(s) for their choice. The reasons presented, not the choice itself, constitute clues as to the individual's current level of moral reasoning.

Table 10.9 details the dilemma faced by young men during the Vietnam War, with responses rated by developmental level. Guidelines for you to use in developing your own dilemmas appear in Table 10.10. Discussing

Table 10.9. The Moral Dilemma

During the Vietnam War, young men of draft age were faced with a moral dilemma: "Should I go to fight, or should I resist the draft by hiding or fleeing to another country?" The types of responses they made were an indication of the level of moral development at which they operated.

Level	"I should go to fight because . . ."	"I should resist because . . ."
1. Punishment/Obedience	"I will go to jail if I don't."	"My friends will ostracize me if I don't."
2. Instrumental/Relativist	"The government will pay me to go."	"My friends will provide me with asylum."
3. Good boy/Nice girl	"My parents will be proud of me."	"My friends will approve."
4. Law and order	"It's the law."	"It's my duty to resist illegal activities."
5. Social contract	"It's in the best interests of the country of which I'm a member."	"It's in the best interest of the country of which I'm a member."
6. Ethical	"It's right to put down the dangerous Communist infiltration."	"It's morally wrong for us to be involved, and I'm willing to take the consequences of my action."

Table **10.10.** Building Moral Dilemmas

Consider the following suggestions in writing your own
dilemmas for classroom discussion.

1. The situation should focus on the lives of students, the course content, or contemporary society. The dilemma should be genuine.

2. The dilemma should involve a central character or primary group of characters around whom the dilemma is focused. Students make moral judgments about what the central characters should do.

3. The dilemma must involve a choice for the central character, who should have two action alternatives that represent a clear conflict. Neither should be an unquestionably "right" choice.

4. Some of the issues around which moral dilemmas can be written include: social norms, civil liberties, life, sex, personal conscience, contracts, property, roles, authority, punishment, and truth.

your students' responses in terms of moral stages is one way to integrate ideas about moral development into your classes. Furthermore, having students see that other moral positions are possible enhances their understanding of the types of responses available to them. We have found such discussions appropriate for a variety of class settings and content areas.

A number of issues related to human development have been presented in this section, and several classroom implications have been outlined. To begin to integrate these concerns into your teaching, consider the questions that follow:

1. What are some informal or formal ways you have for assessing the cognitive levels of your students?

2. What formal operational skills do your students need to complete the course successfully?

3. What course procedures you currently use or might develop are likely to foster formal operational thinking?

4. Are there ways you can work in class with people who do not have a relatively well developed set of formal operational skills? Is it possible to integrate more information at the concrete operations level into your course?

5. In what ways does your course allow students to meet the identity-formation and other needs that Erikson outlines?

6. Do you or could you make provisions to help "new students" make a better transition into your course? Could you use their life experiences to enhance the teaching of the course?

7. What aspects of the course could be used to increase or sharpen

the level of moral reasoning used by students? What ethical issues could be raised in conjunction with the course content? How might students deal with these?

Summary

In this chapter, three planning processes for thinking about course redesign were presented. They are based on an analysis of student and instructor skills, ideas in the creative thinking literature and knowledge about human development. Each makes somewhat different assumptions about what is needed to redesign a particular course, yet taken together they provide an integration of the types of issues one should consider when planning a course.

There are four phases in the instructor- and student-skills planning process. In the first phase, several general content and noncontent goals are identified for a course. Then the general goals are refined and made more specific. In the third phase, important instructor and student skills required to achieve each goal are developed. Finally, several alternative course procedures and the instructor and student skills needed for each are identified. How well the student and teacher skills demanded by your goals match those of particular instructional procedures provide the basis for planning classroom activities.

Creative problem-solving techniques suggest that solutions are best selected after considering a range of alternative ideas. One method for considering alternatives is a technique called attribute listing. In it, the major attributes of a current course are listed, and then alternatives to each attribute are generated. Various combinations of the alternatives are arranged as a stimulus to picking those that might work best.

The cognitive, personality, and moral development of students is important in thinking about classroom design issues. The ideas of Piaget, Erikson, and Kohlberg were outlined and their classroom implications presented. Teachers need to attend to the levels at which students reason in order to facilitate understanding of course content. Personality development becomes an issue for students trying to formulate an identity and determine how certain courses and programs of study fit into their life plan. Moral development is important in that students can benefit from discussions of the moral and ethical issues that face them and their disciplines. Instructors can help students reach certain developmental stages or can enhance the abilities of those already beginning to handle the demands of certain stages. Typically, this requires the use of interactive classroom procedures.

References

Arbuthnot, J., and Faust, D. *Teaching Moral Reasoning: Theory and Practice.* New York: Harper & Row, 1980.

Boobcok, S.S., and Child, E.O., eds. *Simulation Games in Learning.* Beverly Hills, Calif.: Sage Publications, 1968.

Bergquist, W.H. and Phillips, S.R. *A Handbook for Faculty Development.* Washington, D.C.: Council for Advancement of Small Colleges, 1975.

Coleman, J.S., The President's Science Advisory Committee. *Youth: Transition to Adulthood.* Chicago: University of Chicago Press, 1972.

Conger, J.J. *Adolescence and Youth: Psychological Development in a Changing World.* New York: Harper & Row, 1973.

Crawford, R.P. *Techniques of Creative Thinking.* New York: Hawthorne Books, 1954.

Duska, R., and Whelan, M. *Moral Development: A Guide to Piaget and Kohlberg.* Ramsey, N.J.: Paulist Press, 1975.

Elkind, D. Adolescent cognitive development. In J.F. Adams, ed., *Understanding Adolescents.* Boston: Allyn & Bacon, 1968.

Erikson, E.H. Identity and the life cycle. *Psychological Issues,* 1959, *1* (1), 25-30.

Erikson, E.H. *Identity, Youth and Crisis.* New York: Norton, 1968.

Feeney, K. A program to assist re-entry students. Unpublished manuscript, Richmond, Virginia, 1980.

Goldschmid, M. *The Learning Cell.* Montreal: Centre for Learning and Development, McGill University, 1971.

Grasha, A.F. Observations of relating teaching goals to student response styles and classroom methods. *American Psychologist,* 1972, *27,* 144-47.

Grasha, A.F. *Practical Applications of Psychology.* Cambridge, Mass.: Winthrop, 1982.

Hall, L. *New Colleges For New Students.* San Francisco: Jossey-Bass, 1974.

Horn, R.E. *The Guide to Simulations/Games for Education and Training,* 3rd ed. Lexington, Mass.: Information Resources, Inc., 1977.

Johnston, J.M. *Behavior Research and Technology in Higher Education.* Springfield, Ill.: Charles C. Thomas, 1975.

Keller, F.S. "Goodbye teacher." *Journal of Applied Behavioral Analysis,* 1968, *1,* 79-89.

Kenniston, K. Youth as a stage of life. *American Scholar,* 1970, *39,* 631-54.

Kenniston, K. Youth and its ideology in S. Arieti, ed., *American Handbook of Psychiatry,* vol. 1. New York: Basic Books, 1974.

Knowles, M. *Self-directed Learning.* New York: Association Press, 1975.

Kohlberg, L. *The Philosophy of Moral Development: Essays in Moral Development.* New York: Harper & Row, 1981.

Kulik, J.A.; Kulik, C.L.; and Carmichael, K. The Keller Plan in science teaching. *Science,* 1974, *183,* 379-83.

Lidz, T. *The Person: His and Her Development Throughout the Life Cycle.* New York: Basic Books, 1976.

Maier, N.R.; Solem, A.R.; and Maier, A.A. *The Role-Play Technique.* La Jolla, Calif.: University Associates, 1975.

Manaster, G.J. *Adolescent Development and the Life Tasks.* Boston: Allyn & Bacon, 1977.

Mattox, B.A. *Getting it Together: Dilemmas for the Classroom*. San Diego, Calif.: Pennant Press, 1975.

McKeachie, W.J. *Teaching Tips: A Guidebook for the Beginning College Teacher*. Lexington, Mass.: D.C. Heath, 1978.

Milton, O. *Alternatives to the Traditional*. San Francisco: Jossey-Bass, 1972.

Munsey, B., ed. *Moral Development, Moral Education, and Kohlberg*. Birmingham, Ala.: Religious Education, 1980.

Novak, J.D., and Murray, H.T. *The Audio-Tutorial Approach to Learning Through Independent Study and Integrated Experiences*. Minneapolis, Minn.: Burgess Publishing Company, 1969.

Piaget, J. *The Psychology of Intelligence*. New York: Harcourt, Brace, and World, 1947.

Rogers, C.R. *Freedom to Learn*. Columbus, Ohio: Charles E. Merrill, 1968.

Runkel, P.; Harrison, R.; and Runkel, M. *The Changing College Classroom*. San Francisco: Jossey-Bass, 1967.

Sheehy, G. *Passages: Predictable Crises of Adult Life*. New York: Dutton, 1976.

Tough, A. *The Adult's Learning Projects: A Fresh Approach to Theory and Practice in Adult Learning*. Austin, Tex.: Learning Concepts, 1979.

Werner R., and Werner, J. *Bibliography of Simulations: Social Systems and Education*. La Jolla, Calif.: Western Behavioral Sciences Institute, 1969.

Chapter 11
Toward a Definition
of Effective Teaching

"If you're so smart, tell me what effective teaching is!" On more than
one occasion, we've been asked this question at workshops and seminars
on college teaching, although usually the words used to frame the question are a bit more polite. At times the questioner is engaged in honest
inquiry and simply wants another opinion. On other occasions, the intent
of the question is to "stump the expert" or to engage in interpersonal
communication games Eric Berne and others call "Gotcha" or "Yes, that's
a good idea, but . . . " Early in our careers, we tried to provide an answer
to this question by describing aspects of teacher attitudes and behaviors
that appeared to be relatively effective or ineffective. Unfortunately,
this turned out to be a "lose-lose situation." If we did not get hooked
into an interpersonal communication game, we certainly were engaged
in a debate with people who held different points of view—and, we might
add, points of view that were rather reasonable. Such discussions, however,
seldom clarified the issue of defining effective teaching. Instead, they

demonstrated to us that there are often as many definintions of effective teaching as there are people trying to define it, and that the issue often becomes an emotional one, with high stakes involved.

Our institutions, faculty, and students all suffer from a lack of clarity and consensus on the characteristics of good teaching. Although it is not desirable to hold to a single model of good teaching, it is desirable to have a systematic *approach* to defining and assessing individual methods of teaching. Until now, such an approach has not been articulated, but in the remainder of this chapter we will present suggestions for a process that can help you define effective teaching. This definition will be personal, in that it will apply to you in your unique situation, but it also will include broadly applicable criteria and will account for the needs of your institution. Furthermore, it will clarify which classroom behaviors are consistent with your definition and will encourage your involvement with others in defining and assessing your criteria. Before presenting this approach and asking you to consider it in more detail, we will review some of the current attempts at defining effective teaching. *An examination of what we believe to be their strengths and liabilities will indicate why an alternative approach to interpreting effective teaching is needed.*

Approaches to Defining Effective Teaching

Personal Viewpoints

All teachers have some thoughts about what constitutes effective teaching. The question "In your opinion, what are the characteristics of effective teaching?" elicits a variety of responses. Ask it of yourself, and check your response against those that follow. Some were provided by people in teaching workshops, and others by individuals who have written books about teaching. When taken together, they provide a rich sample of the variety of personal viewpoints that are possible.

> I'm not sure I can tell exactly what it is, but I do know one of the outcomes of teaching effectively. When things are going well in the classroom, you feel good about the class and the students. I mean, whenever you do something that they like, they let you know and this makes you try harder. I don't think this feeling is tied to any one teaching procedure or teacher characteristic. It can arise from a number of things that somehow just seem to click [workshop participant].

> [This book] . . . is called *The Art of Teaching* because I believe teaching is an art, not a science. It seems very dangerous to me to apply the aims and methods of science to human beings as individuals. . . . Teaching is not like inducing a chemistry reaction: it is

much more like painting a picture, or making a piece of music, or on a lower level like planting a garden or writing a friendly letter. You must throw your heart into it, you must realize that it cannot be done by formulas or you will spoil your work, and your pupils and yourself [Highet, 1950, p. 2].

There are practical ways of dealing with students which stimulate and facilitate significant and self-reliant learning. These ways eliminate every one of the elements of conventional education. They do not rely on a carefully prescribed curriculum, but rather on one that is largely self-chosen; instead of standard assignments for all, each student sets his own assignment; lectures constitute the most infrequent mode of instruction; standardized tests lose their sanctified place; grades are either self-determined or become a relatively unimportant index of learning [Rogers, 1969, p. 9].

An effective teacher is organized and clear in the information that is presented. He or she also has the ability to interact well with students inside and out of the classroom. I think that these characteristics are the things that make for effective teaching [workshop participant].

Thus, we hold that the chief functions of teachers are to engage in interpersonal relationships which are healthy and growth-producing and to provide environments which foster this type of interaction for students [Stanford and Roark, 1974, p. viii.].

He embodies what he says—and more. He instructs by his decisively personal activity and teaches as a consequence of his life style. He challenges, invokes, leads in critical assessment and humanizes because he himself includes these qualities: he is a rich—and enriching—human being [Langford, 1975, p. 10].

First, in teaching as in writing, a person can go wrong in all the right directions. There must be discipline in teaching, but discipline goes over into rigidity as easily as informality becomes sloppiness. ... Second, generosity is surely an essential of good teaching. ... Giving of self—personality and character—as well as energy, time, skill, and knowledge are required. ... Third, energy is often an outstanding characteristic of the effective teacher. Teachers are aware of the energy required when they come away drained from an effective class. ... Fourth, variety is another central attribute of effective teaching. Fifth, though it may seem too small a detail to be included among these general observations, the use of examples and illustrations is too important to be left out. ... Sixth, however it comes and is maintained, enthusiasm is essential. ... Seventh ... I think there are other virtues in teaching more important than clarity and the power to organize. "There are some enterprises," Melville wrote, "in which a careful disorderliness is the true method." Eighth, honesty is important. [Teachers] should never set considerations of right or wrong aside for long or let their choices be unaffected by such considerations. . . . Finally, a wise teacher develops his sense of proportion. He knows more, has more to balance, and balances more skillfully. . . . [Eble, 1972, p 37-53] .

Effective teaching can only be judged against some set of criteria. For me it is how much the student learned. I don't care what you have to do to get the students to acquire information in the course. As long as you can show that they are getting it—then you are effective [workshop participant] .

For the most part it doesn't make a damn what kind of program a school has or what kind of methods a particular teacher uses or the kind of equipment available or what kind of room it meets in. What does make a damn, and a great big grandmother of a damn, is what kind of man or woman calls himself or herself "teacher." [Johnson, 1972, p. 10] .

Undoubtedly, there are ideas in these quotes with which you agree and disagree. We suspect that some interesting discussions might occur if you could confront those individuals directly. One advantage of personal viewpoints is that they provide us with a broad perspective on the nature of teaching effectiveness—particularly if we are willing to sample and listen to a variety of ideas. Unfortunately, as Chris Argyris and others who have examined how we develop and change personal beliefs note, we are not as open-minded and accepting of alternate points of view as we might think. This is particularly true for issues that arouse affect and that do not have concrete answers. What constitutes effective teaching is certainly one of these issues. In his research, Argyris finds that people do not accept other points of view easily. Rather than accept criticism of our favorite positions, we are more likely to distort the information others give us to try to make it fit with what we already believe. If this fails, we will more than likely reject the new information. Thus it becomes difficult to convince anyone that your point of view is correct.

Not everyone, of course, distorts or rejects the opinions of others in discussions of effective teaching. But we have found the tendency present more often than not. As teachers, most of us have an idea about what it takes to "do it right." It is easy to get locked into practices that work for us, and it is natural to think that they might work for others as well. Discussions of effective teaching typically place people with what they think are correct points of view in a debate, a debate that both sides want to win. Such interactions seldom produce an appreciation for someone else's point of view.

Discussions of personal viewpoints of effective teaching would proceed more effectively if people wanted to understand and did not feel compelled to defend their own positions. Furthermore, the discussions would accomplish more if the personal ideas presented were grounded in or made reference to criteria for good teaching that were outside of personal experiences. Personal definitions typically lack outside sources of verification, and they are seldom well thought out. They are usually just a collection of unrelated ideas, and they lack a rationale that binds them together. Because they lack consistency, it is easy to punch holes in them.

Quantitative Approach

My first encounter with faculty evaluation occurred in the Spring of 1954 when it was rumored about campus that faculty members had been "rated." Being by nature both curious and suspicious, I went to the dean to inquire about the mythical scale and where on it my accumulated merits had registered. His response was a bit baffling. "Four point six," he said "on a scale where 'one' isn't complimentary and 'five' is a level of performance beyond which there is no better." "What does '4.6' mean?" I asked. He couldn't answer that question directly, but he did inform me that ten of my senior colleagues, whose identity would remain anonymous, were asked to rate all other faculty members on a scale of 1 to 5. My score was an average of the ten raters' estimates. It was a sort of "holistic" approach in that this one rating on this continuum represented the summation of my teaching qualities, scholarly contributions and community services. When I pressed for an interpretation of "4.6," or for an elaboration of my strengths and weaknesses, the dean quietly reaffirmed his earlier contention that only those who made the actual judgments could answer my specific questions, and his pledge to anonymity prevented him from directing me to them. He did make a final statement to the effect that had my rating been at the lower end of the scale, I would have had nothing to worry about. This was a most interesting comment because no one had asked to see my student ratings, or a sample of my publications, or a record of my professional developments, or a listing of my community contributions and activities [Bevan, 1979, p. 1].[1]

Jack Bevan's experiences are not unusual in higher education. We have made progress in assessing teaching, but the assessments are still sometimes interpreted and acted upon in unusual ways. Jack Bevan's experiences illustrate the quantitative approach to defining teaching effectiveness. Ratings are taken on characteristics people believe represent effective teaching. Such attributes can be determined quite informally. An individual teacher or administrator might decide that there are "certain things good teachers ought to do." Or a committee might debate the merits of certain teacher traits over a period of several months. Their consensus (or majority vote)

[1] J.M. Bevan, "Faculty Evaluation and Institutional Rewards," in William R. O'Connell, Jr., ed., *Improving Undergraduate Education in the South* (Atlanta, Georgia: Southern Regional Education Board, 1979), pp. 1-2. Reprinted by permission of the publisher and author.

about the attributes of good teaching is placed on an instructor rating form. Students, peers, or administrators would then use the form to give a judgment of the teacher's performance. Most of the time the judgments are converted to mean scores, and a teacher finds herself a 1.3, a 4.5, a 5.7, or some other number on various traits. When this process is made more formal, various reliability and validity checks are made on the information gathered. Sometimes a statistical technique called *factor analysis* is used to refine further the original set of traits. An example of the types of teacher characteristics this approach yields and questionnaire items associated with them appear in Table 11.1.

Table 11.1. Common Dimensions Associated with Teacher Behaviors: Dimension Descriptions and Sample Items

---

A. *Hildebrand and Wilson, 1970*

  1. *Analytic/synthetic approach:* The teacher knows the theoretical background and recent developments in the subject from several points of view. The ability to discuss a variety of ideas and to illustrate the relationship among them in order to increase the students' broad-based understanding of the area is stressed.
     Items: (a) Discusses points of view other than his own. (b) Contrasts implications of various theories. (c) Discusses recent developments in the field. (d) Presents origins of ideas and concepts.

  2. *Organization/clarity:* The teacher is diligent in planning the lectures, with clear objectives to provide an organized picture of the information.
     Items: (a) Explains clearly. (b) Is well prepared. (c) Gives lectures that are easy to outline. (d) States objectives for each class session.

  3. *Instructor/group interaction:* The teacher allows students some responsibility in contributing to the educational process through discussion and the mutual sharing of ideas. The instructor is concerned about the class's response to her teaching.
     Items: (a) Encourages class discussion. (b) Invites students to share their knowledge and experiences. (c) Invites criticism of her own ideas. (d) Knows if the class is understanding her or not.

  4. *Instructor/individual student interaction:* The teacher is approachable and interested in students, and treats them with respect.
     Items: (a) Has a genuine interest in students. (b) Relates to students as individuals. (c) Is accessible to students out of class. (d) Respects students as persons.

  5. *Dynamism/enthusiasm:* The instructor is energetic and stimulating, conveying the impression that he enjoys "turning students on" to his subject.
     Items: (a) Is a dynamic and energetic person. (b) Seems to enjoy teaching. (c) Is enthusiastic about his subject. (d) Seems to have self-confidence.

B. *Isaacson, McKeachie, Milholland, et al., 1964*

  1. *General teaching ability:* Teaching abilities that tend to form a consistent pattern across different instructional styles.

Regardless of how the traits are determined, the score on a rating scale defines the degree of effective performance. Whether one is below average, average, or above average is relatively simple to determine with such scales. You only need compare your "number" to the range of the rating scale digits and decide how much below or, one hopes, above the midpoint of the scale you are. Or your scores can be compared to the mean score of colleagues within your department or college. People are judged relatively effective or ineffective depending on where their numbers fall.

Because everyone is assessed against the same standards (on the same traits) and the process yields numerical scores, it appears that the definition of effective teaching is quite objective. So-called objectivity is seen as desirable these days, when budgets are tight and more faculty might not

---

Items: (a) Material is put across in an interesting way. (b) The intellectual curiosity of the students is stimulated. (c) Things are clearly explained. (d) The teacher is skillful in observing student reactions.

2. *Overload:* The amount and difficulty of the work assigned.
Items: (a) Assigned very difficult reading. (b) Asked for more than students could get done. (c) Assigned a great deal of reading.

3. *Structure:* The ability of the instructor to organize and plan a course.
Items: (a) Decided in detail what should be done and how it should be done. (b) Followed an outline closely. (c) Had everything going according to schedule. (d) Planned the activities of each class period in detail.

4. *Quality:* The concern the teacher has for the quality of classroom-related work.
Items: (a) Told students when they had done a particularly good job. (b) Complimented students in front of others. (c) Criticized poor work.

5. *Group interaction:* The nature of the interpersonal interactions in the classroom.
Items: (a) The students in this class were friendly. (b) In class, I felt free to express my opinions. (c) Students argue with one another or with the instructor, not necessarily with hostility. (d) The students frequently volunteered their own opinions.

6. *Student-teacher rapport:* The nature and quality of the interaction between student and teacher.
Items: (a) The teacher listened attentively to what class members had to say. (b) The teacher was friendly. (c) The teacher was permissive and flexible. (d) The teacher explained the reasons for criticism.

Sources: (Part A) K.E. Eble, *The Recognition and Evaluation of Teaching: Project to Improve College Teaching* (Washington, D.C.: American Association of University Professors and Association of American Colleges, 1970), p. 6. Reprinted by permission. (Part B) R.L. Isaacson et al., "Dimensions of Student Evaluations of Teaching," *Journal of Educational Psychology* 55 (1964): 344–351. Copyright 1964 by the American Psychological Association. Adapted by permission of the publisher and author.

survive in the system. The fear of litigation over personnel decisions also makes institutions favor a quantitative definition.

Yet things are not as objective as they might appear. The subjective biases, values, and attitudes of the people making the ratings and personnel decisions cannot be ignored. *Underlying the numbers are many different points of view about the important traits teachers should possess.* In the research literature, there seems to be some agreement that organization and clarity of presentations, enthusiasm, and abilities to interact with students are desirable teacher attributes. Yet even with these, there is some debate as to how important each really is. For example, Kenneth Eble notes that it is difficult to see the organization, clarity, and enthusiasm in the play *Waiting for Godot*. It is, however, considered by many a masterpiece that teaches people much about themselves and others. Research in the area of cognitive psychology demonstrates that we are quite capable of forming our own organization out of information we receive. It may not be necessary to have a teacher do this for us.

Fixating on traits also ignores the point that teaching situations vary. The important issue is not what general traits are important. Rather, our concern must be with what traits are appropriate for various teaching situations. To focus on a given set of traits may lead us to assume that they are a master key that will unlock the problems in every classroom situation.

If certain attributes are clearly related to effective teaching, then it should be possible to teach people how to adopt them. It might be reasonable to show someone how to become better organized and clearer in presenting information, but we wonder if enthusiasm can be learned as easily.

Finally, it is not always the case that people want an above average performance on certain traits. Research by Charles Levinthal, Leonard Lansky, and Ernie Andrews shows that a student's preferences vary considerably for certain instructor traits. Some students, for example, do not prefer instructors to be too highly organized, enthusiastic, or proficient at classroom discussions. Yet a rating of what students observe in the classroom tells us nothing about their underlying values for particular characteristics. To be perceived as effective, a teacher may not have to be above average for some students on certain characteristics.

A similar point applies to personnel decisions. People on promotion, tenure, and reappointment committees, department heads, deans, and others who must act on the numerical data have their biases. They may feel that certain traits should count more and others less in evaluating teaching.

Thus the quantitative definition is not as objective as it might initially appear. The problems suggest that subjective biases place a role in both the design of the rating system and its interpretation. In our experience, it is not any easier to obtain consensus or institutional clarity on effective teaching with this approach than it is with the personal viewpoint approach.

Definitions Based on Learning Theories

Theories of learning often suggest classroom procedures and teacher behaviors that presumably facilitate students' learning along the lines prescribed by the theory. A detailed presentation of behaviorist, cognitive, and humanistic theories was given earlier. Here, we simply want to indicate how each approach might define effective teaching.

The *behaviorist approach* is based on the idea that a student's learning should be programmed in relatively small steps. A student is rewarded for demonstrating competency in each basic step. Although a variety of procedures can be used to achieve competency, the instructor plays an important role in developing an environment in which it can occur. An important part of the instructor's work is to develop behavioral objectives for the student to master. These objectives are quite specific and might indicate the amount of content to be learned and the degree of mastery the student should demonstrate. Alternatively, they might specify the types of skills a student should be able to perform. Examples include "The learner will list the first six rulers of England in order and the dates of their coronations" and "The learner will use the formula for a one-way analysis of variance to solve a problem presented by the instructor." The form such behavioral objectives take may vary, but the intent is to give the student specific expectations. *According to the behaviorist view, effective teaching is demonstrated when the instructor can write objectives relevant to the course content, specify classroom procedures (e.g. pacing, reinforcement) and student behaviors needed to teach and learn such objectives, and show that students have achieved the objectives after exposure to the instruction.*

An emphasis on problem solving, planning processes, and effective decision making is a major part of *cognitive theories* of learning. Unlike the behaviorist approach, which emphasizes how teachers should structure the environment to promote learning, cognitive theories emphasize how instructors should help students become more effective problem solvers and decision makers. The goal is to improve the methods students use to think about issues. To do this, instructors might begin by assessing existing cognitive characteristics of students and design instructional procedures that are compatible with them. Or a teacher might organize and present information in ways that force students to discover for themselves the answers to issues. *From a cognitive point of view, effective teaching is demonstrated when instructors use classroom procedures that are compatible with a student's cognitive characteristics, can organize and present information to promote problem solving and original thinking on issues, and can show that students are able to become more productive thinkers and problem solvers.*

Humanistic theories of learning emphasize that it is important for people to become exposed to content and feelings in learning environments. The development of a learner's self-concept, ability to trust other people, and sensitivity to the needs and concerns of others are also integral parts of the learning process. Classrooms must emphasize content, but they cannot ignore the personal and interpersonal development of the learner. Teachers do not tell students everything they have to learn or how to learn it. Rather, the teacher facilitates or acts as a catalyst for the students' learning. The goal is to encourage and support self-initiated and self-discovered learning. To do this, teachers must take less of an expert and formal authority stance. In many cases, they must become learners along with their students. They model in their personal behaviors values related to caring about others, the importance of self-knowledge, and of open and honest inquiry into one's feelings about content, and an appreciation and understanding of that content. *Humanistic teaching is effective when teachers can demonstrate that students have acquired content that is relevant to their goals and needs, that they can appreciate and understand the thoughts and feelings of others better, and that they are able to recognize their feelings about the content. The instructor must also be able to demonstrate the personal qualties described to facilitate or otherwise act as a catalyst for students' learning.*

Definitions of effective teaching based on theories of learning have the advantage of being backed by empirical data about the learning process. Thus they are not based as much on personal biases as are the first two approaches. The personal and quantitative points of view suggest that certain teacher characteristics are important to possess, but do not relate these characteristics to the ability of students to learn. The behaviorist, cognitive, and humanistic views specify how and why certain instructor and student behaviors are important for learning to occur.

A further advantage of this approach is that it looks for evidence of effective teaching in both the instructor's and the students' behaviors rather than in the instructor's behaviors alone. The idea that the teaching-learning process involves an interaction between teachers and students is clearly specified, as is the idea that faculty and students must share responsibility for learning.

There are disadvantages to the learning theory approach as well. In practice, very few instructors neatly fit any one model. A survey by Tony Grasha of the teaching practices used in the state of Ohio showed that 85 percent of the teaching methods in use fit the lecture-discussion format and that relatively few instructors could be described as teaching from the perspective of an integrated theory of learning. Most operated from personal biases about learning, making it impossible to apply to their instruction a definition of effective teaching based on any theory of learning. Thus for most instructors the definitions based on learning theory are not very useful in practice.

Another disadvantage of the learning theory approach is that people have biases about the personal acceptability of current theories. This is not so much a problem of the theory as it is of the teachers, but it does effect the usefulness of the approach. Our consulting experiences suggest that the procedures specified by various learning theories are often unacceptable to people *not* using them. For example, some behavioral procedures have students teaching and grading each other. "The blind leading the blind" is a comment often heard. Humanistic procedures may use small groups of students discussing issues. Sometimes the discussions are unsupervised by the instructor. "Group and grope" labels are sometimes applied by colleagues who never do such things. Because the learning perspective recognizes that students have a responsibility for what and how they learn, instructors may have to step into the background on occasion or may absent themselves from a class session altogether. Unfortunately, for more traditional teachers such practices are not teaching. As one person said, "Teaching is getting up in front of a group and sharing with them your insights into a topic. I can't see how it is teaching unless the instructor is present to personally guide and direct the session." Until more people become familiar with theories of learning and their classroom applications, such biases will persist. Unfortunately, these biases make it difficult for instructors basing their instruction on a theory of learning to gain acceptance for the legitimacy of their methods.

Defining Effective Teaching

Problems Common to the Approaches

Thus far we have outlined three major approaches to defining effective teaching and their relative advantages and disadvantages. We now want to articulate and examine several issues that are shared by the three approaches. Any alternate way of defining effective teaching must account for both the individual and the common weaknesses of existing definitions.

The issues common to the personal, quantitative, and learning approaches are a result of the assumption that underlies all or part of how they define good teaching. *They either assume that there are common ideal characteristics of effective teachers or they list particular skills and abilities of a prototype good teacher.* They may specify certain personality characteristics, such as enthusiasm, warmth, empathy, and honesty. Or the ability to develop clear and organized presentations, lead class discussions, write behavioral objectives, or model self-inquiry may be indicated. Such things suggest *ideally* what an effective teacher is like. They describe a prototype that does not necessarily apply to a high proportion of the production models that log time in the classroom. This leads to several problems:

- *Current definitions tell us what several ideal characteristics, skills, and abilities might be, but not how to acquire them.* For example, we could describe the characteristics of a piece of steel and what is is able to do: It is hard, durable, resistant to rust, and it is used to make support beams for bridges and automobile parts. But certain chemical and manufacturing processes made it that way. To understand good steel—or effective teachers—we need to focus on certain processes that will create them. There is nothing in current definitions that suggest ways people can acquire certain traits or abilities. For some traits and abilities, it is even difficult to see how they could be acquired. Are honesty, empathy, and enthusiasm easily taught? And—even if the traits and abilities are easily learned—how does an instructor decide which ones are right for his or her teaching?

- *Current definitions may overwhelm those trying to enhance their teaching effectiveness.* Most of us approach the improvement of our teaching in small steps. Yet if we encounter the characteristics of effective teaching listed in Table 11.1 or those highlighted by the other definitions, we can easily become overwhelmed. Discussions with faculty suggest that the more complicated the teaching process gets, the less people are likely to become willing to explore it. One reason is that it takes too much time, and institutional rewards do not always make it worthwhile. On the other hand, to develop a teaching style around current definitions would surely take a lot of time and energy. Not only would it take time away from other activities— there is the chance of failing. We find that some teachers are afraid of trying to enhance what they do because they have low expectations of their chances of success.

- *Current definitions can lead to "blaming the victims" for "defects" within them.* We know from attribution theory that people have certain biases when they try to decide what went wrong in a situation. All other things being equal, we will blame another person before accepting responsiblity ourselves. Thus students and adminstrators confronted with a classroom problem are likely to blame the teacher. Furthermore, they will look for some defect in the skills and traits of the teacher to account for the problem. We are sure you have heard a conversation like the following: "What's wrong with Professor Jones's teaching?" "Well, for one thing, he's not very organized or enthusiastic. And, if you want to know the truth, he's also not . . . " Thus students who do not perform well "blame the teacher." Administrators who hear occasional complaints about a teacher typically look for some defect within that teacher. Or, when promotion, tenure, and reappointment decisions must be made, decision makers suddenly find a number of uncorrectable defects. The large number of attributes, skills, and abilities inherent in current definitions make it easier to label a particular defect.

This is not to say that teachers are not responsible for certain teaching-learning problems. Rather, we must determine first how much of the problem is caused by the teacher and how much is caused by other factors in the situation. Whether we like it or not, behavior is always a product of the interaction of the person and the environment. Students and administrators are part of the environment and thus must share the "blame" for whatever problems exist in the classroom.

- *Current definitions place the burden for developing effective teaching practices solely on the instructor.* They specify the practice of effective teaching mostly in terms of instructor traits and behaviors. Effective teaching becomes for the most part the instructor's responsibility. This conception fits nicely with the values in higher education of faculty initiative, independence, and the ability of the scholar-teacher to solve his or her classroom problems. In such an atmosphere, it is quite easy for students, administrators, and other decision makers to see themselves as responsible for improving things—particularly when the teacher is blamed for the problems that exist. Yet students and administrators are resources that any teacher needs to enhance classroom behaviors. Instead of "persecuting" a hapless "victim," they too need to be involved in whatever "rescue operation" will make the process better. Faculty, students, and administrators need to see themselves as members of an interdependent system in which everyone shares the responsibility for good teaching.

An Alternative Approach

Our approach to defining effective teaching does not specify common or ideal characteristics, skills, and abilities that teachers or their students must possess. We do not believe that it is helpful to make a priori assumption about what good teaching is or is not. Rather, we take the view that it takes many forms. To define it, each of us must perform a personal analysis of what we want to accomplish in the classroom and the methods we believe are the best to use. This analysis must include a look at ourselves, our institutions, our students, and other unique aspects of our educational environments. This analysis is like a journey that different people take to the same final destination. Each of them may start in a different place. They may use various routes and means of transportation to get there. Some may even get lost temporarily along the way. The important point is that the final destination is eventually reached because the routes and vehicles were personally selected as the right ones to take.

The outcome of this personal analysis is a definition of effective teaching that applies to your unique circumstances. Aspects of your definition may overlap with those of other people, or you may find that no one shares your perspective. But the analysis allows you to justify why you are doing certain things and their major outcomes. Although you may end up embracing one or more of the definitions we examined earlier, it will be because the systematic analysis of your teaching circumstances led you there, not because some expert said that good teachers should do certain things.

In the next section of this chapter, we present a planning process that will help you develop a personal definition of effective teaching. The components of this process are listed in Table 11.2. Each part is discussed in detail. As we present the rationale for each component, consider how you might respond. You might do this simply by thinking about the issues we raise, or you may want to write your responses to each part on a separate sheet of paper.

A Planning Process

Developing teaching-learning assumptions. The first step in the process outlined in Table 11.2 is to list seven to ten of your assumptions about teaching and learning. As we see them, assumptions are the beliefs we have about the causes of behavior. These beliefs are generally related to the things we take for granted about why we and other people behave as they do. In the context of the classroom, they represent our personal storehouse of knowledge about the teaching-learning process. Thus they are a collection of truths, half-truths, myths, prejudices, biases, theories, and other opinions about why teachers and students behave as they do. You are probably aware of some of your assumptions, having articulated them in Chapter 1. Whatever our assumptions, they guide and direct our personal actions as teachers. If I assume that all students are basically lazy and will only work if the teacher rewards their actions, my classroom procedures will probably reflect teacher control and rewards. On

---

Table 11.2. A Planning Process for Defining Effective Teaching

---

1. *Developing teaching-learning assumptions*

   - What are seven to ten assumptions you make about the teaching-learning process?
   - How does each belief meet the three criteria for helpful assumptions that follow?

     Helpful assumptions:

     > are based on clear educational goals and values that were selected after considering and testing alternative points of view
     >
     > are consistent with university, college, and department goals and values
     >
     > are related to the information in the literature on teaching and learning

   - Based on your analysis of your beliefs, which assumptions will you keep, and which ones will you modify or add to your list?

2. *Linking your assumptions to classroom methods, process, and procedures*

   - For the assumptions you already hold and have decided you want to continue to make, list the specific things you currently do in the classroom to meet those assumptions.
   - Can you think of any things you might do that would better represent your current assumptions about the teaching-learning process?
   - For assumptions you modified or developed based on the analysis in the last section, what are things you could do that would represent these assumptions?

3. *Determining and assessing outcomes*

   - What outcome measures are suggested by your teaching-learning assumptions and their corresponding classroom methods?
   - After gathering appropriate data, what action steps should be taken? Consider some of the following as possibilities: (a) Give the situation more time to produce effects. (b) Leave things as they are. (c) Modify certain assumptions or their corresponding classroom activities. (d) Check whether students have the skill or are applying enough effort to make things work. (e) Gather additional information.

4. *Collaborating with other people on your teaching plans*

   - Discuss your teaching plans and feedback from your classrooms with other people. Use their advice to help modify or change what you are doing.

---

the other hand, if I assume that students want to grow and develop and can do this alone, my classroom procedures will probably reflect less direct instructor control over the class.

Our assumptions are so powerful that they may lead us into rather rigid ways of teaching, like those prevalent in the early history of higher education in the United States. The flexibility that is so needed when courses, student populations, and our disciplines change may be lacking. We may not be willing to check our assumptions or to test their adequacy when circumstances vary. Furthermore, our assumptions may keep us from examining alternative points of view. "Don't bother me with the facts; my mind is made up!" is not an unusual posture taken by people when teaching issues are discussed. A major cause of these problems is a failure to examine our assumptions and to adopt new ones when needed.

The assumptions we make are like a double-edged sword. They guide and direct our actions, but they can do so in both helpful and unhelpful ways. In either case, they are important contributors to our classroom goals, procedures, and processes. Thus the place to begin to develop a personal definition of teaching is with our assumptions. In particular, we need to decide whether to keep current assumptions or develop new ones that will enhance our capabilities as teachers. In our experience, assumptions about the teaching-learning process that enhance our capabilities meet the following three criteria:

- *Our assumptions should be based on clear educational goals and values that we selected after considering and testing alternative points of view.* Useful assumptions about the teaching-learning process should reflect the outcome of personal reflection on goals and values that are important to us. Unfortunately, most instructors teach as they are taught. Often the goals and values inherent in their instruction are those of role models. Sometimes such goals and values fit their circumstances and are helpful. Yet there are times when they do not. For example, we have seen instructors attempt teaching methods such as lecturing only because they were taught that way. They are not particularly good at lecturing, yet they persist. One response they give us for their behavior is "I really don't know any other ways that would be more effective." The goals and values inherent in such approaches are not selected after a careful consideration and testing of alternatives. They are adopted simply because they are handy.

- *Our assumptions should be consistent with university, college, and department educational goals and values.* An advantage in higher education is that teachers have control over the processes and content of their classes. Thus, selecting goals and values that are important to us is something we are encouraged to do. Yet as teachers we do not live in a vacuum. The assumptions we make about teaching and learning may run counter to the goals and values of our institutions. There must be some check on this. Otherwise, it is not unheard of for people to encounter resistance to their classroom activities. And, for someone who is seeking promotion, reappointment, tenure, or a salary increase, this conflict produces problems.

Consider for a moment some of the following assumptions participants in sessions we have run have listed as important to them. We think you will easily see why they produced problems. One teacher assumed it was good for students to assess their learning against the values of Christianity. This instructor taught in a public school that had no religious affiliations. Another instructor assumed that students learned best by working alone with very little direct guidance from the instructor. This teacher taught in an open admissions college where many of the students had poor academic skills. At an Ivy League school, this assumption might not have produced as much trouble for her as it did in the open admissions college.

These two examples are of course somewhat extreme, but not uncommon. Those that are less extreme can also create certain degrees of tension among teachers, students, faculty colleagues, and administrators. There are limits to how much a classroom can reflect only our personal goals and values. These goals should be represented, but so should some of the goals and values of the institution. Otherwise our assumptions may not help our institutions achieve the mission for which they were founded.

- *Some of our assumptions should have a relationship to the information in the literature on teaching and learning.* We find more than a few teachers who are unaware of the existence of a literature on college teaching. Jack Noonan, for example, conducted in-depth interviews with one hundred college teachers from a variety of institutions and disciplines with the exception of education. He noted that most were dedicated to their profession and their students. Yet 90 percent had not read an article or book on teaching. Giving some of our assumptions a base other than our personal biases is helpful. It makes our assumptions a bit more authentic then they otherwise might be. And, most important, reading the literature to discover some things that are worthwhile believing increases our understanding of the teaching process.

In workshop settings and seminars on teaching, participants respond to the first two questions in the planning process: "What are seven to ten important assumptions you make about the teaching-learning process?" "How does each belief meet the three criteria for helpful assumptions?" In such settings, people are given presentations on teaching and opportunities to read books and articles on teaching and to discuss their assumptions with other participants. Thus it is relatively easy for them to assess how closely their assumptions are related to educational goals and values and the literature on teaching. Responding to the third question in the planning process, "Having assessed your beliefs against the three criteria for helpful assumptions, what would you keep, modify, or add to your list?'' is not too difficult. A sample of the responses from several participants in a workshop are presented in Table 11.3 to illustrate what happens after such an analysis. *We suggest that people consider modifying an assumption if it meets only two of the three criteria. If it meets none or only one of the three, we recommend that alternative assumptions be developed.*

Reading this book alone does not give you the resources to respond to the first part of the planning process that workshop and seminar participants have. In particular, assessing your assumptions against the literature on teaching and learning may present a problem. You may want to check your library for relevant journals, magazines, and books on the teaching-learning process as well as return to this analysis after finishing this book.

Linking your assumptions to classroom methods, processes, and procedures. After determining what teaching-learning assumptions are worthwhile, you should have classroom activities that are compatible

---

Table 11.3. Sample of Responses to Part 1 of the Planning Process

---

What are seven to ten assumptions you make about the teaching-learning process?
(Responses were taken from different individuals.)

- Students learn best when they are rewarded for their efforts.
- Teachers are seen as more effective if they present information with enthusiasm.
- Students learn course content best in the privacy of their study areas.
- Teachers need to keep absolute control over a classroom.
- Students should have some say in what it is they want to learn in a course.
- Students need the presence of a live instructor in order to benefit from information that is presented.
- Students learn best by "doing."
- Learning proceeds best if students collaborate with each other.

How does each belief meet the three criteria for helpful assumptions?
(An analysis for three of the assumptions described above is presented.)

- *Students learn best when they are rewarded for their efforts.* I decided this was something that was necessary in the classroom early in my career. I simply noted students tried harder when course grades were stressed. But, I don't think I tested other alternatives to this belief. This assumption I think is quite consistent with university, college, and department goals and values. It's a strong part of our system of higher education. I once read an article on teaching and learning and I believe the behavioral point of view would support this assumption.

- *Teachers need to keep absolute control over a classroom.* My teachers in gradu-

with them. The content of our courses, the assignments we give students, our classroom behaviors, how we evaluate students, and the particular methods and processes we use should relate to our assumptions. The classroom provides a vehicle for the expression of our teaching-learning assumptions. To determine how your current assumptions are reflected in the classroom and how any new ones you developed based on the analysis in the last section might be, do the following:

- For the assumptions you already hold and have decided you want to continue to make, list the specific things you currently do in the classroom to meet those assumptions.

- Can you think of any things you might do that would better represent your current assumptions about the teaching-learning process?

- For assumptions you modified or developed based on the analysis in the last section, what are things you could do that would represent these assumptions?

The statements and questions listed often provide a fast yet useful way to determine if our classroom activities reflect our teaching-learning

---

ate school tended to take this point of view. I guess I simply picked it up from them. I don't think that it violates any of the goals and values of my institution but I know that some people don't agree with me. I haven't read anything on teaching that suggests this is supported by the evidence. In fact, Carl Rogers's book *Freedom to Learn* suggests that my assumption is incorrect.

- *Students learn best by "doing."* I've adopted this assumption after hitting my head against a brick wall trying to get students to learn certain concepts only by lecturing to them. I think the assumption is consistent with my institution's goals and values. For learning applied concepts and skills, the literature suggests that practicing them is necessary.

Based on your analysis of your beliefs, which assumptions will you keep, and which ones will you modify or add to your list?
(Responses of people who made the three assumptions described in the last section are presented.)

- *Students learn best when they are rewarded for their efforts.* I don't see any reason to change this assumption at this time. This assumption meets the criteria for useful assumptions well.

- *Teachers need to keep absolute control over a classroom.* Based on my criteria, I think I'm on shaky ground keeping it as it is. I might be more consistent with the literature if I assumed that teachers need to create structures that facilitate the students' learning. Such structures should be flexible and allow for students to have some say in what they want to do. I'm going to modify this assumption and test out how it works in practice.

- *Students learn best by "doing."* I don't see any reason to change. I'm pretty much on target with each of the three criteria.

assumptions. A sample of responses from participants in our workshops and seminars appears in Table 11.4. In such settings, we ask people to have at least one other person check their responses. We do this because we believe it is important to have another opinion about whether our assumptions and classroom behaviors are consistent. Chris Argyris has adequately documented the extent to which people will say they do one thing yet in practice behave differently. Another view on what we are doing and how consistent we are is thus needed. In data gathered from such settings, we find that people discover that one-fourth to one-third of the assumptions they make are not totally consistent with their classroom activities. Although you may not do the analysis in a workshop or seminar setting, it is still a good idea to have another person check your beliefs about such things. An informal discussion over lunch or a cup of coffee is as good a way to do this as any other.

Our assumptions and corresponding classroom activities and instructor behaviors when interwoven provide us with part of our personal definition

---

Table 11.4. Relating Classroom Methods, Processes, and Procedures
          to our Assumptions

Responses of three people whose assumptions were described in Table 11.3 are listed below.

- *Students learn best when they are rewarded for their efforts.* I use the grades on the midterm, final exam, and the term paper as a reward at the present time. It occurs to me that I could do a better job of this. Perhaps I could have a conference with each student to discuss his or her progress in class. I could verbally reward them at such a conference. I might also consider praising them a bit more when they speak in class and make a good point.

- *Teachers need to keep absolute control over a classroom.* I decided to modify this to an assumption that teachers need to create structures that facilitate the students' learning. These structures should be flexible and allow for student input. What I might do to implement this latter assumption is to use a system of contracts in the class. The students will negotiate with me for a certain amount of work they want to do and we'll determine what kind of grade should go with varying amounts. I might require a minimum amount of work for a C and whatever else they do to get a higher grade they need to suggest and to get my approval. The class I want to try this in has about 18–21 students so it shouldn't be too hard to implement.

- *Students learn best by "doing."* There are a number of things I do. Every class session has a short exercise that gives the students a chance to try several of the skills we discussed. I also ask application questions on the exams so they can apply what they know to situations I create for them. I can improve what I do here by adding a practicum experience to the course in the future. I'll see if I can get the students placed for 3–5 hours a week in an agency setting where their counseling skills might be used.

---

of effective teaching. If asked how we define good teaching, we can provide a definition that is based on: (a) personal assumptions that reflect clear personal educational goals and values and that are consistent with institutional goals and values and the literature on teaching and learning, and (b) a clear relationship among our assumptions and classroom methods, processes, and procedures. To complete our definition, we would have to specify how effective our teaching is in practice. That is, answers to the question "Effective for what?" need to be articulated. To do this, we must know what outcomes our teaching produces. Ideas in the next part of the planning process should help you determine this.

Determining and assessing outcomes. If it is done competently, our teaching should produce certain effects. To assess its effects we need to maintain a broad perspective. To do so, we must first examine the possible outcomes of good teaching. Then we must determine which of these outcomes our teaching *should* influence. Finally, we must check to determine whether our ideas about outcomes are correct.

The possible outcomes of teaching can take several forms. We have listed several of them in Table 11.5, along with appropriate measures of those outcomes. As we note in the table, examples of these outcome measures can be found in other chapters of this book. Our list is, of course, not complete; we are sure that you have others in mind that you could add to the list.

Our purpose in providing a list of alternatives is to suggest ways you might overcome a bias some people have in seeking evidence of effective teaching. We note a tendency for some people to focus almost exclusively on content achievement as measured by course exams. There are problems with using this as a sole determiner of effective teaching. For example:

- *Content achievement is not always appropriate for all the assumptions and classroom activities we have.* Not everything we do in the classroom must relate to content achievement. Students can learn other skills and abilities as well. The ability to collaborate, work independently, or seek and effectively use library resources are things various classroom activities encourage. An examination of some of the assumptions and activities listed in Tables 11.3 and 11.4 suggests alternative outcomes.

- *A student can perform adequately in a course utilizing things in addition to the instructor's influence or knowledge of the course material.* These factors include the student's general academic ability and intelligence, the student's study habits, knowledge acquired from previous courses, the difficulty of the exams, subjective biases of the graders, the writing style of the student on essay exams,

Table 11.5. Possible Outcome Measures of Effective Teaching

Measure	*Data Sources*
Student content achievement, including factual knowledge, competencies in using various skills, and ability to meet specific course objectives	Classroom exams and quizzes like those described in Chapter 7.
	Criterion-referenced exams similar to those described in Chapter 7
	Standardized achievement exams for discipline developed by Educational Testing Service and other sources.
	Professional board exams in fields like architecture and health sciences.
Variations in learning styles of students	Instructor observations and self-reports of students on their behavior in class.
	Use of learning style measures like those described in Chapter 5 to assess cognitive and social learning styles.
Quality of student life in the classroom	Use of questionnaires and/or interviews that assess students' responses to various aspects of the classroom environment, including course procedures, instructor behaviors, textbooks, other course materials and resources, relevance of course to their programs of study, and general satisfaction with course. Examples of how to do this appear in Chapter 7.
Performance of students in later life—how well they do in occupational and other settings	Interviews and questionnaires sent to graduates of programs
	Comments of employers on students' progress in jobs that specific classes trained them for by providing certain skills.
	Responses of community and professional people familiar with the accomplishments of students.
	Significant achievements in later life that various sources, including the former student, agree are related in part to particular courses, instructors, or programs of study.
Application of concepts	Classroom exams that stress application of concepts and principles.
	Performance of students on simulation exercises in class that demand the use of concepts.
	Performance of students in practicum experiences as rated by supervisors.

Measure	*Data Sources*
Ability to think creatively and to improve problem-solving and decision-making skills	Classroom and/or standardized tests that assess creative thinking and problem-solving skills.
	Ratings made by peers, instructors, employers, or other sources of students' ability to develop new solutions to problems.
	Performance in classroom simulations and role-playing activities that demand such skills.
Variations in values and self-concept and career changes as a result of instructional processes	Self-reports of students.
	Information from standardized measures of values and occupational preferences.
	Observations of student performance in classroom simulations, role plays, and other activities that suggest variations in self-concept and personal values.
Ability of instructor to achieve goals and objectives for class through the use of particular classroom methods, process, and procedures	Use of goal-method analysis and other assessment procedures described in Chapter 8.
Quality of instructor's life in the classroom	Self-reports on perceptions of satisfaction with various aspects of the classroom role.
Effects of instruction on other people	These people include students, colleagues, administrators, and others who have been affected directly or indirectly by a particular class. Included here are new courses that were added to a curriculum because of one successful course, recognition the school received because of a particular course offering, willingness of people to major in a field because of the quality of the instruction, and teaching methods and course designs that led to outside funding.
Variations in instructor's teaching styles as a result of using particular teaching-learning assumptions and corresponding classroom methods, process, and procedures	Use of self-reports or peer observations.
	Use of teaching style measures and informal assessment devices described in Chapter 11.
Use of new classroom procedures and methods to accomplish instructional goals	Descriptions of course designs, syllabi, the materials used, and the reports of students and other qualified observers as to their quality.
Increase in teacher's knowledge and understanding of discipline and teaching issues.	Self-reports of teachers, colleagues, and students.
	Comparisons of teaching methods before changes with those used afterward.

exam cues given by the instructor during class, and whether the student has acquired a positive or negative "halo" in the instructor's mind. Any one of these factors can attenuate a relationship between our assumptions, classroom activities, and teacher behaviors, and student content achievement.

- *The amount of content learned is a rather ambiguous entity.* What does it mean to say that our classroom tests measure content? There are many aspects of content, including factual knowledge, understanding of concepts, creative use of facts and concepts, application of facts and concepts, and the ability to think critically. Content achievement is related to the specific goals and values we have, which are reflected in our teaching-learning assumptions and classroom procedures. Thus we need to specify the type of content we want students to achieve and whether we want them to apply it, regurgitate it, or use it to create new ideas. Otherwise our exam scores tell us very little about what students have achieved.

- *The amount of student content achievement is not always under the control of the teacher.* To fix the "cause" or "responsibility" for learning with the teacher may be an inappropriate assumption. Ohmer Milton notes that in the final analysis, learning occurs within the learner, and responsiblity for learning can reside only in him. Teaching is not the transfer of knowledge or understanding from the brain of the instructor to a number of brains that belong to students. The assessment of content achievement is best done by examining all the resources students have access to for learning content. Such things as classroom notes, textbooks, course outlines, examinations, outside readings, study habits, and personal motivation to learn play a role in content achievement. The teacher is only one element in this process.

Because of these considerations, we hope that you select content achievement as only one possible outcome of the process of good teaching. Furthermore, it is best to examine more than the teacher's role in students' acquiring content. Students have a major part of the responsiblity for content achievement.

Finally, the list of possible outcomes in Table 11.5 also includes effects of good teaching on the instructor and other individuals. We believe that effective teaching affects people besides the students in the class and has a large number of potential outcomes.

Having examined several possible outcomes of effective teaching, we must decide which of them are appropriate for our teaching-learning assumptions and corresponding classroom activities. Sometimes this determination is rather straightforward. The assumption that students learn best by "doing" and the corresponding use of practicum experiences suggest that evidence on the application of course concepts would indicate appropriate outcomes. Similarly, the assumption that learning is a collaborative activity and that discussion groups and group projects should increase cooperative skills might be assessed. The use of a learning style instrument to measure collaboration or increases in the quality of group projects over time might represent appropriate outcome measures. At other times we might need to use our imaginations or consult with other people to link outcomes to our teaching-learning assumptions and classroom activities.

The last step in the process is to gather the necessary data. We can hope that the information will support our assumptions and their appropriate classroom activities. If not, we need to ask ourselves several questions: "Is the problem with the assumptions I'm making?" "Am I using the classroom activities appropriately?" "Am I giving my teaching-learning assumptions and their corresponding classroom activities enough time to produce an effect?" "Is the source of the problem with the students' level of skill or effort given to the class?" We may need to gather additional information from a class to answer some of these questions properly. We must not assume, however, that the lack of supporting data automatically means that we are failing in implementing our plans. *Outcome data should not be viewed as black or white—that is, as either supporting or not supporting what we are trying to accomplish.* More often than not, it lies in the gray areas between total support and nonsupport. Before abandoning what we are attempting, we should first try to make "mid-course" corrections in our teaching-learning assumptions or the methods, processes, and procedures we use to implement those beliefs, or both.

Using evidence to make "mid-course" corrections is best done if our outcomes are examined on a periodic basis. We might do this two or three times during an academic term or school year. It will keep us sensitive to the outcomes we want to achieve and allow us to adjust our teaching to increase the chances of achieving them. Becoming effective in teaching is a developmental process; we are never completely developed as teachers. Periodic feedback can serve to guide our teaching along lines that are consistent with our teaching-learning assumptions, or it can suggest things we might do to modify those assumptions and corresponding methods, processes, and procedures.

Collaborating with other people. At various points in our discussion of this planning process, we have suggested that other people be consulted. We believe that collaboration is such an important part of planning to enhance one's teaching that such contacts should be planned. In workshops and seminars we emphasize that people should not hope that such things will occur naturally. Rather, we encourage people to establish regular contacts with colleagues and other interested individuals to discuss their teaching plans and any data they may receive.

There are several reasons for our asking that you do this. *In our view teaching is not a private enterprise or a mysterious art form that no one else can understand.* Earlier we suggested that students, administrators, and other colleagues might provide valuable insights into your teaching processes. Teaching involves some observable skills and abilities that other people can see and comment on. In other areas of professional concern we discuss our activities rather easily, and with considerable benefit. Consider research and scholarship for a moment. The research-scholarship model is a collaborative activity. We discuss our ideas, theories, hypotheses, and experiments with students, colleagues, journal editors, and close friends. Their comments often lead to modifications in what we are doing. Such collaboration is a part of the process for conducting research and other scholarly activity. We must make it more a part of the process for enhancing our teaching as well.

Another important reason for collaboration is that it enhances our ability to make changes in our teaching. The process we have described of working from teaching-learning assumptions to classroom activities and then to outcome assessment is quite complicated. Whatever its benefits, it is not easy to implement. Use of the process is assisted by having a group of supportive people with whom to discuss your plans and your progress in completing them. One of the things we have learned from the study of personal growth and development in therapy, business, and educational settings is that successful efforts are typically done in collaboration with others. Bill McKeachie, for example, has shown that people do not make large changes in their teaching by working alone. In his study, the group that showed negligible amounts of improvement was teachers who discussed their teaching with no one else. Significant amounts of improvement were noted for those individuals who consulted with colleagues. Our work with faculty supports this finding. It is difficult to make large changes in one's instruction by working alone. Not only do we need someone off whom to bounce our ideas, but we need at times a sympathetic shoulder to cry on.

There are several forms that such collaboration can take. Periodic informal discussion with colleagues over lunch or at other convenient times is useful. Some campuses have teaching-learning consultants who assist faculty, and meeting regularly with a formal consultant may prove extremely beneficial. Some departments and colleges have faculty complete "growth contracts" that specify proposed changes in teaching and other activities. The contracts are developed and monitored in collaboration with other colleagues. They can easily be modified to work on a definition of effective teaching. Finally, the management of some colleges and departments uses a "management by objectives" approach. Here individual faculty members develop a set of work-related objectives for an academic year, typically with the department head. Establishing objectives for enhancing teaching along the lines suggested in this chapter is easily integrated into such discussions. In the final analysis, the form of collaboration you choose depends on finding something with which you are comfortable.

Conclusions about the planning process. We have covered much ground in attempting to examine approaches to effective teaching. The planning process we outlined may be one way to overcome some of the deficiencies in existing models. Its major strength is that it provides a systematic approach for defining and enhancing one's teaching. Because what you do can be traced back to various teaching-learning assumptions, you have some criteria to fall back on. It becomes much more difficult to be accused of being arbitrary in your classroom procedures. The use of various outcome measures focuses us on evidence for good teaching that is grounded in various accomplishments. Because a variety of outcomes might follow from your teaching, you are not likely to be forced to defend your teaching on the basis of a single outcome measure. Collaborating with other people in the planning process also helps build support and a certain amount of consensus for your approach among colleagues. They are more likely to see as legitimate your particular approach to the classroom.

There are in our view also several disadvantages to this approach. It takes time and energy to implement. Depending upon the reward structure of one's institution, sometimes the payoff for spending time on teaching is not very high. Thus this method may not be used in favor of a more intuitive approach, such as "teach as you were taught." Because it suggests a developmental process, people are never finished with it. The need to respond to data on an ongoing basis means that one must periodically redefine classroom activities. In our experience, the need to monitor teaching constantly is seen by some as a burden. We have tested the components of this approach in our consulting work, workshops, and seminars, but it needs more extensive use before firm conclusions regarding its usefulness can be reached. More information is needed about how it provides help for effective teaching. Although we are encouraged by the response thus far, additional information is certainly needed.

Summary

Several approaches to defining effective teaching have emerged. There are approaches based on personal viewpoints, quantitative distributions of teacher traits, and theories of human learning. Each has certain advantages and disadvantages in helping us define good teaching.

The *personal viewpoint* represents those ideas that experts in the field of teaching and learning and anyone else with an opinion have about good teaching. Sometimes, it seems that there are as many definitions as there are people trying to define it. Such definitions range from concerns about student learning to lists of ideal traits that instructors must possess. An advantage of this approach is that it provides us with a rich and broad set of perspectives on the nature of teaching effectiveness. A disadvantage is that the views lack consensus and lead people to defend their point of view rather than accept alternative views.

The *quantitative approach* assesses the extent to which instructors possess various traits that define effective teaching. Typically people receive scores that rate them as below average, average, or above average on particular attributes. The quantitative approach appears to be objective, but such appearances are deceptive. Underlying the numbers are many different points of view about the important traits teachers should possess. Fixating on traits also has the disadvantage of not recognizing that teaching situations vary. Thus certain traits cannot be seen as a universal master key that will unlock all teaching problems. The advantage of having so-called objective data on teaching from this approach is offset by these problems.

Theories of learning often suggest classroom procedures and teacher behaviors that presumably facilitate students' learning along certain lines. The *behaviorist approach* to learning suggests that effective teaching is demonstrated when the instructor can write objectives relevant to the course content, specify classroom procedures (e.g. pacing, reinforcement) and student behaviors needed to teach and learn such objectives, and demonstrate that students have achieved the objectives afterward. From a cognitive view, effective teaching is demonstrated when teachers use classroom procedures that are compatible with a student's cognitive characteristics, can organize and present information to promote problem solving and original thinking on issues, and demonstrate that students are able to become more productive thinkers and problem solvers. *Humanistic teaching* is effective when teachers show that students have acquired content that is relevant to their goals and needs, can appreciate and understand the thoughts and feelings of others better, and are able to recognize their feelings about the content. The instructor should also be able to demonstrate that he or she has the personal qualities described to facilitate or otherwise act as a catalyst for students' learning.

Definitions of effective teaching based on theories of learning have the advantage of empirical data about the learning process to back them up. Disadvantages include the fact that in practice very few instructors neatly fit any one model. Another disadvantage is that people have biases regarding the personal acceptablity of current theories. This is a problem when people who do not use these approaches are in a position to comment on the acceptability as a teacher of a colleague who does. It sometimes makes it difficult for someone who bases his or her instruction on a theory of learning to gain acceptance for the legitimacy of his or her methods.

In addition to their individual problems, the approaches have several issues in common. They either assume that there are common ideal characteristics of effective teachers or list particular skills and abilities of a prototype good teacher. Thus they describe what the ideal is but seldom offer good advice on how to acquire such traits. Current views also may overwhelm people, because they appear to complicate the issue of teaching. Furthermore, people who do not have certain traits perceived as desirable may be seen as having "defects" within them. Finally, current definitions place the sole burden for developing effective teaching practices on the instructor. They ignore the fact that good teaching is the responsibility of teachers, students, and administrators, who form an inderdependent system.

We suggest that one way to overcome some of the problems with current views is not to make a priori assumptions about what good teaching is or is not. Rather, we take the view that there are many forms of good teaching. To define it, each of us must perform a personal analysis of what we want to accomplish in the classroom and the methods we believe are the best to use. To facilitate this analysis, we suggest that a planning process be used that includes the following elements: developing teaching-learning assumptions, linking your assumptions to classroom methods, processes, and procedures, determining and assessing the outcomes of your instruction, and collaborating with other people on your teaching plans.

References

Argyris, C. Theories of action that inhibit individual learning. *American Psychologist*, 1976, *31*, 636-54.

Argyris C., and Schon, D. *Theory in Practice*. San Francisco, Calif.: Josssey-Bass, 1974.

Bevan, J.M. Faculty evaluation and institutional rewards. In W.R. O'Connell, Jr., ed., *Improving Undergraduate Education in the South*. Atlanta, Ga.: Southern Regional Educational Board, 1979.

Eble, K.E. *The Craft of Teaching*. San Francisco, Calif.: Jossey-Bass, 1976.

Eble, K.E. *Professors as Teachers*. San Francisco, Calif.: Jossey-Bass, 1972.

Grasha, A.F. Survey of teaching practices in higher education in the state of Ohio. Program planning report, mimeographed, 1976.

Grasha, A.F. The role of internal instructor frames of reference in the student rating process. *Journal of Educational Psychology*, 1975, *67*, 451-60.

Highet, G. *The Art of Teaching*. New York: Alfred A. Knopf, 1950.

Hildebrand, M., and Wilson, R.C. Effective university teaching and its evaluation. In E. Eble, ed., *The Recognition and Evaluation of Teaching*, Salt Lake City: Project to Improve College Teaching, 1970.

Isaacson, R.L.; McKeachie, W.J.; Milholland, J.E.; Lin, Y.; Hofeller, M.; Baerwaldt, J.W.; and Zinn, K.L. Dimensions of student evaluations of teaching. *Journal of Educational Psychology*, 1964, *55*, 344-51.

Johnson, R.E. Cited in Don Flourneoy, ed., *The New Teachers*, San Francisco, Calif.: Jossey-Bass, 1972.

Langford, T. The conveyance of personal knowledge. *Excellence in University Teaching: New Essays*. Columbia, S.C.: University of South Carolina Press, 1975.

Levinthal, C.F., Lansky, L.M. and Andrews, O.E. Student evaluations of teacher behaviors as estimations of real-ideal discrepancies: A critique of teacher rating methods. *Journal of Educational Psychology*, 1971, *62*, 104-09.

McKeachie, W. Improving your teaching. In W. McKeachie, ed., *Teaching Tips: A Guidebook for the Beginning College Teacher*. Lexington, Mass.: D.C. Heath, 1978.

Noonan, J. Personal communication, 1978.

Rogers, C. *Freedom to Learn*. Columbus, Ohio: Merrill, 1969.

Stanford, G., and Roark, A.E. *Human Interaction in Education*. Boston, Mass.: Allyn & Bacon, 1974.

Index